GLORY AT
A GALLOP

GLORY AT A GALLOP

Tales of the Confederate Cavalry

WILLIAM R. BROOKSHER
DAVID K. SNIDER

BRASSEY'S

Washington · London

Library of Congress Cataloging-in-Publication Data
Brooksher, William R.
  Glory at a gallop: tales of the Confederate cavalry / William R.
Brooksher, David K. Snider.
     p. cm.
  Includes bibliographical references and index.
  ISBN 0-02-881081-3 Trade paperback ISBN 1-57488-002-0
  1. Confederate States of America. Army. Cavalry. 2. United
States—History—Civil War, 1861–1865—Cavalry operations.
  I. Snider, David K. II. Title.
E546.5.B75 1993   93-13242
973.7'3—dc20

10 9 8 7 6 5 4 3 2 1

To Avil and Gail
Who believed—sometimes!

Contents

Preface   ix

Prologue: The Best Cavalry in the World   xiii

Cast of Leading Characters   xvii

I   A Noble Band of Circuit Riders   1

         Jeb Stuart's Famous First Ride Around McClellan

II   A Stampede in Kentucky   18

         John Morgan's First Kentucky Raid

III   Storm in the Morning   33

         Nathan Bedford Forrest's Capture of Murfreesboro,
           Tennessee

IV   Three Times 'Round   46

         Stuart's Second Circuit Around McClellan

V   Fightin' Means Killin'   71

         Forrest's Long Midwinter Raid Against the Union's Western
           Tennessee Supply Line

VI   A Visit to Holly Springs   87

         Earl Van Dorn's Destruction of the Huge Union Supply
           Depot at Holly Springs, Mississippi

VII   Lay Your Wires to Kill Him   99

       Morgan's Second Raid into Kentucky's Bluegrass Country

VIII   The "War Child" Rides   114

       Joseph Wheeler's Remarkable Cavalry Operations
         at Stone's River

IX   To Steal a General   127

       John Mosby's Kidnapping of Union General
         Edwin H. Stoughton

X   Too Late to Gettysburg   140

       Stuart's Long Ride and Late Arrival at Gettysburg

XI   Long Ride to Oblivion   155

       Morgan's Marathon Raid into Indiana and Ohio

XII   Ride Down the Valley   173

       Wheeler's Sequatchie Valley Raid to Isolate Chattanooga,
         Tennessee

XIII   Until Forrest Is Dead   185

       Forrest's Crushing Defeat of Samuel D. Sturgis
         at Brice's Crossroads

XIV Take No Prisoners   200

       Mosby's Guerrilla Cavalry Raid on Philip H. Sheridan in the
         Shenandoah Valley

XV   A Perfect Piece of Rascality   213

       Wade Hampton's Daring Raid to Steal the
         Union Army's Herd of Beef

XVI Devil on the River   225

       Forrest's "Rebel Navy" Raid on Johnsonville, Tennessee

Epilogue: Glory at a Gallop   236
Bibliography   239
Index   245

Preface

The genesis of this book goes back twenty-four years. It began as a casual conversation in 1969 at Whiteman Air Force base in Missouri where we both were stationed. As friends and fellow missile crew officers in an intercontinental ballistic missile unit, however, we did not naturally flow into a discussion of cavalry, much less one about the Confederate horse cavalry. What created the spark was a common interest in military history and the importance of individuals as leaders. This interest was further refined to the South during the Civil War, particularly to the watershed era of the Confederate Cavalry and to the small but outstanding group of men who attained fame in leading it. As career military men and native sons of the South, we then and there decided to put our own spin on selected people and events representing the best aspects of the Confederacy's unparalleled horse soldiers. Our first article on the Confederate Cavalry was published in 1973, about four years from the time of our original conversation.

What has transpired since then has been for each of us a literary, personal, and professional odyssey. Our writing and publication efforts, carried out through time and normally over long distances, have been reasonably successful; our personal friendship and literary collaboration have prospered; and we both have completed rewarding military careers and moved on to civilian professions. Seldom do people of kindred spirit and similar interests have the opportunity to share such a long-term association bonded by enduring friendship and, much less, have products of that association published.

We realize that broad public interest in the Civil War is cyclical but the event itself is indelibly imprinted upon our national character as a force which has had continuing impact on shaping the course of American history. Records of the event remain a rich repository for inquisitive minds and neither scholarly works, popular accounts, nor media treatments of the war have exhausted its incredible array of topics for investigation by those willing to put forth the effort. The Confederate Cavalry in numbers alone represents only a small aspect of the total Civil War, but its influence and the defiant, romantic spirit it symbolized have left a legacy far beyond its size and place in time. It is in this context that our book was written.

The authors owe a special debt of gratitude to five exceptional people who, in their own way, made a specific contribution to this book. The late Bruce Catton provided much needed words of encouragement and inspiration at the beginning of our writing efforts that got us past the initial publication rejections and bolstered our confidence to continue. William C. Davis, former editor of *Civil War Times Illustrated* (*CWTI*) and a respected author in his own right, gave us our big break in 1973 by publishing our first article in *CWTI*—and paying us for it! The late Prof. Robert H. Woody of Duke University taught one of the authors that good history is accurate information crafted with creativity and imagination. Gail Snider provided unfailing support to her husband and typed more manuscript pages through the years than anyone wishes to remember. Avil Brooksher willingly accepted many hours of solitude and provided continuing moral support and encouragement during her spouse's long hours of research and writing. In addition, we want to thank Don McKeon, Vicki Chamlee, and Michelle Shableski of Brassey's for their patience and willingness to help; and Maria Cornejo of Macmillan for her excellent work in editing our manuscript. Finally, we owe a debt of gratitude to our friends and military associates who gave us encouragement over the years.

Eight of the chapters in this book were originally published as articles in *CWTI* and are used with permission. "A Noble Band of Circuit Riders," originally published as "Stuart's Ride—The Great Circuit Around McClellan," appeared in the April 1973 issue; "Three Times 'Round," published as "Around McClellan Again," in August 1974; "A Visit to Holly Springs" in June 1975; "The 'War Child' Rides" in January 1976; "Devil on the River" in August 1976; "A Stampede in Kentucky" in June 1978; "Ride Down the Valley," published as "Bold Cavalry Raid: Ride Down the Sequatchie Valley," in March 1983;

and "A Perfect Piece of Rascality" published as "A Piece of Rebel Rascality," in June 1984. Four chapters originally appeared in *Military Review*: "Fightin' Means Killin'" (March 1975); "Lay Your Wires to Kill Him" (November 1975); "Until Forrest is Dead" (June 1976); and "To Steal a General" (September 1977). The two chapters entitled "Storm in the Morning," originally published as "Surrender or Die," and "Too Late to Gettysburg," originally published as "Errant Riders Misbegotten Errand," were first printed in the February 1985 and June 1989 issues, respectively, of *Military History* and are reprinted with permission of *America's Civil War* magazine published by Empire Press of Leesburg, Virginia, a Cowles Media Company. "Take No Prisoners" was published by *Soldiers* in September 1987. The authors wish to express their appreciation to the editors and publishers of these magazines for granting us permission to use the articles. These articles have been revised, some substantially, for inclusion in this book.

The Best Cavalry in the World

Cavalry, if one stretches the definition of the word to its limits, has in some form been a dominant feature of warfare throughout most of recorded history. The identity of the first man to discern the utility of substituting animal power for human power in combat is buried irretrievably in anonymity. The reasons for its development and continuing popularity are, however, readily identifiable. Cavalry means speed, flexibility, and great mobility to a commander. With it, he can reposition forces rapidly, scout or raid deep behind enemy lines, or bring overwhelming power to bear quickly on a vulnerable point. It also permits the individual soldier to shift some of his burden to a living or mechanical beast and move with speed and in comparative comfort. Psychologically, it singles him out as something special, for there can be no doubt, as he grandly rides past the "grunt" slogging through the mud or dust, the cavalryman is a cut above the ordinary.

This mental and visual preeminence is not sufficient to exclude him from the miseries of combat, however. The cavalryman hurts, suffers, and dies like all other members of the profession of arms. The nature of his mission often forces him far from the comfort provided by the closeness of friendly supporting forces. Dashing forward to scout or disrupt an enemy movement, he frequently finds himself an island in a sea of enemies. Sometimes, he dies alone with no friend to comfort his passing or to remember where he lies.

In Virginia there is a quiet, shady, little glen occupied only by a tombstone. On it is carved:

> The Yankees came in a thousand bands,
>   To ravage our fair Virginia lands,
>   This lonesome and secluded spot,
> Was all this goddamned Yankee got.

Nevertheless, romanticism is there too. The nature of cavalry is such that its activities readily lend themselves to the use of superlatives in their description. There is nothing of the mundane in a cavalry charge! Instead, the vision of a long line of mounted horses at full gallop, riders leaning forward behind flashing sabers racing the urging notes of a wildly sounding bugle, seizes the imagination, conjuring a spectacle of grandeur and glory beyond the reach of ordinary men. Yet, ordinary men they have always been. And, down through the ages, these ordinary men doing extraordinary things built the cavalry legend.

Cavalry exploits through the centuries have tended to fire the imagination. Who can be immune to heroic tales of men who have made nations tremble and often fall? Or, to the aura of fear and foreboding left hanging over vast areas by freewheeling bands of merciless riders whose daring made them rulers without crowns? Or, to the surging power of conquest, impelling the riders leading the forces carving empires out of wilderness? History is filled with examples: War chariots thundering through the Middle East repeatedly subjugated nations under the iron heel of pharaoh or king. Swooping silently out of the restless dunes of the desert, bands of fierce nomads astride fleet camels have for millennia left the bones of caravans bleaching under the sun's shriveling glare. War elephants swaying down out of the Alps created fear and doubt among the Imperial Legions of Rome; and their counterparts half a world away drove armies before them in the steaming jungles of South Asia. Armies of nomadic horsemen pouring over the bleak steppes of Central Asia crashed through the portals of Christendom, causing that venerable institution to quiver in abject fear. Knights mounted on heavily armored horses were the scourge of the battlefield in medieval times as humankind sank into such an abyss of ignorance, warfare, and rapine that the period is aptly labeled the Dark Ages. Pony soldiers coursing through the endless sea of grass that was the American West formed the cutting edge of a vast movement that conquered a continent, in the process subduing an adversary that had no peer on horseback. And, in this century, the gray *panzers* of the *Wehrmacht* screeched out of foreboding forests to run rampant over Europe in an incomprehensibly short time, only to melt away a few years later before the khaki-clad tankers of Gen. George S. Patton as they sliced through the continent's heart.

Despite having taken some rather bizarre forms and having often been used in peculiar ways, the word *cavalry* most often evokes an image of a man on horseback. Certainly, it is in this form that this mode of warfare has indelibly impressed itself on the minds of most. Mechanical cavalry is of recent origin and other forms of this method of warfare were long ago neatly stored to gather dust in the deep recesses of history. Horse cavalry, as a military institution, evolved slowly but steadily over the centuries. In doing so, it went through many stages, adapting to new weapons, tactics, and conditions until it reached its apogee during the American Civil War, the first total war and the last great conflict before the advent of automatic weaponry.

Although both sides in this war used cavalry extensively, the Confederacy was particularly adept in its employment. Many reasons could be cited for Southern supremacy in its use, but all would stem from a fundamental one—the type of individual who composed the gray cavalry. The average Confederate had been born to the horse and gun. Accustomed to a life of riding and shooting, war meant only a change in locale and game. The skills he had developed over the years coincided beautifully with the demands now placed upon him. Fiercely independent, proud to a fault, and possessed of boundless confidence in his ability, he embraced "the cause" with an almost evangelistic fervor as he galloped off to defend honor and country. These traits were encouraged by the cavalry's leaders. Confederate Maj. Gen. J. E. B. Stuart acknowledged this when he said, "We must substitute esprit for numbers. Therefore I strive to inculcate in my men the spirit of the chase." So, often ragtag in appearance and frequently lacking in arms and equipment, the Rebel cavalryman compensated by utilizing these traits. Improvising, taking incredible risks, and acting with sublime audacity, he carved himself a preeminent niche in cavalry's history.

The qualities that made the Southerner such a superb cavalryman stemmed from an attitude and view of life that tended to chafe under the restraints of military discipline. Consequently, Confederate cavalrymen almost always lacked spit and polish and were likely to regard the demands of discipline away from the battlefield as something to grudgingly tolerate and perform perfunctorily, if at all. Most of their officers came from the same mold and had no difficulty accepting this state of affairs. Its effect on European officers serving with the Confederacy and accustomed to iron discipline was markedly different, as this confrontation between French Prince and Maj. Gen. Camille Armand J. M. de Polignac, CSA (Confederate States of America) and a Rebel private illustrates.

Southern troopers, with their normal disdain for correct military usage, fell into the habit of referring to their units as layouts or she-bangs. One day a private, searching for his organization, sauntered up to de Polignac, waved his hand in semblance of a salute, and asked, "Which way to Colonel Censer's layout?"

"To Colonel Censer's what?" asked the uncomprehending French cavalry veteran.

"To Colonel Censer's layout," the Rebel repeated as if speaking to a slightly retarded child. "You know it, it belongs to your shebang."

"Well, damn my eyes to ze deep blue hell!" de Polignac shouted in a paroxysm of aggravation. "I have been militaire all my life. I was educate for ze army. I have hear of ze compagnie, ze battalion, ze regiment, ze brigade, ze division, and ze army corps, but goddamn my soul to hell eef evair I hear of ze layout or ze shebang before!"

Despite the contemptuous attitude reflected in this encounter, the discipline was there when it counted. These hard-bitten, resourceful troopers rode their opposition into the ground as long as their slowly disintegrating nation could support them. Time after time, Union advances stumbled, stalled, or failed as bands of gray horsemen raced behind them to cut off the supplies necessary to their existence. Blue armies in camp were often forced to fight for forage as Rebel riders incessantly harassed their patrols and outposts. When they moved to battle, the Federal armies had to fight their way through a screen of opposing horsemen, constantly watching their flanks and rear to guard against surprise. So persistent and unpredictable were these wild-riding horsemen that many Union generals could give the opposing army only partial attention as they struggled to stave off disaster from all points of the compass. Union Maj. Gen. William T. Sherman, their implacable opponent, said of the gray-clad riders, ". . . war suits them, and the rascals are brave, fine riders and dangerous subjects in every sense. . . . They are the best cavalry in the world."

Cast of Leading Characters

Nathan Bedford Forrest (1821–1877): An uneducated but successful planter and slave trader from Tennessee, Forrest enlisted in the Confederate Army as a private in 1861. A brilliant tactician and gifted strategist who applied basic war-fighting skills with imagination and ruthless ferocity, he quickly rose through the ranks to become a lieutenant general by the end of the Civil War. Forrest's exploits in battle became almost legendary and established him as one of the most feared of all Confederate cavalry leaders. *Forrest's Cavalry Corps–Army of Tennessee; Army of Mississippi*

Wade Hampton (1818–1902): A South Carolina landowner and legislator, Hampton was one of only three Confederate officers (Forrest was another) who became a lieutenant general without formal military education. A man of great physical strength and courage, he was best known as a brigade commander in Jeb Stuart's Cavalry Corps of the Army of Northern Virginia and later commanded all of Lee's cavalry. Following the war, Hampton was elected governor of South Carolina (1876–1878); then he served in the U.S. (United States) Senate until 1891. *Hampton's Cavalry Corps–Stuart's Cavalry Corps; Army of Northern Virginia*

Robert Edward Lee (1807–1870): One of Virginia's most revered sons, Gen. Robert E. Lee was perhaps the finest field commander in American history. His uncanny understanding of the nature of conflict as it unfolded during the Civil War provided insight into the value of horse cavalry and allowed him to use it to remarkable advantage. Under Lee's command, the Confederate Cavalry achieved a fleeting pinnacle of prestige never again to be duplicated as the advent of technology inexorably changed the face of modern warfare. *Confederate Commander in Chief*

John Hunt Morgan (1825–1864): Morgan, Kentucky's contribution to the list of famous Confederate Cavalry commanders, was a man of limited military experience best known for a series of wild raids in Kentucky, Indiana, and Ohio. Handsome, shrewd, and fearless, Morgan inspired almost fanatical personal loyalty in his men and rose to the rank of brigadier general. Noted for his use of an expert telegraph operator to intercept and disrupt Federal communications, Morgan's cavalry created havoc in the Western theater of the war until he was captured on a raid into Ohio and imprisoned in the Ohio State Penitentiary. *Morgan's Cavalry–Buckner's and Wheeler's Corps, Army of Tennessee; Army of Mississippi*

John Singleton Mosby (1833–1916): Originally assigned to Jeb Stuart's cavalry as a scout, Virginian John S. Mosby went on to form an independent cavalry command of partisan rangers which numbered approximately eight hundred men at its peak. An ingenious, fearless leader with a flair for daring and spectacular acts, he operated primarily in the Virginia countryside using bands of from twenty to eighty men in fast-moving offensive thrusts to upset enemy plans. Mosby's cavalry detachments were known for their ability to disintegrate in the face of possible capture and reform later in different locations and were so effective in their area of operations that they became known as Mosby's Confederacy. *Mosby's Rangers–Company A, Forty-third Battalion, Partisan Rangers; Army of Northern Virginia*

James Ewell Brown "Jeb" Stuart (1833–1864): Born in Virginia and educated at West Point, Jeb Stuart became the Confederacy's premier cavalry commander, an almost legendary figure against whom all others were measured. A gallant, charismatic man, his personal flamboyance was matched by skill and boldness as exemplified by two daring rides in 1862 around the entire Union line. Major General Stuart became an increasingly controversial figure until his death in 1864, but his corps was regarded as the "eyes of Lee's army" and represented the horse cavalry well at its high point in history. *Stuart's Cavalry Corps–Army of Northern Virginia*

Earl Van Dorn (1820–1863): A native of Mississippi and graduate of West Point, Van Dorn was frequently at the center of controversy in both his personal and professional life. After a series of assignments in the Confederacy's Western theater, he was given a cavalry command which he used brilliantly to destroy the huge Federal supply depot at Holly Springs, Mississippi. After proving himself an able cavalry commander, Major General Van Dorn's life and career were cut short at his Spring Hill, Tennessee headquarters by an angry husband's bullet. *Van Dorn's Cavalry–Army of Mississippi*

Joseph Wheeler (1836–1906): A West Point graduate from the State of Georgia, "Fightin' Joe" Wheeler was one of the Confederacy's ablest cavalry officers, commanding in over a hundred battles. By age twenty-six, he had attained the rank of brigadier general and was commanding a cavalry brigade in the Army of Tennessee. He later attained the rank of lieutenant general and commanded all the cavalry of the Mississippi. After the war, Wheeler was elected to the U.S. House of Representatives from Alabama, served as a major general of the U.S. Volunteers in the Spanish–American War, and was retired as a brigadier general in the U.S. Army. He was the only officer to command a corps in both the Union and Confederate Armies. *Wheeler's Cavalry Corps–Army of Tennessee, Army of Mississippi*

CHAPTER I

A Noble Band of
Circuit Riders

Cavalry's full military potential
is realized only when it is employed with skill and audacity at the
precise moment Dame Fortune winks at the right man. Such a
moment arrived on the banks of the Chickahominy River in
Northern Virginia late in the spring of 1862. The recipient of her
favor was Virginia's laughing cavalier, Brig. Gen. James Ewell Brown
("Jeb") Stuart. Capitalizing on his opportunity, he set an example that
for months to come would cause the Rebel cavalry to be the bane of
every Federal commander's life and the darling of the Confederacy.

As that spring had ground slowly toward summer, Maj. Gen.
George B. McClellan's Army of the Potomac, 100,000 strong, moved
into position on both banks of the Chickahominy River and stood
before Richmond. Confident he possessed the strength to deliver a
decisive blow to the Confederate capital, the meticulous Federal general moved slowly, content to hold his attack until he had marshalled
his forces precisely.

McClellan, who had graduated number two in his class at West
Point, had won two brevets during the Mexican War. Following the

1

war, he served ably in the Engineers, demonstrating outstanding competence, but became discouraged by the lack of opportunity. Transferring to the cavalry in the hope of more rapid advancement, he was selected to study European armies. During his tour, he observed the Crimean War, closely watching the siege of Sebastopol and filing a long, detailed report of the activities he observed. His experience there made a lasting impression on him and would be reflected in many of his later actions. Returning home, he found opportunity still extremely limited in the peacetime army. Discouraged by the bleak prospects, he left it in 1857 to become an engineer for the Illinois Central Railroad, soon rising to a vice presidency. He eagerly returned to the service at the outbreak of war, however, quickly gaining national recognition that led to his appointment to command the Army of the Potomac. He proved a disappointment. He quarreled incessantly with senior civilian leaders, maneuvered more than he fought, and meddled in politics, an arrogant popinjay incapable of decisively commanding an army. His dallying tactics caused the media to tag him with the unflattering nicknames "Mac the Unready" and "The Little Corporal of Unsought Fields."

While "Little Mac," as his troops called him, organized and maneuvered his army, the tide of war that had been running in the Union's favor slowly began to ebb. The Army of Northern Virginia had just gained a new commander, Gen. Robert E. Lee, son of Revolutionary War hero, "Light Horse Harry" Lee. Like his opponent, he was a West Pointer who also graduated second in his class, but there the similarity ended. He had served brilliantly in the Mexican War, playing a major role in the victory at Cerro Gordo and distinguishing himself at Chapultepec where he was wounded. Following the war, he served a tour as superintendent of West Point, followed by duty with the Second Cavalry in West Texas. Returning east because of family problems, Lee led the marines who captured John Brown at Harper's Ferry. Later, declining an offer of command of the Union Army, he cast his lot with his native state, becoming commander of the Army of Northern Virginia on 1 June 1862. This man, who considered duty "the most sublime word in the English language," became the idol of the South, and his stature remains undiminished to this day. Of him, Viscount Garnet Wolsely said, "He is stamped upon my memory as being apart and superior to all others in every way."

Lee understood that to await perfection in warfare was to court disaster. So, with characteristic decisiveness, soon after taking command and while McClellan dallied, he moved to strike a blow of his own. When it fell, it brought the Union to the brink of defeat and ultimately led to the dismissal of his Union opponent.

Lee was acutely attuned to the fact that an army on the defensive rarely wins a war. Victory demands bold determination, imaginative execution, and a willingness to take carefully calculated risks, despite the potential for loss that is always present. These considerations led him to decide it was essential for the Confederate Army to take the offensive. Although heavily outnumbered, Lee believed the situation was such that he could successfully attack McClellan and possibly destroy his army. Such an attack would require the major portion of his army to move up the Shenandoah Valley and merge with Maj. Gen. Thomas J. ("Stonewall") Jackson's troops. He could then bring the combined forces crashing down on McClellan's right to the north of the Chickahominy, roll it up and, with luck, crush the entire Union Army. This plan could succeed, however, only if he knew precisely the strength and disposition of McClellan's right wing. The only sure way to determine this was by conducting a cavalry reconnaissance in strength. Lee summoned Jeb Stuart.

No man was better suited for the task. Stuart, a West Pointer, was a veteran of Indian fighting in Texas and Kansas. On temporary duty in the East, he had volunteered as Lee's aide-de-camp and accompanied him to Harper's Ferry. Once there, he went in first and read the government's ultimatum to John Brown prior to the assault in which he performed with distinction. Although only twenty-nine years old, Stuart was already on the way to building a reputation as a superb leader of light cavalry and would emerge from the war as its most famous cavalryman. Extremely popular in the South, he was not handsome or particularly imposing physically. In fact, he was so much the opposite he had been nicknamed "Beauty" as a cadet at the academy. He did, however, possess a magnetic quality of leadership that quickly and permanently earned him the unswerving loyalty of those who served under him. His infectious good humor, love of excitement, thirst for glory, and daring nature, coupled with a keen mind, made him an ideal commander of mounted troops.

When Lee called him to his headquarters at Dabbs Farm on 10 June, Stuart undoubtedly reported eagerly. Earlier he had submitted a scheme for dealing with McClellan and probably expected a strategy

discussion regarding implementation of his plan. Instead, he discovered that he had been summoned to discuss the execution of another:
Lee unfolded his own plan, quietly explaining his need for information concerning the Union right wing. He told Stuart that his job
would be to lead a raid on the Federal right to obtain the required
intelligence. Stuart responded enthusiastically. He assured his commander he could not only accomplish what Lee desired but also suggested his mission could easily be extended to include a sweep
around McClellan's entire army.

Lee's reaction to the brash offer of his lieutenant is unknown. It is
certain, however, that he did not expressly forbid it. While the written orders issued to Stuart amply cautioned against actions that were
ill-advised, they were sufficiently vague to allow him all the leeway
he needed. In part, they directed the young cavalry chief ". . . not to
hazard unnecessarily your command or to attempt what your judgment may not approve; but be content to accomplish all the good
you can without feeling it necessary to obtain all that might be
desired." For a man like Stuart, they were a license to steal!

Stuart immediately dispatched orders to his command identifying
the cavalry units that would participate: Colonel Fitzhugh Lee's First
Virginia; Col. William Henry Fitzhugh ("Rooney") Lee's Ninth
Virginia, both units augmented by companies of the Fourth Virginia;
Lt. Col. William T. Martin's Jeff Davis Legion, augmented by the
South Carolina Boykin Rangers; and two units of the Stuart Horse
Artillery under Lt. Jim Breathed—twelve hundred of the
Confederacy's, and perhaps the world's, finest cavalry troopers. Each
man was ordered to prepare rations for three days and to draw sixty
rounds of ammunition from ordnance. They were directed to assem-
ble at Kilby's Station near Richmond to await further orders. Their
destination was revealed to no one.

Stuart's senior staff were a mixed bag. Fitzhugh Lee, a nephew of
Robert E. Lee, was a West Pointer who graduated forty-fifth in his
class, barely escaping expulsion at the hands of his famous uncle who
was superintendent at the time. Posted to the West, he had been badly
wounded in the Indian Wars and was serving as an assistant instructor
at the academy when war broke out. He would later be governor of
Virginia, consul general in Havana, Cuba, and one of two men to
serve as a major general in both the Confederate and Union armies.
His cousin and Robert E. Lee's eldest son, Rooney, was a Harvard
graduate who had entered the Regular Army in 1857 as a second
lieutenant, Sixth Infantry. He took part in the Utah Expedition, then

resigned in 1859 to run White House, a plantation on the Pamunkey River which he had inherited. Martin was a graduate of Centre College in Kentucky and a successful lawyer. He was described by a biographer as ". . . a man of moral as well as physical courage, and he did not hesitate to take unpopular stands in following his own best judgement." Chief among these unpopular stands was his opposition to secession until the Civil War began.

At 2:00 A.M. on the twelfth, Stuart awakened his troopers with the command, "Gentlemen, in ten minutes every man must be in his saddle!"

In the bright moonlight bathing the Virginia countryside, horses were quickly saddled and units formed into a column of fours. Stuart, black plume flying from his hat, hummed a tune as he slowly made his way to the head of the column to join his staff. At five o'clock the command began to move. As the long column broke into a trot, an officer left behind called out to Stuart, "When will you be back?"

From the head of the northward jogging troopers, a laughing Stuart's answer drifted to the rear, "It may be for years and it may be forever."

Torrential rains had inundated the area for several days prior to the start of the mission. Now, they gave way to the stifling heat of late spring, allowing the blazing sun beating down on the sodden earth to create a steam bath atmosphere. Sweltering in the muggy air, the sweat-soaked Rebels advanced steadily northward along Brooke Turnpike past fields filled with waving grain and woodlands green with heavy foliage. Scouts had long since been dispatched to range far to the front and right to guard against surprise and to obtain any available information regarding the enemy. At Turner's Tavern, the riders veered left, crossing the Richmond, Fredericksburg, and Potomac Railroad, hoping to give the impression that they were on their way to reinforce Jackson. Late in the day, they passed west of Ashland Station and at nightfall went into a quiet, fireless bivouac just below the South Anna River near Winston's Farm. They were twenty-two miles north of Richmond.

Once the troops were settled for the night and scouts sent to survey Federal activity on the right, Stuart and Rooney Lee rode off to visit Lee's father-in-law, Col. Henry Wickham. They made the twenty-five mile ride late, arriving after midnight. Lee spent the remainder of the night visiting with the Wickham family while Stuart slept in a chair. Shortly before daylight, Stuart roused himself and returned with Lee to camp. There, the scouts reported no enemy activity.

At daybreak, the men were quietly roused and ordered to mount up. Once formed, the column turned sharply eastward toward Hanover Court House. Now, Stuart told the Lees and Martin that he had orders to scout the Federal right. He neglected to mention that in the back of his mind lay a plan to circle the Union army.

As the day advanced, the force moved rapidly through the rolling countryside behind a unit commanded by Lieutenant W. T. Robins, Rooney Lee's adjutant. As they wound along past farmsteads, residents rushed to the roadside to wave and call encouragement to the passing troopers. The slouching, grinning riders waved and shouted back as casually as if they were on a quiet Sunday outing instead of headed for combat. Their jocularity abruptly subsided and the festive atmosphere evaporated, however, as they neared Hanover Court House. Ahead they saw their first "bluebirds," a portion of Robert E. Lee's old command, formerly the Second, now the Sixth U.S. Cavalry, under Lt. Edward Leib.

Leib had left his Old Church camp at about six o'clock in the morning on the thirteenth, under orders to scout the road as far as Hanover Court House. He had traveled to within about a half mile of his destination when he spotted the Rebel advance. Unsure of their identity, he decided to be cautious. Leaving his troops hidden in the edge of a wooded area, he moved slowly forward along a small creek until he observed a party of six Confederates approaching on the opposite side of the stream. When they saw him, they immediately turned back to join the main body of raiders. Their action left no doubt in Leib's mind—the horsemen were Confederates. Estimating the Rebel force to be about two squadrons, he was not unduly excited, but, deciding caution was still best, he returned to his company and retreated toward Old Church.

Informed of the Union troops in front, Stuart held the advance on the crest of a wooded knoll. He called Fitz Lee to the front and dispatched him to the right with orders to circle behind Leib. As soon as Lee was well on his way, Stuart gave the order to advance but held to a deliberate pace, expecting to force Leib into Lee's flanking force. Unfortunately for the raiders, Lee ran into trouble in the form of a swampy area and was delayed long enough for the Union troops to pass him before he could regain the road.

Stuart continued to move forward slowly, deploying half a company as skirmishers to clear points he felt to be dangerous. In this manner, the advance continued to Hawes Shop near Totopotomoy Creek. Here the road passed into a deep, narrow ravine with sides that were heavily covered with pine and laurel; terrain so restrictive that troops could move forward only in a column of fours. Now, Lieutenant Robins reported that Union cavalry was up ahead and was prepared to receive an attack.

Rooney Lee, whose Ninth Virginia was in the lead, sent flanking parties to both sides and ordered his leading squadron under Capt. S. A. Swann to charge with sabers. Swann moved off at a trot until, rounding a curve in the road, he saw Leib's command drawn up directly in front of him. He immediately ordered, "Charge!" Without hesitation, the Rebels dashed ahead making the morning echo with their piercing yells. This sudden charge was too much for the Federals who broke and scattered in confusion. Swann gave chase for about a mile before the road became so narrow and heavily choked with brush that, fearing an ambush, he had his bugler sound "Recall."

Leib now sent his commander, Capt. William B. Royall, a message, "Confederate troopers raiding. Two squadrons strong. Nothing to worry about." It was about eleven-thirty and he had still not seen the main Confederate force. And, it would be another three hours before senior Federal officers would know that Rebel cavalry was behind their lines.

The ford over the Totopotomoy was undefended, although it offered an excellent defensive position. This, in Stuart's opinion, amounted to a strong confession of weakness by the enemy. More important, it provided the key bit of information Lee wanted: The Federal right wing was in the air and the ridge between Totopotomoy Creek and the Chickahominy River was unguarded. Stuart now had all the intelligence Lee needed and could have turned back, his mission a complete success. To have done so would not have been Jeb Stuart's way.

Leib continued to fall back toward Old Church. About a mile before reaching it, he was joined by Captain Royall and a second company of cavalry. Royall took command and prepared to meet the advancing Rebels. While he waited, he was reinforced by a part of a third company.

With Robins again in the lead, the Confederate force moved forward rapidly, skirting fields, leaping fences and ditches, clearing woodland areas, and occasionally picking up a straggler. Not far from Old Church, the lead topped a low hill and saw Royall's troops drawn up in line of battle prepared to take a Rebel charge. Again, the terrain was such that the attack could only be made in a column of fours.

Rooney Lee ordered Capt. William Latane's Fifth Squadron to make the attack. Sabers drawn, the squadron charged uphill, along a narrow road heavily wooded on both sides, and into the open field where Royall waited. The Federal troops took the charge standing in line across the road. They had time to fire their pistols one time, almost harmlessly, before the two lines met with a crash. With sabers flashing in the dust and yells ringing in the air, the two forces swayed back and forth in hand-to-hand combat for a few moments. Then, the Federal cavalry broke and wheeled away in retreat. After a few hundred feet, the discipline of the Regular Army told and the Federals again wheeled into line. Again, they took the surging Rebel charge and, again, they broke. A second time, the Federals stopped their flight and turned to meet the shouting, victory-flushed gray-backs. This was their final stand. Latane's men swept over them, routing the Federals completely. Stuart had paid a price, however, for Latane lay dead. He was to be the only loss of life the raiding party would suffer.

Royall, severely wounded, turned his command over to Leib who withdrew the remnants to the south by way of Cold Harbor Road. Stuart did not pursue him since his route lay in another direction.

Fitz Lee, who had been a member of the Sixth Cavalry before the war, could no longer bear to be left out. Anxious to participate directly in the discomforting of his old unit, he galloped to the front and begged Stuart to let him take the lead. With a laugh, Stuart assented and Lee pushed off quickly. Arriving at Old Church, he led a charge directly into Royall's camp but found himself practically unopposed. The ten Federal troopers who remained were quickly made prisoners, supplies and equipment were confiscated, and the camp burned.

The point of no return for the Confederates had now been reached and Stuart had to make a final decision. Three alternatives were open to him: He could return the way he came; he could attempt to escape to the north; or he could continue and hope to complete a circuit of McClellan's army.

Return meant passing through an aroused enemy, for he had already rolled up their right and passed within sight of McClellan's tents. If he elected to do this, he would probably be intercepted by enemy infantry and most certainly would run into cavalry. Besides, he would certainly be expected to attempt to return by that route. Escape to the north was impossible because the South Anna River was impassable as a result of the recent rains. Left to him was the long route; the enemy had the short one. If he continued, however, once past Tunstall's Station, which was only nine miles away, he would have little to worry about. He would have to cross the Chickahominy River but he had information indicating it was fordable and the enemy could scarcely be expected to anticipate such a move. But, what was probably the clincher was that such a move offered an opportunity not only to wreck part of the Federal communications but also to humiliate McClellan by a "supremely impudent and contemptuous gesture."

Stuart called his commanders into conference and explained his desire to circle McClellan. They silently heard him out, but when asked their opinion, not one agreed with his proposal. All of them, however, assured him that he had their full support in any decision he reached. True to his compulsive nature, Stuart turned his horse toward Tunstall's Station.

Shortly before three o'clock in the morning, Brig. Gen. Philip St. George Cooke, the Federal cavalry commander and Stuart's father-in-law, who was camped three or four miles from where the first skirmish had occurred, was informed of the Rebel raid. A native Virginian, his decision to remain with the Union caused his son-in-law to remark caustically, "He will regret it but once, and that will be continuously." Cooke was an 1827 graduate of West Point and a veteran of the Black Hawk War, the Mexican War, and the Utah Expedition. He had also spent some time exploring the Far West and had been a U.S. observer during the Crimean War. He would spend fifty years in the U.S. Army and was about to undergo the most severe embarrassment of his long career.

Under the impression that he was about to be attacked, he ordered "To Horse" sounded and dispatched some units of the Sixth Cavalry under Maj. Lawrence Williams forward to meet the enemy. Williams moved out at 3:30 P.M. and was soon in contact with Confederate pickets who rapidly withdrew when fired upon. Initial contact was reported to Cooke who ordered Williams to hold his position and report any additional information he could obtain.

Meanwhile, Cooke had received information that perhaps as many as five regiments of Confederate infantry were accompanying the cavalry strike. This threat was significant enough that, although he had several units in position, he hesitated to move them even though the quality of the intelligence he was receiving was suspect. Finally, at five o'clock, Col. Gouverneur K. Warren's Fifth New York Infantry was ordered up to support Cooke and, if necessary, repel an attack on his flanks. Warren, a native New Yorker, topographical engineer, and former professor of mathematics at West Point, first moved up about four miles; then Cooke ordered him to continue to the vicinity of Old Church.

Cooke now directed his cavalry forward but discovered they were without rations and forage. This situation forced him to stop everything and send the First Cavalry and Col. Richard H. Rush's Regiment to obtain the necessary supplies, with further orders for them to move forward in two hours. Cooke then, by his account, ". . . returned to my tent to get a cup of coffee, not being well and having a long ride in the morning since taking food."

Finally, at about eight o'clock, Cooke got underway. He was accompanied by Brig. Gen. William H. Emory, another topographical engineer. Emory had been second in command during the Northwest Boundary Dispute of 1844–46. He had served with distinction during the Mexican War, winning two brevets. After the war, he had remained in the area as a presidential commissioner to establish the boundaries created by the Gadsen Purchase. Cooke and Emory joined Warren and Williams near Old Church at about ten o'clock.

Cooke then sent Emory, with Colonel Rush's cavalry, toward Tunstall's Station while holding the main force in position. This action resulted in the strength of the Union counterforce standing by idly, discussing various possibilities, attempting to evaluate intelligence of questionable reliability, and scouting the nearby countryside in an effort to determine Stuart's intentions while a considerable amount of valuable time was wasted. Cooke also hesitated because he was convinced the Confederate cavalry was supported by infantry, even though both Warren and Williams insisted there was no substantial evidence to support such a conclusion. Finally, to complete the confusion and uncertainty, Cooke heard from Brig. Gen. Fitz John Porter, a loyal supporter of McClellan's who would later, and regarding other circumstances, be unfairly charged with disloyalty, disobedience, and misconduct before the enemy, court-martialed, and cashiered from the service. Porter's fuzzy instructions directed Cooke to bring all the information he could get, to hold his own and maintain his position, and not to attack a superior force. In the midst of this confusion and uncertainty, the night slipped away. At last, between three and four o'clock in the morning of the fourteenth, Cooke ordered his troops to move forward in pursuit of Stuart.

The Confederates, ecstatic over their success up to this point, were pressing on guided by men from New Kent who knew every inch of the countryside intimately. So rapid was their pace and unexpected were their tactics that they themselves regularly provided the surprised Federals with the first news of their arrival. Although no major action occurred prior to the Rebels reaching Garlick's Landing, the ride was not without incident. Stragglers were constantly taken prisoner, a wagon loaded with champagne and wines was instantly converted for the use of the thirsty riders, another wagon loaded with Colt revolvers was eagerly appropriated by the poorly armed Rebels, and once a body of Federal cavalry threatened briefly but, after taking a good look at the gray column facing them, elected to withdraw without offering combat.

At Garlick's Landing, Union Lt. Joseph S. Hoyer had encamped for the night with nine troopers, fifteen teamsters, and a wagon train. At about six o'clock in the evening, while the men and animals were feeding, they suddenly found themselves confronted by a platoon of Rebels deployed as skirmishers. Hoyer was ordered to surrender. Ignoring the Confederate demand, he quickly formed his personnel into line and opened fire. His spunky response to their challenge caused the gray skirmishers to rapidly pull back out of range. They were immediately replaced by a squadron of Rebel cavalry. The Rebel riders simply poured over the Union camp killing three, making several prisoners, and driving the remainder into the brush. The victorious raiders then burned about thirty wagons and two schooners.

The remainder of the Confederate force was now nearing Tunstall's. From a hill overlooking the station, they saw several Federal soldiers lounging about, oblivious to the fact that they lay directly in the path of the Rebel advance. Lieutenant Robins hurriedly formed the advance guard and, with a wild yell, led them in a charge down on the unsuspecting Union troops. Several Federals immediately scattered with individual Rebels in hot pursuit. Robins galloped directly up to the station building where a captain of infantry and thirteen of his men stood unarmed. Only one man offered any resistance, but before he could run to his musket and ram a charge home, Robins was upon him. A sweeping blow of Robins's saber that passed near his head convinced the infantryman that he had made a serious error in judgment. He recovered promptly, however, by leaping into a ditch and disappearing. His immediate quarry lost, Robins turned back to meet the captain who was approaching, sword in hand, to surrender himself and his company.

All resistance disposed of, Robins's troops cut the telegraph line and set to work obstructing the railroad while the remainder of the column came up. They had managed to get a tree down across the tracks and had placed an oak sill about a foot square and fourteen feet long beside it, when they heard the whistle of an approaching train. Robins yelled for the raiders to take cover and prepare to fire. They barely had time to get into positions on both sides of the tracks before a Union troop train swept into view. Spotting the obstruction, the engineer applied full steam, bringing the train roaring down on the Rebel force. As it whipped past, sweeping the obstruction aside, the graybacks poured a volley into the engine and cars killing the engineer and killing or wounding several troops. They were unable to stop the hurtling Iron Horse, however, and it shot on toward White House. Stuart, watching the rattling train disappear, expressed confidence that its arrival at White House would certainly result in a serious collision because of the extraordinary speed with which it had departed the scene.

The train lost, the Confederates set to work firing the bridge over Black Creek and burning a large number of wagons that were parked at the station. Considerable time was spent in this effort and the last Rebels did not leave the area until about eleven o'clock at night. As they rode off, their departure was illuminated by huge fires that bathed the countryside in flickering yellow light.

The Confederate movement had been so rapid and so unpredictable that the completely confused Union force had been unable to even slow it down. So all-pervasive was the doubt and uncertainty of the Federal troops that a force of twenty-five came under a flag of truce to surrender to Martin's rear guard under the impression they were surrounded. In fact, the column had already passed more than a mile beyond them.

The heat, fast pace, extremely poor road conditions, and lack of rest were beginning to tell on the gray troopers. In fact, the artillery horses were so exhausted that they had been unable to bring the weapons up in time to be effective at Tunstall's Station. Even so, rest was out of the question. The raiders had simply run out of options. Capt. John Esten Cooke put it succinctly in chicken eatin' terms, "It was neck or nothing." The column had to push on.

Robins again led the way behind the New Kent scouts, moving to New Baltimore near Talleysville where he halted to await the arrival of the remainder of the force. At New Baltimore, the Rebels were delighted to find that an enterprising Yankee had established a store to capitalize on the trade of travelers passing between McClellan's army and the supply point at White House. Empty haversacks were quickly refilled and the Confederates gorged themselves on the store-keeper's stock of crackers, cheese, canned fruit, and sardines.

Brig. Gen. John F. Reynolds now assumed an active role in the pursuit. Reynolds, the son of a newspaperman and friend of Pres. James Buchanan, was greatly respected by his troops. A man of courage and a skilled tactician, he had earned two brevets in the Mexican War. His brigade of infantry, supported by a portion of the Eleventh Pennsylvania Cavalry, arrived at Tunstall's Station near midnight. He was joined by General Emory and Rush's Lancers at two o'clock. It appeared to them that Stuart was probably not much more than two hours and four miles ahead of the Federal force. Part of this force was almost fresh and all of it fresher than Stuart's jaded troopers. Yet, for some inexplicable reason, and contrary to what one would expect from Reynolds, no pursuit was attempted.

Finally, at daybreak, Emory sent out patrols with orders to scout the countryside in an effort to find Stuart's trail. At eight o'clock, he received word that the trail had been found. He concentrated his cavalry force and sent Rush, who commanded a unit made up of the social, athletic, and military elite of Philadelphia and the only lancers to see action in the war, forward after Stuart. Then, in a little while, he received additional information that Stuart's force consisted of four regiments of cavalry and a battery of artillery. This caused him to order a regiment of infantry and the Eleventh Pennsylvania Cavalry forward in support of Rush. Shortly after this group departed, he was joined by General Cooke who had completed his march from Old Church. Leaving Tunstall's Station to Cooke, Emory went forward to direct a last desperate attempt to catch the raiding Rebel column.

A full moon shed its light over the Confederates as they left New Baltimore. Approaching exhaustion, troopers fell asleep in the saddle only to be startled awake by the weird shadows cast by the silvery moonlight. In their eyes, bushes suddenly took the shape of enemy pickets, clumps of crooked trees became vedettes and night noises turned into the sound of approaching enemy columns as nerves frayed from tension and fatigue. Everything turned out to be the trick of a tired mind, however, for no enemy activity of any sort was encountered as they moved dazedly through the hot Virginia night.

Dawn was spreading its first pale streaks of light when the Rebel advance reached the banks of the Chickahominy River to find themselves staring disaster in the face. The stream was a raging torrent, barely contained within its banks. Crossing appeared to be a hopeless proposition. Nevertheless, Rooney Lee and some of his troopers forced their horses into the water and, after a terrific struggle with deep mud and tangled roots, made the opposite shore. The difficulty with which they crossed indicated that it was unlikely that even a major portion of the column could make it across. Realizing the hopelessness of the situation, Lee, who was determined not to remain separated from his command, plunged back into the boiling waters and returned, almost drowning in the process. His rash action erased any lingering doubt that, unless something out of the ordinary was done, the Rebel force could not hope to escape by the route they were following. In a desperate attempt to stem or bridge the boiling current, axes were obtained and several large trees chopped down, but they were swept away like twigs the instant they touched the churning water.

Rooney Lee, staring out across the torrent, was approached by Esten Cooke who asked, "What do you think of the situation, Colonel?"

Lee, in his usual tone of voice, calmly replied, "Well, Captain, I think we are caught."

Lee was not alone in his sentiment. Rebel troopers, their actions reflecting their trapped feelings, covered the bank of the river in every imaginable posture. Some sat on the ground, half-asleep but still holding their bridle reins; some slept in their saddles; others ate or smoked or stared aimlessly across the river; practically to a man they reflected an air of resignation. Some few continued to attempt to cross the stream but, in about two hours, only some seventy-five made it. Then, Stuart arrived on the scene. He spoke a few quiet words to Rooney Lee before dispatching a courier to Gen. Robert E. Lee to ask him to buy some time for them by creating a diversion on the Charles City Road. Stuart then spent a few moments staring at the impassable stream, twisting his heavy beard, deep in thought. At last, he ordered the troopers to follow him and loped off down the river in search of another crossing.

After traveling a short distance, Stuart found the abutments of Forge Bridge. The bridge had been destroyed earlier, but the abutments were still strong and separated by only thirty to forty feet of open water. An old warehouse standing nearby offered sufficient material to construct a temporary bridge. Stuart immediately set a group of men to work dismantling it while others, using a skiff they had found, started to devise a suitable bridge. While they worked, the cannons were wheeled into a defensive position and Fitz Lee was sent out with a strong rear guard to prevent surprise. While all this activity was going on, John Mosby reported that Stuart was ". . . lying down on the bank of the stream, in the gayest humor I ever saw, laughing at the prank he had played on McClellan."

In a remarkably short time a footbridge was finished. The Confederates immediately started to file across holding the reins of their horses who swam alongside. A footbridge by no means satisfied Stuart, however. He was determined to bring out everything he had taken in or to die trying. So, while part of the column crossed, work continued feverishly to broaden and strengthen the bridge sufficiently to support the artillery. Setting the example, Stuart took a position in the skiff himself and hummed a song as he nailed boards into place. At last, the bridge was complete and the artillery rumbled across. Finally, at 2:00 P.M., the last man, Fitz Lee, rode across the river and the bridge was set on fire.

As the gray column was disappearing into the trees, Rush's Lancers charged up to the bridge and fired a futile volley that whistled harmlessly through the leaves. They were exactly ten minutes too late. It was all over for the Federal troops north of the Chickahominy. All that was left to them was a long, weary ride back to camp to face the criticism and investigation that would follow.

The Confederates still had problems, however. They had actually crossed only one branch of the river and were on an island. Fortunately, the remaining branch was fordable, but the crossing was in terrible condition and, to Stuart's disgust, an artillery limber had to be abandoned.

The column then pushed out into a swampy area, herding a large number of prisoners on captured mules in front of it. Many prisoners rode two to a mule and, frequently, there were falls into the shallow, muddy swamp water. The cursing, complaining prisoners had a thoroughly unpleasant time of it. One of them, when confronted with his third swamp in succession, demanded in a voice filled with indignation, "How many damned Chicken Hominies are there in this infernal country?"

Although the greatest danger to Stuart's command was now over, it was still within the power of the Union forces to punish them. They were about thirty-five miles from Richmond and at least twenty miles within enemy lines. They could not avoid passing within sight of Federal gunboats on the James River and Maj. Gen. Joseph Hooker, who held the line of the White Oak Swamp, could easily have thrown a force of infantry in front of them. But, except for a few desultory and ineffective rounds from the gunboats, no further attempt was made to interfere with the progress of the Rebel column.

As the jubilant Stuart rode along en route to report to General Lee, Esten Cooke approached him. Still a bit shaken by the narrowness of their escape over the Chickahominy, Cooke said, "That was a tight place at the river, General. If the enemy had come down on us, you would have been compelled to have surrendered."

"No," Stuart disagreed. "One other course was left."

"What was that?" Cooke asked.

"To die game," came the curt reply.

General Lee listened, no doubt with delight, to the report of his young lieutenant's raid. One hundred sixty-five prisoners had been turned over to the provost marshal. Two hundred sixty horses and mules, along with a large quantity of captured arms and equipment had been placed at the quartermaster's disposal. Most important, however, Stuart confirmed Lee's suspicion that the Union right wing was in the air. Now, Lee was certain of the feasibility of his plan.

Strangely enough, the significance of what had happened seems never to have occurred to McClellan. In his official report submitted to the secretary of war in August 1863, "Little Mac" summarily dismissed the significance of the raid, saying, "The burning of two schooners laden with forage and fourteen government wagons, the destruction of some sutler's stores, the killing of several of the guard and teamsters at Garlick's Landing, some little damage done at Tunstall's Station, and a little *éclat* were the precise results of this expedition." How utterly wrong this was should have been apparent to him when the Confederate Army descended on his right wing and defeated it soundly at Cold Harbor on 27 June.

The South was wild with joy when Stuart's troopers rode into Richmond on the fifteenth. Robins reported, "The Southern papers were filled with accounts of the expedition, none accurate, and most of them marvelous."

Stuart's praises were sung to high heaven and his reputation as an outstanding cavalry leader assured. Continued success would later cause Union Maj. Gen. John Sedgewick, a veteran of the Mexican War and of six years of fighting Indians with the First Cavalry, to remark, "Jeb Stuart was the greatest cavalry officer ever foaled in America."

That Stuart was pleased with himself is beyond doubt. Telling Maj. Gen. James Longstreet, a Department of Northern Virginia division commander, about his ride, Jeb remarked that he had left one general behind on the trip. Longstreet asked him to identify the unfortunate soul who had fared so poorly. With a twinkling eye and a joyous laugh, Stuart replied, "General Consternation."

The success of Stuart's circuit of the Union Army did more than give Lee the information he desired. It reinforced the South's spirits. And, although the actual physical damage was not critical to the Union effort, it strengthened the notion in Washington that McClellan was too frequently embarrassed. Both Lee and McClellan were, in truth, guided by noble aspirations, but the watchword was action. Stuart's wild-riding troopers, described by Fitz Lee as a noble band of circuit-riders, drove this point home with distinct clarity.

CHAPTER II

A Stampede in Kentucky

The significance of Jeb Stuart's ride around the Army of the Potomac was not lost on other Confederate cavalry leaders eager to add to their laurels. None was more eager than the transplanted Alabamian who commanded a portion of Maj. Gen. E. Kirby Smith's cavalry guarding the Cumberland Gap, Col. John Hunt Morgan. In many ways, Morgan was cut from the same cloth as his Virginian counterpart. Like Stuart, this six-footer was a flashy dresser and always superbly mounted, studiously presenting the air and manner of a polished gentleman. But unlike Stuart, his military background was somewhat skimpy, although he had seen action in the Mexican War as a first lieutenant with the First Kentucky Cavalry. Leaving the service after the conflict, he occupied his time between wars as a merchant in Lexington, Kentucky. With the advent of hostilities, he quickly left this more mundane calling, leaping at the opportunity to return to the military. Like the West Pointer, Stuart, he possessed an innate talent for leading cavalry. He quickly demonstrated a knack for employing this natural ability to offset his lack of training and shortage of experience. Daring, shrewd, and fearless, he was determined to make his mark and make it soon.

Morgan was such a staunch advocate of developing a plan for invading Kentucky that he stubbornly and aggressively pushed for it at every opportunity. He argued forcefully with anyone in authority who would listen, that any positive move in that direction by the Confederacy would rouse this sleeping giant to the Rebel cause. The mere act of invading, he insisted, would result in thousands of Kentuckians rallying to the Southern banner. In an effort to prove his point, he badgered Smith for approval to conduct a cavalry raid into the area. Such a raid would, Morgan maintained, allow him to obtain recruits and horses, better equip and arm his men, reconnoiter a route for invasion, prove the enemy's weakness, and demonstrate the willingness of Kentucky's citizens to support the South. Now, he had what he needed to win the argument and enable him to prove the feasibility of his plan. Pointing out that Stuart had just impudently ridden around Maj. Gen. George B. McClellan's entire army, he sarcastically noted that ". . . it was a slur on the Blue Grass, the finest horse country in the world, to leave great riding to Virginia!"

Fortuitously for Morgan, Union actions had created an atmosphere conducive to such a raid. For whatever reasons, Maj. Gen. Henry W. Halleck, commanding the Department of Mississippi, had failed to capitalize on his stunning victory at Corinth. Instead of aggressively pursuing the advantage he had gained, he muddled around and made the worst decision available to him. He split his army.

Halleck had the forces of both Major General U. S. Grant and Maj. Gen. Don Carlos Buell available to him. Grant wanted to strike at Vicksburg, the last Rebel stronghold on the Mississippi River. But, Halleck would have none of it. Instead, he ordered Grant to hold in place and dispatched Buell to take Chattanooga. Buell moved out sluggishly and promptly got into trouble. His poorly executed attack ground slowly forward for a bit, then stalled out south of his objective.

With Grant tied down and Buell thrashing about ineffectively, Confederate leaders began thinking about the offensive and looked about for an opening that would permit them to grasp the initiative. One of the spots their searching gaze came to rest on was Kentucky, lying somnolently in the loose grip of Brig. Gen. Jeremiah T. Boyle's relatively small, poorly led Union force. To add to Confederate prospects, Boyle had little to recommend him as a commander. He was a border lawyer and slaveholder who had remained loyal to the Union, gaining his current rank as a result of his political contacts in President Lincoln's administration. Following the battle at Shiloh, he had been assigned to Kentucky where, for all practical purposes, he functioned as the governor. In this capacity, he had succeeded in earning the enmity of most Kentuckians because of his high-handed method of dealing with them.

Morgan did not miss the significance of the situation either. He immediately intensified his campaign to gain approval for his proposed raid into Kentucky. The favorable situation and Morgan's persistence proved too much for Kirby Smith. He finally agreed.

Not one to miss the significance of a date, on the Fourth of July, Morgan led his troops at a long gallop out of Knoxville and plunged into the rugged Cumberland Mountains headed for Sparta, Tennessee. The command consisted of Morgan's own Second Kentucky Cavalry, with Lt. Col. Basil W. Duke's Regiment, Capt. Richard M. Gano's Texans, and Col. A. A. Hunt's Georgia Battalion, a total of 867 men.

Raggedly uniformed and armed with an astonishing variety of rifles and shotguns, the raiders were a singularly unimpressive-looking military organization. In truth, their appearance would not have been inaccurately described had they been called rabble. And, the state of their discipline in most respects closely paralleled their appearance. The little they did possess they owed to the unflagging efforts of George St. Leger Grenfell, a veteran of both the British Army and the French Foreign Legion, and Morgan's adjutant without commission. This war-loving English military adventurer, who had seen combat in the Mediterranean area, the Crimea, India, Italy, and South America, was appalled at the state of Southern training and discipline. He had promptly made its improvement a personal challenge. He had labored mightily to mold the command into a disciplined military unit but had met with a notable lack of success. Nevertheless, despite the misgivings he must have felt, he would soon discover that lack of spit and polish had little to do with the fighting spirit or abilities of these free-spirited riders.

The raiders came under hostile fire the moment they entered the heavy forests of the Cumberlands. These mountains were infested by an unknown number of men who lived in the twilight zone of war. To a man, they were ruthless, wanton killers, more wild beast than human, owing allegiance to nothing, the war permitting them to rob and kill without fear of reprisal. As a sideline to their normal business of theft, rape, and murder, they missed no opportunity to assassinate any member of either army unfortunate enough to come within range of their long rifles.

Winding their way through the dark wooded valleys and over the deceiving ridges of the Cumberlands, the gray riders were constantly faced with the chilling terror of sniper fire from these murderous out-laws. Typically, the only warning the riders got of the presence of one of these predators was the hiss of a bullet tearing through the heavy summer air accompanied by the nasty snap of a rifle. Then, before the smoke of the shot could dissipate, the would-be killer would melt into the rough country, leaving no more trail than a ghost. Fortune was with the raiders, however. After enduring three days of incessant harassment from their invisible tormentors, Morgan's men rode out of the shadows of the rugged hills into the Cumberland River Valley, miraculously having lost only one man.

Lacking the detailed knowledge he needed of the country they were entering, Morgan had searched for and been given the name of a man he was assured could provide the expert knowledge he required. The raiders met him en route and added to their company a strange, glowering mountain man, who was akin to, if not one of, the silent killers that had harassed their passage through the Cumberlands.

An outlaw of wide fame, Champ Ferguson was a dedicated killer of Yankees. He had gained his justly deserved reputation after his wife and daughter had been molested by some Union soldiers and Home Guardsmen. As soon as he had learned of the atrocity, Ferguson embarked on a mission of revenge. Without delay, this grim mountaineer, who knew every inch of eastern Kentucky inti-mately, ferreted out every one of the assailants. As each went to ground, this hulking harbinger of death closed on him and merci-lessly snuffed out his life.

Ferguson's uncertain background and appetite for unbridled vio-lence caused some serious misgivings among Morgan's subordinates, particularly in his brother-in-law, Basil Duke. The commander would brook no objection, however, believing Ferguson's talent as a woods-man and encyclopedic knowledge of the region worth any risk his presence might entail and stuck with his decision to use him as their guide. Duke was forced to accept the fact that his commander was willing to ignore Ferguson's unsavory reputation, but could not bring himself to do so. In fact, he was both chagrined and appalled that his leader would turn a blind eye and accept such an individual. Unable to change Morgan's mind, Duke decided precautionary measures of some sort had to be taken and bluntly told Ferguson he could not, under any circumstance, murder captives.

Greatly offended, this remorseless hunter of men replied, "Why, Colonel Duke, I've got sense. I know it ain't looked on as right to treat reg'lar soldiers tuk in battle thataway."

True to his word, Ferguson not only conducted himself properly but proved to be invaluable as he led the group through the hostile country that stretched before them. The outlaw's skillful performance not only vindicated Morgan's decision but played a significant role in the later success achieved by the raiders.

Wasting no time, Ferguson led the force through Sparta, Tennessee toward the Cumberland River. They arrived there about midday on 8 July and paused to rest. Shortly, they were joined by a returning scout who brought welcome news to Morgan. They informed him that Tompkinsville, Kentucky, less than twenty miles away, was lightly held by 350 men of the Ninth Pennsylvania and a few Home Guards. Delighted with this news, Morgan decided to announce his arrival in the Blue Grass State by surprising and capturing this garrison. Scouts were dispatched to watch the enemy and report any change in their disposition while the remainder of the command, waiting for darkness, went skinny-dipping in the river or loafed in the deep shade of the trees lining the Cumberland's banks.

At eleven o'clock, the Rebels formed up in a column of fours and faded into the summer night. Moving deliberately, they wound forward over rough roads occasionally blocked by fallen trees, holding a pace that would permit them to arrive at their objective in the first pale light of daybreak. Gano and his Texans broke off five miles from the village to swing in a wide semicircle to the rear of the target to block any attempt the defenders might make at retreat. The main column held a direct route, arriving at five o'clock to find their attempt at surprise had been futile. The alert defenders had already drawn up before the town obviously prepared to fight.

Under the gaze of the defenders, Morgan very deliberately formed up his command—Hunt on the left, Duke on the right, the artillery in the center. As the troops settled into position, Morgan slowly looked up and down the line, then nodded almost casually to his bugler. At the first notes of "Charge" the raiders launched straight across the open field separating them from their adversaries. Disregarding an ineffective Union fusillade, the riders held their fire until within sixty yards of their targets, then fired a sudden volley. That was enough. The Pennsylvanians broke and ran only to meet Gano's Texans charging headlong into their rear. Trapped between two walls of gray riders, the bluecoats immediately surrendered. The clock had advanced a mere ten minutes. Morgan had four hundred prisoners, twenty wagons, fifty mules, rifles for all his men, and by his estimate, $500,000 worth of supplies. A pretty good return for the investment of one-sixth of an hour!

Stung to the quick by the unexpected Rebel onslaught, but doubtful as to Morgan's intentions, Union reaction was both sluggish and uncertain. Rather than moving quickly to block Morgan, Boyle confined his troop movements to a small effort to bolster Bowling Green and Munfordville. He then advised his superiors of the Rebel attack and, concerned about his limited strength, requested additional troops.

The raiders left Tompkinsville in the afternoon after sorting through their spoils and rode into Glasgow after midnight. Anxious to prove his contention that recruits were for the asking, Morgan hurried to publish a ringing proclamation urging local citizens to join him. Confident of success, he announced rather grandly, "Kentuckians! I have come to liberate you from the hands of your oppressors." Hard-riding couriers traveling at a long gallop carried this message far and wide but few of the "oppressed" responded.

The distribution of the proclamation underway, the command pushed on to Horse Cave Gorge, arriving at about nine o'clock in the morning. Bushed by the long night of riding, the raiders tried to grab a few minutes' rest while another unique Morgan man displayed his talents. George Elsworth, an expatriate Canadian who had joined the Southern cause, was a telegrapher without peer. He had the uncanny knack of being able to duplicate the "hand" of another operator after hearing him for only a few seconds. This wizard of the telegraph key now put his talent to full use. He cut into the telegraph line and engaged Louisville in conversation to obtain the intelligence Morgan needed. He then sent out a stream of orders, reports, and dispatches concocted by his leader to confuse the enemy. Among them was a report that Brig. Gen. Nathan Bedford Forrest had captured Murfreesboro, Tennessee. In fact, Morgan lacked definitive knowledge of Forrest's exact location or plans. But, in an almost unbelievable fluke of war, Forrest, who was raiding in Tennessee at the time, promptly captured the town as the bogus dispatch had announced.

While Elsworth practiced his magic, the raiders watched as massive storm clouds piled up in the sky and slowly drifted toward them. Nervously watching the storm's white-hot bolts of lightning probe the thunder-shaken countryside, the riders prepared to leave Horse Cave Gorge. One of them, seeing the hissing bolts of raw energy move ever closer to the telegraph wires as the telegrapher hurried to unhook, muttered, "Ole Lightnin' hisself." The name stuck and for the remainder of the war the transplanted Rebel answered to "Lightnin'."

The raiding column again moved hurriedly forward, halting only to allow a small force time to break off and destroy the railroad bridge between Lebanon and Lebanon Junction. Then, late in the afternoon, it surged again in the direction of Lebanon, reaching a covered bridge over the Rolling Fork River just after dark.

Morgan and his staff, well-out in front of the column and unaware of any obstacles before them, casually trotted onto the bridge as if out for an evening's pleasure ride. Suddenly, a yellow tongue of flame flickered toward them from the pitch blackness. As the drumming roar of a gunshot reverberated inside the heavy structure, Morgan felt the tug of a bullet whisk his hat into the darkness. Without concern for their dignity, the raider leaders dashed unceremoniously for cover.

The bridge was of critical importance to both sides. It offered the only respectable river crossing for six miles or so in either direction. Further, the terrain about it was such that it could easily be defended by a very small force. On the shore opposite the raiders, a steep cliff, heavily wooded on top, towered over the bridge.

Morgan, a bit shaken and uncertain of the strength and position of the bridge guard, moved up a howitzer and placed a platoon in readiness. At his command, the river's expanse shook with the sound of the field piece firing. Its round crashed down in the center of the bridge with a terrific blast, sending chunks of wood and splinters flying. The platoon charged behind the cannon's roar to find a large hole in the bridge but no sign of the guard. With only the slightest attempt at resistance, the bridge guard had abandoned this easily defended position. In so doing, they not only missed the opportunity to make the raiders pay dearly for passage, the Federals had handed Morgan a free pass to Lebanon.

Once over the river, the Rebel force formed up and charged down on the city. Game at last, the defenders spread out to meet the assault outside of town. Their effort was too little, too late. The gray wave of furiously charging horsemen rode over them without a pause. In minutes the town belonged to the raiders.

Lebanon gave up enormous stores along with 250 prisoners. The Rebels quickly took all the public property they could and destroyed the remainder. Private property did not fare much better. Morgan had issued orders to protect it, but they were ignored by many needy raiders who simply helped themselves to anything that caught their eye. And, according to a local citizen, did so without ". . . being guilty of proffering pay for anything."

Once again Morgan issued a proclamation, calling this time for ". . . the willing hands of fifty thousand of Kentucky's brave . . ." to join him in destroying ". . . the hireling legions of Lincoln." Once more the response was far less than overwhelming.

Boyle's initial misgivings rapidly grew into outright panic. His frantic state of mind was matched by that of Andrew Johnson, the military governor of Tennessee and future president. Together, they swamped Washington, army headquarters, and neighboring governors with requests, demands, complaints, and questionable intelligence. Messages from Boyle to Halleck, Buell, and the governors grossly overestimated Morgan's strength, pleaded abjectly for help, and talked darkly of Kentucky being overrun. To Washington, Boyle painted a brighter picture, suggesting that with a bit of help he could handle the situation. Johnson, for the most part, contented himself with demanding aid from both the president and the secretary of war; while the governors of Ohio and Indiana added their voices to the chorus, turning the telegraph lines into an electrical Tower of Babel. In the midst of the confusion hovering over the Union leadership, the Federal troops in Kentucky, bolstered by a few men from Indiana and Ohio, were frantically trying to get into position to corral the marauders.

Officialdom's response to the cries for help was, in the view of the supplicants, eminently unsatisfactory. Washington, in the typical bureaucratic fashion for which it remains renowned, contented itself with denying the demands made upon it and asking for more information. Pres. Abraham Lincoln told Halleck to talk to Johnson in an effort to calm him down. Buell ordered Boyle to throw up some fortifications, advised him Morgan's strength had been overestimated, and assured him that he had enough force to handle the Rebels. On the other hand, he privately acknowledged to Halleck that he might have to give Boyle some help. Halleck largely kept his opinions quiet, saying very little to anyone.

Having obtained or destroyed what they wanted in Lebanon, the raiders moved on, passing through Springfield, Harrodsburg, and Versailles. As the main column moved deliberately on its course, smaller detachments broke off from time to time to carry out limited missions. Gano and his hard-nosed Texans dashed behind Lexington to destroy a bridge on the Kentucky Central Railroad, isolating that city from Cincinnati. Capt. Thomas Allen led a group that destroyed all the bridges over the small streams between Lexington and Louisville. Others drove in the pickets guarding the roads to Frankfort while the main column made a slight feint toward the capital.

On the fifteenth, Morgan arrived at Midway and decided to put Lightnin' to work again. Quickly cutting into the telegraph wires, Elsworth began monitoring Union traffic. The telegrapher soon discovered the raiders were in potentially serious trouble. A strong Federal column was moving toward them from Frankfort, a second waited at Lexington, a third was at Cynthiana, and a fourth at Paris. Furthermore, the Union commanders now knew the Rebel strength and had guessed correctly that they were headed for Georgetown. While Elsworth listened, Brig. Gen. William T. Ward in Lexington arranged a movement in conjunction with Col. John Finnell in Frankfort to crush Morgan between them.

Now keenly attuned to his danger, Morgan decided to avert it by taking ". . . the liberty of advising the Federal forces where he wanted them." At his leader's direction, Lightin' assumed the identity of the Midway operator and told Lexington, "Morgan with upward of one thousand men, came within a mile of here, and took the old Frankfort Road, marching, we suppose, for Frankfort. This is reliable."

Ward, a former U.S. representative, accepted the message at face value, relayed it to Frankfort and suggested the force en route to Georgetown be recalled. Elsworth listened to the orders, then broke into the busy circuit, killed the line to Frankfort, and frantically tapped out, "Frankfort to Lexington: Tell General Ward our pickets are just driven in. Great excitement. Pickets say the force of the enemy must be two thousand. Operator." Then the line went dead. As the Federals violently recoiled to meet this unexpected development, the raiders jogged out toward Georgetown.

The composure momentarily shown by the field commanders, who had almost trapped Morgan, was not reflected at other levels. In Cincinnati, newspapers headlined, PANIC AT UNION HQ IN LOUISVILLE; public meetings were held at various locations; and a battery of city police and firemen were dispatched to Lexington. In the hope of gaining control of something, authorities clamped martial law on that unfortunate city. So great was the fear and confusion surrounding the situation, that Lexington's provost marshal said rather grandiloquently, "Everything here seems stagnant and three-fourths of the stores and manufactures are closed; every face wears a sickly, frightened look; men speak to each other of Morgan as though his name were to them that of Richard the Lion-Hearted was to the Saracens."

In Louisville, Boyle's panic was exceeded only by his confusion. He continued to fire off messages in every direction. Washington, Halleck, Buell, and the neighboring governors were all beseeched to send help and warned of imminent Rebel uprisings in the state. The paper-shufflers in Washington fumed, procrastinated, and demanded more information while Buell tried to calm the frantic Boyle by promising him some assistance. The one man who seemed to fully keep his perspective, Lincoln, was convinced the situation had been blown completely out of proportion. Totally exasperated, he wired Halleck, "They are having a stampede in Kentucky. Please look to it."

Forging steadily forward, the column arrived at Georgetown near sundown to find it defended by a force of Home Guards. Morgan immediately demanded they surrender unconditionally or prepare to suffer the consequences. Startled by the brusqueness of the demand presented to him, the leader of the Home Guards hesitated only momentarily. Then, without ever facing his enemy, he turned to his men and made what has to have been one of the more astonishing speeches of the war. Perhaps rising above the occasion, he said, "Morgan, the marauder and murderer—the accursed of the Union men of Kentucky is coming down on us. Behind him in his track everywhere there prevails terror and desolation. In his rear, the smoke of burning towns is ascending, the blood of martyred patriots is streaming, the wails of widows and orphaned children are resounding. In his front, Home Guards and soldiers are flying. Tom Long reports him just outside of town, with ten or twelve thousand men, armed with long beards and butcher knives. I think we had better scatter and take care of ourselves."

Scatter they did. As part of them raced through the town seeking a safe haven, they were spotted by a group of Southern sympathizers who were imprisoned in the courthouse. One of the confined men wriggled as far as possible out of a window and pointed to the Stars and Stripes waving over the building. In words described as sufficient to make a sutler fight, he shouted, "Are you going to desert your flag? Remain, and perform the pleasing duty of dying under its glorious folds, and afford us the agreeable spectacle that you will thus present."

Duke reported, "This touching appeal was of no avail." Morgan's men trotted into town unopposed.

The confusion that engulfed the Federal high command was contagious. The befuddlement that plagued the military was often reflected in the acts of ordinary citizens. The divisiveness of the war only added to the general confusion that prevailed. People living in the same locality frequently had difficulty keeping track of the loyalties of neighbors and acquaintances. An experience of Gano's as he was returning from spreading confusion around Lexington illustrates the sort of embarrassment that often resulted.

Gano had once lived in Georgetown and knew almost everyone in the area. When he was a few miles from the village, he stopped at an old friend's house to feed his men. Word of the presence of supposedly friendly troops in the vicinity was promptly carried into town. On hearing of them, the most committed Union man in the area mounted his horse and left at a gallop to obtain their aid in disposing of Morgan. He charged up to the house sheltering the Rebels, slid his foam-flecked horse to a stop in a shower of gravel, and shouted for their commander. Gano sauntered out and nodded to him.

"Why, how are you, Dick?" the surprised man asked. "I didn't know that you were in the Union Army. I've got something for you old fellow."

Gano assured the man he would be happy to oblige him.

"Where is the commander of these men?" the visitor inquired.

"I am their commander," replied Gano.

"Well, then here's an order for you," the visitor said, handing him a dispatch from Home Guard Headquarters.

Gano slowly read it, then, in a tone of deep concern, said, "Oliver, I should be truly sorry to see you injured. We were schoolmates, and I remember our early friendship."

The Union man stood transfixed as it slowly dawned on him that he had made a terrible mistake.

"Oliver," Gano continued, "isn't it possible that you may be mistaken in these troops? To which army do you think they belong?"

Clearly dreading the answer, Oliver asked in a choked voice, "Why, ain't they Union?"

"Union!" Gano spat. "Don't let them hear you say so, I mightn't be able to control them. They are Morgan's Texas Rangers." And, with that, he led the crestfallen and speechless Oliver off to join a group of prisoners being held nearby.

Morgan took advantage of the paralysis that gripped the Union forces and spent two days in Georgetown resting his command. Having positioned himself nearly equidistant from all opposing forces, he could respond rapidly to any move they might make. He took advantage of this brief respite to send Kirby Smith a message assuring him, if he would invade Kentucky, up to thirty thousand men would join him. He also surmised that he could hold the country outside of Lexington and Frankfort until Smith joined him. He had virtually no basis for making either statement. Contrary to his glowing estimate, the natives had shown little eagerness to follow his colors. Furthermore, it was obviously only a matter of a short time before the Union would overwhelm him unless he moved. As it was, throughout the two days spent in the town, Morgan's men had rested in line of battle and his patrols were kept busy driving away Union pickets.

On the eighteenth, it was clear to Morgan that he had to get out of the state immediately or he'd run the risk of losing everything. He decided to leave. With Ferguson laying out the route, he faked at both Lexington and Paris, then drove straight for Cythiana. His aim was to give the impression that he was headed for Cincinnati while, in fact, he was gaining access to a choice of escape routes.

The raiders were about to discover that Cythiana was a considerably tougher problem than they had encountered to this point. It was situated behind the Licking River and held by four hundred of Metcalfe's cavalry and some Home Guards commanded by Lieutenant Colonel T. J. Landram. The only direct access to it was a single covered bridge on the outskirts of town. Landram had deployed his troops along the riverfront and placed his lone artillery piece, a twelve-pounder, in position to command the bridge. The Federal troops were determined to hold "their" town and were braced for the Rebel attack they anticipated.

As Morgan's column approached, it split apart, the Texans turning north and the Georgians south, to flank the town. Companies E and F of the Second Kentucky moved forward along the sides of the road keeping under cover as best they could. The Kentuckians were welcomed by a hailstorm of Federal bullets as soon as they came into range, but struggled through it to the river's edge. Spreading along the banks and keeping under cover, they were able to direct such a scathing fire at the exposed defenders opposite them that the Yankees surrendered even though no Rebels had crossed the river. Then, to add insult to injury, the Rebels forced the beaten bluebirds to flounder across the shallow river to join them as prisoners.

As this part of the fight played out, A Company tried to force its way directly across the bridge but fell back in the face of heavy enemy fire. They rallied and again attempted to drive across the bridge but reeled back before the blasts of the twelve-pounder and deadly accurate fire from sharpshooters posted in riverfront buildings. Determined to gain their objective, the troopers finally leaped into the river and waded frantically across, holding their arms and ammunition above their heads. As they floundered along, man after man sank into the bloody water as Yankee bullets searched out victims among the struggling band. Despite the gaps in their ranks, the survivors plunged doggedly ahead until they reached the eastern shore. Here they huddled under what scanty cover they could find and opened fire. Still, the Federal sharpshooters continued to pick them off.

Just when it appeared the beleaguered A Company troopers would be forced back into the water, the howitzers came up. The cannon quickly swung into position and opened a steady fire on the town's defenders. This gave the Rebels the edge they needed and, under cover of the barrage, C Company charged. They crossed the bridge at a full gallop, thundering straight up the town's main street, yelling at the top of their lungs and firing at anything blue. This sudden change in the situation and the deadly fire of the riders demanded the undivided attention of the defenders. As they braced to contain this challenge, other forces moved to relieve the suffering of the pinned down A Company.

C Company's success permitted B Company to move into position to enfilade the sharpshooters and lift the cloud of death hovering over A Company's decimated ranks. That unit wasted no time in enjoying their respite. They immediately jumped to their feet and charged into town. As they rushed forward, the Texans and Georgians raced in from both flanks. The three groups quickly converged on the Union cannon and put it out of action. The loss of this support caused the Federals to begin to retreat. As they moved back, the retreating troops fought stubbornly to keep the raiders from overwhelming them. The main Union force moved rather deliberately back until they reached the railroad station. Once there, they barricaded the structure and again made a stand. So fierce was their resistance from this stronghold that the fight threatened to become a stalemate.

At this opportune moment the fierce old Englishman, Grenfell, appeared on the scene. Wearing a bright red cap and waving a drawn sword, he made his way among the attackers to take the lead. Cursing, cajoling, and threatening, he rapidly formed up the attackers and led a wild charge on the station. The Federals threw their all into a last effort to avoid defeat. It was to no avail. Plunging reck-lessly through a sheet of stinging lead, the Rebels broke into the blue bastion as its defense crumbled. The defenders simply could not contain the final Confederate effort. Afterward, however, Grenfell could attest to the stubbornness of their resistance as he looked at the horse shot from under him and counted eleven bullet holes in his own uniform.

The beaten survivors retreated rapidly to the east, just ahead of a furious Confederate pursuit. Determined to allow no one to escape, Morgan's men pressed hard and eventually captured most of them, although their commander managed to outdistance his would-be cap-tors. The Union lost a total of 510 men, both killed and captured, in the engagement. As in other towns, large stores of supplies and equipment fell into Rebel hands. What they could not immediately use or take with them was quickly burned.

Rapidly wrapping up their business in Cythiana, the riders trotted out of town at two o'clock in the afternoon. They pushed steadily through the countryside, along a route laid out by Ferguson, toward Paris. About five miles outside their destination, they were met by the city fathers who surrendered the town. Taking advantage of an opportunity to rest, the raiders paused to await word from their scouts. They did not have long to wait. Soon scouts came riding in to report that a force of about twenty-five hundred men under Brig. Gen. G. Clay Smith was bearing down on them from Lexington.

The Rebel command, feeling the pressure of pursuit, got underway early the next morning. They pushed steadily ahead all day, following a route that took them to Winchester where they crossed the Kentucky River just before their pursuers. They continued their march through the summer darkness until four o'clock in the morning when they arrived at Richmond and halted for much needed rest. Holding there for twelve hours, Morgan's force then moved forward under cover of darkness, arriving at Crab Orchard at daylight. They rested for a few hours and moved again, arriving at Somerset at sundown the next day.

Clay Smith, for reasons known only to him, had not pressed the pursuit, but had contented himself with simply tailing the raiders. Other Union forces were acting with more determination, however, as additional blue troops moved rapidly toward the fleeing raiders. Col. Frank Wolford was pressing hard from the south and a large force was rushing toward them from Louisville. The commanders of these troops were fully aware of Morgan's strength and, if given time, were confident they could obliterate him.

Time was the one element Morgan had no intention of providing, though he still had work left to do. Somerset contained large stores of arms, ammunition, clothing, blankets, and shoes. The raiders hastened to turn these supplies into a conflagration before time ran out. As the destruction progressed, Morgan told Lightin' to hook up, he had some telegraph traffic to send. Elsworth quickly cut into the line and soon his flying fingers were tapping out a series of "complimentary" messages. Both Washington and Louisville were recipients of these unwelcome, sarcastic, and chiding wires that undoubtedly raised hackles everywhere they landed. And, none must have smarted more than Morgan's farewell to Boyle. It read, "Good morning, Jerry! This telegraph is a great institution. You should destroy it, as it keeps me too well posted. My friend Elsworth has all of your dispatches since July 10 on file. Do you wish copies?"

Their work done, the raiders swung to horse and followed their laughing leader out of town. They marched to Stagall's Ferry, crossed the Cumberland River, and disappeared into the green-blanketed mountains that had hidden their approach.

The Rebels had spent a total of twenty-four days behind enemy lines, ridden over one thousand miles, captured seventeen towns, and destroyed hundreds of thousands of dollars' worth of Union supplies and arms. Over fifteen hundred Home Guards had been scattered, twelve hundred Regulars captured and paroled, and three hundred recruits added to Rebel rolls. In addition, Morgan had completely equipped, armed, and mounted his force. Federal weakness in the region had been clearly demonstrated with the results that Kentucky and its neighboring states were pervaded with gloom and no little fear. The cost to Morgan had been about ninety men.

Recriminations for the Confederate success started among Union officials early in the raid and continued well after it ended. The silent Halleck, once summed up by Secretary of the Navy Gideon Welles as one who ". . . originates nothing, anticipates nothing, . . . takes no responsibility, plans nothing, suggests nothing, is good for nothing . . ." had no trouble spotting the problem this time. In an indignant message to Buell, he informed him, "The stampede among our troops was utterly disgraceful." He also ordered him to have the matter thoroughly investigated to identify officers deserving dismissal. The list available to choose from was more than ample, for at crucial points most of the Union leaders had succumbed to panic, timidity, and fear. In doing so, they became sheep—easy prey for the lean, gray wolves who rushed among them.

CHAPTER III

Storm in the Morning

A sagging of Union expectations in the summer of 1862 was countered by a sudden glow of vitality that suffused the South. Northern military leadership had fumbled badly across the board, resulting in a sharp decline in the willingness of the northern populace to support their nation's efforts. Where only two months earlier confidence had been so high that recruiting stations were closed, bewilderment and panic had now taken over. Manpower was no longer plentiful and Secretary of War Edwin Stanton was forced to earnestly appeal to the Northern states for more soldiers as the North's ability to prosecute the war came into question. So bad was the situation that only the indomitable will of Abraham Lincoln held the faltering blue armies and wavering nation together. These same circumstances that had permitted Col. John Hunt Morgan to romp through Kentucky also opened the way for another Rebel foray to the South.

When Maj. Gen. Don Carlos Buell finally broke his fascination with repairing the Memphis and Charleston Railroad and began to move in earnest toward Chattanooga, Tennessee in mid-June, Gen. P. T. G. Beauregard decided to make a move of his own. He began by ordering a rising cavalry star, Col. Nathan Bedford Forrest, to that location. Forrest's initial orders were no more than to take charge of several cavalry units there and to organize them into an effective fighting force.

On receipt of these orders, Forrest promptly relinquished command of his "Old Regiment" and made preparations to assume his new command. He chose ten men to assist him in his assignment, including his brother Bill. This group set out from Tupelo, Mississippi on a humid, rainy morning in early June of 1862. Traveling steadily toward Chattanooga, passing well south of Buell's army as it laboriously churned along the railroad, they arrived at their destination at the end of the third week of June.

Forrest, the son of an impoverished backwoods blacksmith who had been forced to assume responsibility for a large family at age sixteen, had become a success despite considerable odds against him. Rising from these humble beginnings, he had parlayed hard work and native shrewdness to achieve success as a plantation owner and slave trader. By his account, he was a millionaire at the time the Civil War began. A native Tennessean committed to the Southern cause, he had enlisted as a private in Josiah White's cavalry in June 1861. His enlisted service was short-lived, however, as a result of the governor asking him to raise a battalion of cavalry. He did so and was commissioned a lieutenant colonel as commander of Forrest's Tennessee Cavalry Battalion in October 1861. Despite a total lack of military training, he moved up rapidly, demonstrating an innate ability to successfully direct military operations. Possessed of a terrible temper and a driving dedication to success, this grim-countenanced warrior would rise to lieutenant general and earn a reputation as one of the premier cavalry leaders of the war. After the war, his dedicated opponent, Maj. Gen. William T. Sherman said of him, "After all, I think Forrest was the most remarkable man our Civil War produced on either side."

Forrest found his new command a motley group. Except for Terry's Rangers, the Eighth Texas, who had fought with him before, almost all the troops were disaffected and badly in need of both training and supplies. The new commander wasted no time in immediately putting those characteristics that earned him both fear and respect to effective use in resolving the problem that faced him. By alternately cursing them, praising them, and threatening to shoot them himself if his orders were not carried out, he rapidly jolted his new troops into a unit possessing some degree of order and discipline. It became an outfit with a reasonable prospect of being able to fight effectively. Once past the initial stages, Forrest planned to use action to complete the training they so sorely needed and the enemy as his source of supplies to equip them. Unwilling to waste time, he plunged into action as quickly as possible, following his underlying philosophy and guiding principle that everything his troopers did would ultimately bring harm to their opponents. He had no inclination toward niceties, technicalities, or formal organizing.

At the end of June and, by sheer luck of the draw, in conjunction with John Morgan's raid through Kentucky, Forrest was ordered into Middle Tennessee. Specifically, he was directed to observe the progress of Buell's army, take whatever action he could to hinder its movement pending Chattanooga's reinforcement, and break or disrupt Buell's communications network.

These instructions, simple as they were, assigned Forrest a task that most military leaders would have considered out of the question. Forrest's command consisted of one thousand stale, poorly trained and disciplined troopers suffering from low morale. In addition to his troubles, the organization was characterized by internecine quarrels over priority of rank. When informed of the mission, a senior Confederate officer abruptly dismissed the idea of ordering a token force to a position two hundred miles from their base of support with the intent to delay an army of thirty thousand as ". . . rash, inconsiderate, and likely to lead to disaster." Events would soon demonstrate this estimate to be no fair appraisal of the capabilities of Bedford Forrest. It failed to take into account that this man did not do, or even think of doing, what other commanders would most likely do in a campaign or battle.

On 10 July 1862, Forrest's command moved out. It was a blistering hot day in an exceptionally dry season in eastern Tennessee. As the column trotted through the parched countryside, they were engulfed in a cloud of clinging clay dust churned up by their mounts. The boiling dust marking their passage soon covered them in a heavy layer, turning the column into a uniform earth color and adding to the discomfort of the unremitting heat. Maintaining a mile-eating pace despite the crushing heat, they progressed rapidly, reaching and crossing the Tennessee River at midmorning. The river's cool water gave the sweating men a brief respite from the stifling heat and choking dust, but their misery resumed as soon as it fell behind.

A few miles beyond the river, a new misery was added as the column began to ascend the heights of Walden's Ridge. The steep incline was covered with thick underbrush that soon destroyed the order of the march, turning the force into a ragged mass of cursing, sweating men and straining animals. Forrest granted no respite, however, and by late afternoon the last elements had trickled over the summit. Dropping down the other side, the reformed column began to wind across the Sequatchie Valley, moving well north of the Federal Army, edging eastward toward Chattanooga. As dusk approached, the Rebel command began a gradual climb to the summit of the Cumberland Mountain Plateau, the weary riders grateful to escape the heat of the valley below. Night found them bivouacked around a faded frame courthouse in the tiny mountain hamlet of Altamount, Tennessee.

Dawn broke clear and mild on the eleventh. Forrest's column greeted it in the saddle. The first rays of the morning sun found them trotting into Beersheba Springs, a decaying resort once used by the aristocracy of the lower South as a summer refuge from the ravages of Yellow Fever. Mrs. Armfield, wife of the town's founder, greeted the men warmly and provided each mess orderly a supply of coffee. In an impatient, snappy mood, Forrest did not tarry. He turned the column down the Cumberland Mountains toward McMinnville. As evening shadows closed about them, the raiders arrived at Rock Martin's, between Sparta and McMinnville, where two companies of Spiller's Battalion of Tennessee cavalry under Maj. Baxter Smith and two independent companies of Kentucky cavalry waited to join them. Forrest's command, now fourteen hundred strong, pressed on to McMinnville, going into camp there late that night.

The first shafts of light were just streaking the morning sky on the twelfth when Forrest called his key staff officers to his smoldering campfire. Coffee was poured all-round and, as it smacked their stomachs, their leader informed them he intended to capture Murfreesboro, Tennessee. He directed them to make necessary preparations for a rapid march over the forty-six miles of Tennessee's rolling hills that separated them from their objective and to be prepared for an immediate assault on the garrison when they arrived. They were told there would be only one short rest stop at Woodbury in order to water the horses. With the order to make ready for departure at 1:00 P.M., the officers were dismissed. As they walked into the breaking day, other events were unfolding that would startle both them and their opponents.

Over in the once "dark and bloody ground" that had become Kentucky, Morgan slowed his wild dash through the Bluegrass long enough for his man, Lightnin' Elsworth to send a message to the federal provost marshal at Lexington. This "dispatch" reported that Forrest had taken Murfreesboro, was moving on Nashville, and warned that Morgan and Forrest would soon be acting in concert. By sheer coincidence, the gods of war smiled on Morgan's little game, for shortly a raging Forrest would transform the first part of Morgan's fabrication into brutal truth.

On the morning of the twelfth, Murfreesboro's inhabitants and the Union soldiers stationed there awakened to an apparently peaceful day, unaware of the bolt of lightning about to strike them. This little town, situated a short distance to the east of Stone's River and the Nashville and Chattanooga Railroad, had been largely untouched by the war. Lulled into complacency by its relaxed atmosphere, the Federal garrison had been dispersed throughout the area. Five companies of the Ninth Michigan Volunteers and one squadron of the Fourth Kentucky Cavalry under Lt. Col. John G. Parkhurst were camped about a mile east of town near the Liberty Turnpike; the Ninth Michigan Infantry and a detachment of the Seventh Pennsylvania Cavalry under Col. William Duffield occupied the eastern edge of town, including the courthouse and jail; and the Third Minnesota Infantry and Hewett's Kentucky Battery of four guns under Col. Henry C. Lester, who was also garrison commander, were situated about one and one-half miles from town on the east bank of Stone's River. The total force was about equal in number to Forrest's command.

The lackadaisical attitude of the garrison's commander had permitted the Union forces to become dangerously separated and had also allowed discipline to slip. Duties were perfunctorily performed and frequent quarrels and brawls erupted among the troops. A command-wide state of indifference and lethargy was the first impression of Brig. Gen. Thomas T. Crittenden when he arrived on the twelfth to relieve Lester. His initial reaction and worst fears were quickly confirmed as he made his first inspection of the completely relaxed garrison. His immediate irritation at what he considered an inexcusable state of affairs was slowly replaced by a growing feeling of unease as the vulnerability of his command became apparent. His findings and intentions were summed up later when he commented, "I found things negligently and loosely done at the post and attempted to remedy all the negligence I saw there."

A nephew of the famous Sen. John J. Crittenden, the general was a lawyer with an extremely limited military background. Born in Alabama, he had relocated to Missouri where he practiced law prior to the Mexican War. He volunteered his services when war broke out and served as a lieutenant of Missouri volunteers. He returned to his

law practice following the war and was living in Indiana at the outbreak of the current hostilities. Joining the Union, although he had
many relatives who went with the Confederacy, he had fought at
Philippi, Carrick's Ford, and Shiloh prior to moving to command at
Murfreesboro.

Although Crittenden had quickly and accurately summed up the
state of his command, perhaps because of his limited experience, he
failed to act with a sense of urgency to set things right. Despite his
misgivings, he saw no reason not to wait until the next day to reorga-
nize and concentrate his forces. For the time being, he contented
himself with doubling the number of patrols going out each day
along the five turnpikes radiating from town. Unknown to him, from
force of long habit all patrols returned to the comfort of town each
night, leaving the roads unguarded. Firmly in the grasp of circumstance, the uneasy general went to bed that night oblivious to the
peril racing toward him.

At 1:30 P.M. on the twelfth, Forrest drew up his command in formal readiness and rode slowly in front of them. The air was balmy,
the men were rested, and Forrest was at his best. He confirmed
Murfreesboro was their target and told them they would cover about
forty-six miles at a rapid pace and then immediately begin an attack.
Smiling, he went on to say that Murfreesboro would be his forty-first
birthday present and first victory as a brigadier general. He then
waved them forward. With a cheer swelling through the ranks, the
column trotted off into the summer afternoon.

Throughout the afternoon and evening the gray riders moved
steadily through the rolling foothills. As darkness closed in, a gentle
breeze fanned men and animals as they jogged along. In this peaceful
stillness the anger and agony of war seemed a bitter unreality. Images
of homes, wives, and children crowded pleasantly into their thoughts.
For a brief moment, the power of the mind obliterated the savagery
of reality. But, as it always does, reality returned. At eleven o'clock,
the gray troopers rode into Woodbury, about nineteen miles from
Murfreesboro.

As soon as the column halted inside the town, Forrest was engulfed
by a swarm of furious women. From the ensuing clamor, he was able
to discern that the federal provost marshal at Murfreesboro, Capt.
Oliver Cromwell Rounds, had incarcerated most of the local men in
the Murfreesboro jail and the ladies were demanding that he promptly do something about it. After listening patiently, he assured the
women their menfolk would be home before the next sundown. With

that, the women filled the Rebels with food and tales of Yankee perfidy. The raiders rested for two hours, slowly realizing the fatigue that had crept upon them. At 1:00 A.M. on 13 July, Forrest's forty-first birthday, the command was on the road again.

Anticipation mounted as the riders moved forward, seized in the grip of uneasiness that precedes combat. After three hours, Forrest's men were five miles out of Murfreesboro. At this point, Forrest commanded the troopers to halt, dismount, fix saddles, and tighten girths. In a few moments, fatigue forgotten, the raiders moved slowly forward with their commander in the lead. It was characteristic of Forrest to put himself at the extreme forefront when approaching an encounter because he did not entirely trust even the best scouts.

As the command neared the town, scouts reported a fifteen-man Union picket just ahead. Forrest quietly directed Col. John A. Wharton, a Tennessee born, Texas educated lawyer who had fought with distinction at Shiloh, and a small detachment to circle behind the blue soldiers and capture them before they could sound the alarm. Moving quickly but silently though the darkness, Wharton's men approached the pickets hoping to be taken as Union cavalry. When challenged, they responded that they were a company of Seventh Pennsylvania Cavalry en route to join their command in Murfreesboro. The ruse came off successfully. The pickets were surrounded and captured without a shot being fired.

With surprise working to his advantage, Forrest decided to use his main force to attack the town and Duffield's forces. Col. J. K. Lawton was ordered to position his regiment between Lester's troops and the town. His job was to engage Lester at long distance and hold him at the river until the full force could strike him. At 4:30 A.M., his troop dispositions made, Forrest commanded his warriors forward at a gallop.

Murfreesboro was in the deep sleep of early morning. The only souls stirring were a few early-rising cooks chopping firewood. Inside the jail at the center of town, James Paul, a Confederate spy, and Capt. William Richardson, a Confederate officer, both of whom had been informed that they were to be executed as spies, were sharing a cell. Richardson was shaken awake by Paul who told him, "Listen! Listen!" Moving to the window, they listened as a strange noise rapidly permeated the night. The sound was akin to that of an approaching storm as the hooves of more than a thousand horses traveling at a free gallop beat upon the turnpike. Standing on a box in their cell, the prisoners watched the blurred shapes of men and horses swirl through the darkness and listened to the drumming of hoof-beats intermingled with the blood-curdling Rebel yell, the roar of double-barreled shotguns, and the staccato snaps of revolvers. While most of the Confederate advance wave charged by, several stopped at the jail and began working to get inside.

The Federals stationed inside the jail and the prison yard, seeing they were about to be surrounded, suddenly turned vindictive. Several of them rushed into the passageway in front of the prisoners' cells and attempted to shoot them. The prisoners saved themselves from this vicious attack by crouching in the corner by their cell doors where the Federals could not bring their guns to bear on them. It quickly became apparent to the guards that they must vacate the jail or be captured. Before leaving, however, one fired some papers and shoved the flaming bundle beneath loose planks in the flooring of the hallway. He then fled with the string of keys. The fire spread rapidly, threatening to engulf the prisoners before Forrest's men would be able to bend the grating on the heavy metal door sufficiently for them to be dragged under a lower corner flat on their backs. As the rescue effort was in progress, Forrest rode by and was told of the attempts to shoot and burn the prisoners and that the guilty guards had taken refuge in the nearby courthouse. In a deadly quiet voice, he told his troops, "Never mind. We'll get them later."

Forrest's attack was working well. Lawton's Georgians finished with the jail while Morrison's Georgians and four companies of Rangers surrounded the courthouse. Squads of Texans quickly began searching taverns and houses looking for the provost marshal but set-tling for any Yankee they could find. Forrest watched the search's progress from his horse as he rode slowly about, his dark features making him look a bit like a gray-clad Satan in the fitful light cast by burning buildings. Finally, a shaking lady of the town told Forrest that the much sought out Capt. Oliver Cromwell Rounds was most likely in the home of one of the town's more reputable ladies. Forrest directed the house to be searched immediately, and Rounds was reportedly found between two featherbeds. Laughing raiders jerked him from the house in his nightshirt, mounted him on a horse, and galloped him down the main street of Murfreesboro, the nightshirt flapping in the breeze.

By this time, the thoroughly aroused town was in a wild uproar. Citizens streamed into the streets in their excitement with little regard for their own safety. One lady described the scene, "We sprang from our beds and rushed to the windows to see the streets full of gray-coated, dusty cavalrymen, while . . . bang! bang! bang! was heard in every direction. The glad cry of 'our boys have come' rang from one end of the town to the other, and staid, elderly citizens clapped their hands in delight . . . that day when the rebels burst so suddenly upon us was the happiest day experienced by the citizens of Murfreesborough during the war."

Meanwhile, Wharton's Rangers charged into the tents of the Ninth Michigan, firing in all directions, sending befuddled Union soldiers scampering over each other. However, in the confusion of the initial charge, four of Wharton's companies had become separated, mistakenly rushing into town with the Georgians. This weakened Wharton sufficiently to prevent him from immediately overwhelming the Michigan troopers and gave them time to rally behind a makeshift barricade of wagons. From this position, they poured heavy fire into the attacking Rangers, forcing them to fall back. Wharton, painfully wounded, withdrew his men four miles back on the Woodbury Pike. Unknown to Forrest, his rear was left uncovered by Wharton's withdrawal.

In other action, Maj. Baxter Smith, with a battalion of Tennesseans and Kentuckians, surrounded and captured the Seventh Pennsylvania Cavalry just as they were preparing to mount. Then, following Forrest's orders, Smith swung his force out on the Nashville and Lebanon Pike to cut off any Federal retreat in that direction. Simultaneously, Lawton maneuvered his regiment between the Union forces under Lester and the town proper. Lawton was in a precarious position, however, because his men were exposed to Lester's artillery.

Back in the center of town, Morrison's Georgians and the four companies of misplaced Rangers were having difficulty with the courthouse. This solid structure was proving able to withstand the best the attackers could bring to bear since they had no artillery. Determined to take it, they charged several times but each time were driven back. Forrest finally arrived on the scene and changed the assault tactics. He organized storming parties and told them to go forward in single file. The lead man in each party was given an axe, and the party was instructed to keep it in the air until the doors were battered down. This relay effort did the trick and the doors gave way. The defenders hung on stubbornly, however, until they were driven into the arms of their captors by the stench of smoke from smoldering fires, fueled by cloth and manure and lit for that purpose. Among those captured was General Crittenden who was severely criticized later, probably unfairly, for his lack of preparation. In any event, this action ended his career. He was finally exchanged in October and resigned from the service the following May.

The town was now in Confederate custody. Forrest summoned the former prisoner Captain Richardson, and the two walked down the line of sullen Union prisoners. As they slowly passed the first man, Forrest said, "They tell me these men treated you inhumanely while in jail. Point them out to me."

Richardson told him there was but one man he wished to call to his attention, the one who had set fire to the jail. Forrest instructed him to do so. Sometime later, when the list of private soldiers was being called out, this man did not answer. The name was repeated— still no answer. Before it could be called a third time, Forrest commanded in a cold voice, "Pass on. It's all right." There was a brief silence, then the roll call continued.

His position in the town secure, Forrest turned his attention to the Federal forces under Lester who had formed a line of battle and were fitfully skirmishing with Lawton's Regiment which blocked access to the town. As he moved to engage Lawton, Lester left a hundred men strongly fortified behind wagons in his camp by the river. Forrest, with six companies of Tennesseans and Kentuckians, quickly circled to the rear of Lester's line to attack this force. The initial charge at this makeshift fortress was thrown back in confusion and disorder. Forrest angrily reformed the gray horsemen and commanded Smith to lead a second charge. Smith tied his reins to his saddle and, with pistol in one hand and saber in the other, led a determined charge but was again beaten back by withering sheets of Yankee lead. Forrest, now white-hot with rage, regrouped the disorganized troopers, holding them back long enough to deliver a blistering tongue-lashing, swearing he would no longer tolerate such a disgraceful performance in language that even his dullest soldier vividly understood. This time Forrest led the charge himself, hurdling his recently motivated troopers over wagons and rock ledges into the stunned bluecoats. This settled the issue. The reaction of the Yankees was later described by Forrest when he wrote, "They run like Suns of Biches."

As Forrest's men overran the rear guard, Lawton's raiders heard the firing and thought it was an attack on the rear of Lester's line. Lawton immediately ordered a charge that overran Lester's front. The Federal commander soon reformed the broken line, however, and took up a holding position on a hill.

Now aware of Wharton's withdrawal on the Woodbury Pike and the danger this posed, Forrest decided not to attack Lester. He left enough force to hold him in place, sent for Wharton's squadron and moved back to Murfreesboro.

It was now one o'clock in the afternoon, and several of Forrest's staff informed him of the urgent need to get out of Murfreesboro, accurately pointing out the danger of their being cut off by Union forces from Lebanon, Shelbyville, and Nashville. With a cold stare, Forrest dismissed their concern, "I did not come here to make half a job of it, I mean to have them all."

Forrest now spread his forces around the Ninth Michigan still in position on the eastern edge of town. The unit was now under the command of Parkhurst since Duffield had been seriously wounded earlier in the fighting. Forrest ordered Smith's men to dismount and charge the Federal barricades under covering fire provided by the remainder of the force. With the firing at its fiercest, Forrest, under a flag of truce, sent a blunt message forward. Parkhurst looked at it and forwarded it to his wounded commander. Duffield was startled by its contents. It read, "Colonel: I must demand an unconditional surrender of your force as prisoners of war or I will have every man put to the sword. You are aware of the overpowering force I have at my command, and this demand is made to prevent the effusion of blood." Duffield, unaccustomed to the raw language used in the message, was particularly concerned about the "put to the sword" part. While he was contemplating his next action, Forrest was rejoined with Wharton's Texans. Then, to the Rebel's surprise, Duffield surrendered.

While Forrest received the Ninth Michigan's surrender, he sent his adjutant to Lester's hilltop holdout with the same message he had given to Duffield. After reading the message, Lester asked to see Duffield. His request was granted and he was escorted to the wounded officer. The situation confronting Lester was not a comforting one and the suffering Duffield could offer no help or encouragement. To add further to Lester's discomfort, while he conferred with Duffield, Forrest marched his troops past until Lester had seen all of them twice. This display convinced the Union officer that he faced a much superior force and that the baleful Confederate who opposed him was probably both willing and capable of carrying out his threat. Badly shaken by what he had seen and seriously concerned about his situation, Lester asked for an hour's time to think. He was given thirty minutes. He used the time to call his staff together, brief them on what he had observed on his visit to Duffield, and to read them Forrest's ultimatum. Their decision was to surrender. It was now three o'clock on the thirteenth and all Union forces had capitulated.

A few hours later, the lead squadrons of the Confederate force were leaving town. At nightfall, the raiders camped at Readyville, halfway back to Woodbury. As the camp was being set up, Forrest sent scouting parties in all directions to determine the raid's effects and to detect any hostile movements. He knew he was in an extremely precarious position because of his heavy load of prisoners and plunder.

After sending out the scouts and placing guards, Forrest realized he did not have enough men left to drive the captured wagons and artillery. Determined not to be deprived of his booty, he separated the enlisted prisoners from their officers and rode among them to make a speech. He explained his problem to the men and told them, if they would volunteer to drive his wagons and artillery, he would parole every man at McMinnville. To the embarrassment of Crittenden and his officers, a Union trooper yelled, "Three cheers for General Forrest!" In response, the hills rang as Federal enlisted prisoners cheered the Rebel general.

Forrest was as good as his word. At McMinnville, the following day, the enlisted men were set free with two days rations. The officers were sent to Knoxville to be turned over to Gen. Kirby Smith. For all practical purposes, the raid was successfully concluded.

The capture of Murfreesboro marked Forrest's first independent operation as a brigade commander—one General Viscount Wolseley termed a ". . . rare mixture of military skill . . . and bluff." Forrest and his gray horsemen had, in a little over four days, traveled almost two hundred miles, including a forced march of forty-six miles, followed immediately by a daylong battle and another twelve-mile trek loaded with prisoners and supplies, without a break. Approximately twelve hundred Federal prisoners were taken, including the commanding general, his staff, and entire field office. Four pieces of heavy artillery, forty wagons, three hundred mules and one hundred fifty horses were captured. In addition, every Confederate trooper left Murfreesboro fully equipped with personal gear. Almost $300,000 worth of supplies were carried away and another $200,000 worth were burned, including 150,000 rations for Buell's army, which was immediately forced to go on half-rations. The Murfreesboro depot and telegraph were burned and a large segment of the Nashville and Chattanooga Railroad was torn up so completely that it remained disrupted for two weeks following the attack.

The capture of Murfreesboro by a Rebel command which was raw, poorly armed, inadequately equipped, and without artillery created immediate consternation among Federal commanders. Forrest's jarring blow had fallen under the nose of a thirty-thousand-man army and in the direct presence of twelve regiments that had some knowledge of his probable intentions. Col. James B. Fry, Buell's chief of staff, who firmly believed the Federal force at Murfreesboro could have successfully defended the garrison, stated that its capture was one of the most disgraceful examples of neglect of duty and lack of good conduct found in the history of wars.

Stung by the ease with which Forrest had penetrated their territory and the completeness of his victory, the Union moved quickly to forestall a repetition. Local forces in Middle Tennessee were repositioned to protect Nashville from possible attack by the unpredictable Confederate, and tough policies were quickly implemented in an effort to avoid such surprises. As a result, even though the Confederates were able to raid successfully after this, it was extremely rare for any Federal garrison to be taken so completely by surprise.

Forrest's raid was comparatively early in the war and was one of the first such forays made by the Confederates in this theater. Its complete success must have appeared almost miraculous to leaders who fully understood that it had been accomplished by a command that had virtually no confidence in itself or its leader. What many failed to realize was that they had just observed in action the native military genius and consummate leadership ability of Forrest that would grow to legendary proportions.

At Murfreesboro, the magnetism and charisma of the man began to have their real effect on the South. Here, Forrest took his first major step toward joining the pantheon of great Confederate leaders as is indicated by this incident: In Murfreesboro, following the Union surrender, an elegant lady stepped from her veranda and approached Forrest who was quietly sitting on his horse. She carried an ornate silver spoon and a dainty kerchief. Looking up at the commander, she asked, "General, will you back your horse for me?" Forrest swept off his hat, acknowledged her presence and did so. The lady stooped and dipped up a spoonful of dust from where the horse had stood. She carefully covered the spoon with the kerchief, bowed very low to the general and, with no words, returned to her house bearing the souvenir with her.

CHAPTER IV

Three Times 'Round

Along Antietam Creek in southern Maryland on 17 September 1862, the Army of Northern Virginia stood with its back to the Potomac River and slugged it out toe-to-toe with the Army of the Potomac. That day was to be the bloodiest day of a long and bloody Civil War. When dark came, the issue was still in doubt even though the gray army, less than half the size of the blue, had been bled white. The soldiers stayed another day though, and their commanders even considered going on the offensive. At nightfall on the eighteenth, better judgment prevailed, however, and the battered Rebels slipped across the river into the secluded valleys of northern Virginia's Blue Ridge Mountains. Here their commander, Gen. Robert E. Lee, halted them to rest and to rebuild their badly dissipated strength.

Maj. Gen. George McClellan's Union Army had been hurt too, but not as severely as Lee's. Rapid and decisive pursuit of the Confederate Army offered an opportunity for McClellan to crush his opponent and, perhaps, end the war. Decisiveness and rapid action were not in the nature of the supercautious major general, however. His pursuit was tentative despite heavy pressure from Washington. He contented himself by simply probing across the river to find out where his enemy had gone. His search was short one. Gen. A. P. Hill,

46

commander of the famed Light Division, was waiting and promptly tossed the Union force back into Maryland with heavy losses. At that, "Little Mac" decided it was time to rest and regroup.

In the days that followed, both armies took advantage of the chance to relax and recuperate from the bloody experience they had just endured. Nowhere was relaxation and recuperation pursued with greater vigor than at the headquarters of Jeb Stuart, now a major general and commander of Lee's cavalry. He had established himself at The Bower, home of the Dandridge family, near Martinsburg. Their house was one of those large, rambling structures that automatically comes to mind with a thought of the antebellum South. Situated on top of a small hill overlooking a clear mountain stream, its giant oak-covered grounds provided an ideal place for the tents of Stuart's troopers. There, with the mountains, blue in the haze of early autumn, as a backdrop for this peaceful setting, the cavalry slipped into an easy routine.

Duty was light, consisting of routine staff work, some picket duty, and light patrols. Lee's army occupied a line reaching from Martinsburg to Winchester. Stuart had the responsibility of providing a cavalry screen between it and the Potomac along a line running from Williamsport to Harpers Ferry. Thus, there was plenty of free time to enjoy the distractions offered by The Bower.

Life at The Bower became one huge, never-ending party. Stuart's admirers had showered the command with lavish gifts of food, and the surrounding countryside provided abundant wild game to supplement these and the command's regular rations. This unaccustomed abundance was squandered in frequent large dinners that were often augmented by spectacular military reviews staged by Brig. Gen. Wade Hampton's South Carolinians or one of the other units. Ladies' Day was also a regular occurrence; for "Beauty," as Stuart was inappropriately nicknamed at West Point, admired the ladies as much as they admired him. There was plenty of female companionship available at other times, especially from the Dandridge daughters and their visiting cousins. All these women were courted fervently by members of Stuart's staff.

The autumn days were filled with couples strolling in nearby woodlands or boating on the creek. The nights did not lack for excitement either. Stephen Dandridge held open house most nights, gatherings marked by parlor games, charades, and dancing. Music for the dances was provided by the regimental band or, more often, by the banjo of Sam Sweeney and the bones of Bob, Stuart's mulatto servant, backed up by violins. When the music started, the house rocked with singing, laughter, and dancing until the early hours of the morning when the festivities were generally brought to an end with a rousing rendition of "Jine the Cavalry." Life was so pleasant that the war tended to slip into the background or, if it was thought of at all, to be quickly dismissed. Heros von Borcke, a Prussian on Stuart's staff, explained the prevailing mood in his somewhat fractured English, "Let us enjoy ourselves today for we know not that we shall live tomorrow yet."

The frolicking troopers were jolted back to reality on the first of October. Brig. Gen. Alfred Pleasonton, a *beau sabreur*—and the ideal cavalryman to many—leading a force of cavalry supported by infantry, slipped across the Potomac; rolled over Brig. Gen. Rooney Lee's pickets; moved obliquely across his sector; and entered Martinsburg. Even though Lee and Hampton had discussed the possibility of such a development and had made plans to deal with it, their plans had not been executed. Now they were faced with the fact that, not only had their picket line been broken, but a strong Union force had invested a town they were charged with protecting.

Stuart, alerted to the attack by a courier and the sound of firing, rode at breakneck speed toward the sound of combat. When the agitated commander arrived, he found his two brigade commanders some distance from the town attempting to position their forces. And, to add to his unhappiness, he immediately came under sniper fire from the Union attackers. Infuriated by the situation, he summoned his brigadiers. Fixing them with a cold stare, he gave them exactly twenty minutes to eject Pleasonton from Martinsburg. With his commander's fury as encouragement, Rooney Lee quickly began forming up his unit on the Martinsburg–Darksville Turnpike. As soon as they were in formation, he led them in a driving charge toward the town. Hampton, also highly motivated by Stuart's speech, had formed his brigade to the left of Lee's. He, too, led his yelling troopers forward at a gallop.

Pleasonton did not await the pleasure of the Confederate gentlemen but hastily withdrew in good order. Hampton and Lee pressed the pursuit but, although they inflicted some slight loss on his troops, they could not prevent Pleasonton's escape. For his part, Pleasonton had what he came to find. While in Martinsburg, the Union commander had devoted his time to gossiping with the locals. During the course of these "friendly conversations" this veteran of the Mexican

War and frontier duty had managed to pry word of the locations of all the Confederate forces from those he spoke with.

The matter of Pleasonton disposed of and the picket line restored, the Confederates returned to a rousing welcome at The Bower. The cavalrymen resumed their life of leisure but it was to be short-lived. At the higher levels of army and government, pressures were rapidly building that would send them back into combat.

The leaders of the Confederate government in Richmond were worried. Although Lee's army lay between them and McClellan, these men feared another assault across the peninsula. Further, there was always the possibility of a water-borne assault that would out-flank Lee and leave the capital open to attack. While apparently not concerned with this possibility, Lee was anxious to learn McClellan's position and, if possible, what his intentions were. He was also keen-ly aware that McClellan depended on two railroads for his logistic support. Lee reasoned that if he could cut one of these lines, McClellan would not move and Virginia would be free of the threat of invasion through the winter. Cavalry offered Lee the means of obtaining the information he needed and of freezing "Little Mac" in position.

In the North, the results of Antietam and the advent of the Emancipation Proclamation had resulted in a great deal of bickering and maneuvering of the political variety. McClellan played an active role in these disruptive activities, hoping to replace Maj. Gen. Henry Halleck as commander in chief of the Union Army and, perhaps, to gain control of the government. His "outside" activities contributed to discontent in his command and to the growing exasperation of Pres. Abraham Lincoln with his general in the field. Lincoln's urging of McClellan to get on with the war and press the Confederates was answered by a barrage of messages complaining of inadequate sup-port and citing this failure of supply as making it impossible for the army to press the offensive. The president endured these activities, complaints, and excuses to the limit of his patience, then instructed Halleck to send McClellan a message that said, in part, "The President directs that you cross the Potomac and give battle to the enemy or drive him south. Your army must move now while the roads are good."

As had often happened before, Lee moved first. On the same date Halleck sent his message, Lee summoned Maj. Gen. Thomas J. "Stonewall" Jackson and Jeb Stuart to his headquarters for private discussions. As these meetings continued throughout the early part of the week, the army began to take notice. There was a definite feeling that action was in the air and rumors were rife that something big was up. The most persistent of these was that there would be a raid into Pennsylvania.

Late in the day on 8 October, Stuart directed his adjutant, Lt. Channing Price, to have all paperwork requiring his attention ready that night. Except for Price's activity, the night proceeded as usual with dancing until about eleven o'clock. At that point, Stuart called a halt and went to his tent to complete the work awaiting him. He finished at about one o'clock and ordered the music to begin anew. To the sound of the banjo and the bones, the ladies of The Bower were given a farewell serenade.

The music had barely died away before Price learned in detail of the planned expedition. Among the dispatches handed to him was an order from Lee directing Stuart to take a force of twelve hundred to fifteen hundred men into Maryland and Pennsylvania. Broadly, the directions were to proceed to Chambersburg; destroy the railroad bridge over the Conococheague; inflict any additional damage possible; gain all information available regarding the position, strength, and intentions of the enemy; capture state and federal officials for use as hostages; and acquire a supply of horses. Stuart was directed to keep the movement secret and told that Col. John P. Imboden, First Virginia Partisan Rangers, would create a diversion in the vicinity of Cumberland to attract the enemy's attention. The specific manner in which the orders were to be carried out was left to Stuart's discretion.

Early on the morning of the ninth, orders went out to form up the command. It consisted of three divisions of six hundred men each. One commanded by Brig. Gen. Wade Hampton, one of the largest slave and plantation owners in the South, recently turned soldier; the second by General Lee's eldest son, Col. W. H. F. "Rooney" Lee; and the third by the irascible Col. William E. "Grumble" Jones, a grumpy mountaineer Stuart could barely abide and who was later court-martialed by him for disrespect. Maj. John Pelham, who had left West Point to join the Confederacy at the start of the war, was directed to bring two guns from his battery and two from Hart's.

The command was ordered to move out as soon as possible and rendezvous at Darksville that afternoon. When all units arrived at that location, Stuart gave each commander some orders and a copy of an address to the troops. It said:

> SOLDIERS: You are about to engage in an enterprise which, to insure success, imperatively demands at your hands coolness, decision, and bravery; implicit obedience to orders without question or cavil; and the strictest order and sobriety on the march and in bivouac. The destination and extent of this expedition had better be kept to myself than known to you. Suffice it to say, that with the hearty cooperation of officers and men I have not a doubt of its success—a success which will reflect credit in the highest degree upon your arms. The orders which are herewith published for your government are absolutely necessary, and must be rigidly enforced.

The orders of which Stuart spoke, in general, established rules governing seizure of property; rules for receipting for seized property; prohibited individual plunder; provided for seizing persons and their treatment; prohibited straggling; established procedures for caring for seized horses; and prohibited the seizure of private property in Maryland.

The troops then moved forward again. They were in an almost festive mood brought on by the tales of the many veterans in the group who had accompanied Stuart on his earlier ride around McClellan. This mission had been so spectacularly successful from their point of view that they were inclined to believe they could follow the black plume and scarlet cape of their leader anywhere in safety. They did not know, and it probably would not have mattered, that they were going directly into the enemy's country where every hand would be against them.

The command proceeded to Hedgesville, then to the vicinity of the Potomac near McCoy's Ford. They made their approach after darkness and dismounted to avoid being spotted by a Union signal station across the river and to reduce the likelihood of alerting Union pickets guarding the ford. As soon as they had assembled at the crossing, a group of thirty-one men led by two experienced scouts was formed. This group, commanded by Colonel W. C. Butler, was charged with crossing the river on foot in the morning in an attempt to surprise and capture the enemy pickets. The command then settled down in a dark, silent bivouac to await daylight.

At four o'clock the command was awakened. Unable to light a fire and without breakfast, they hurriedly formed up with Hampton in the lead and were followed by Jones, then Rooney Lee bringing up the rear. On point, Butler watched as the first element of the scouting party moved out.

Dawn brought with it a heavy fog that shrouded the river and its surrounding valleys in a thick mist, screening from view everything more than a few feet away. Butler's men drifted through the fog, slipped into the river, and quickly disappeared, melting silently into the grayness. For almost an hour, the waiting troopers on the Virginia shore heard no sound above the swishing of the Potomac as it rushed past them. Then, from the other shore, came a ripple of gunfire. The scouting party had failed in its attempt to surprise the pickets.

At the first sound of the guns, Butler threw the remainder of his party into the river and quickly secured the ford. Behind him, the Rebel column poured into the river and across, striking north toward the National Pike some six miles away. They moved rapidly forward, learning en route that they had narrowly missed a collision with Brig. Gen. Jacob D. Cox's Union division that had crossed in front of them between three and five o'clock that morning. Near Fairview, Hampton's troops, approaching quietly through the heavy fog, surprised and overwhelmed the Federal signal station they had hidden from the previous evening. Their surprise was so complete that they captured all equipment and personnel except two officers who narrowly escaped.

They had been observed by more than the river pickets, however. Capt. Thomas Logan, Twelfth Illinois Cavalry, in command of the pickets at McCoy's Ford had been awakened by a Mr. Jacques at five-thirty in the morning and told that a Confederate force was crossing the river. Logan immediately tried to call in his pickets but, because of Rebel activity, was unable to do so. Realizing his force was insufficient to challenge Stuart, Logan took up a position that would allow him to observe Confederate actions. He maintained contact with them until about nine o'clock. Then, certain they were proceeding in the direction of Mercersburg, he fell back to Clear Springs and placed pickets on all roads leading north.

At seven-thirty in the morning, Brig. Gen. John Kenly, commanding at Williamsport, who earlier in the year had survived a bitter battle with the First Maryland, Confederate States of America (CSA), in Front Royal where he had been severely wounded and taken prisoner, was informed of the raid. Believing the Rebel force headed in his direction, he took action to protect his post and sent a company of cavalry forward to watch Confederate movements. At ten o'clock, he received word that a Rebel force consisting of about twenty-five hundred men and eight pieces of artillery was moving toward Mercersburg. He immediately forwarded this information to Major General D. N. Couch, commanding Third Division, VI Corps, and Brigadier General W. T. Brooks, commanding Second Brigade, Second Division, VI Corps. By midday, McClellan's headquarters was aware that a Confederate force had penetrated Union lines.

Heavily overcast skies covered the raiding column as it moved through rolling hills that were showing the first colors of autumn. At ten o'clock, they reached the Pennsylvania line and halted. Stuart rode down the line, stopping at each division to hear his orders read to the waiting troopers. After the orders had been read to the entire command, the column moved out with a cheer, almost six hundred of the men fanning out on both sides to sweep the country clean of horseflesh.

The threatening weather and the season combined to help the raiders. Good weather would have resulted in the farmers being scattered about the countryside; but on this day the somber skies had most of them inside. It was also threshing season and at most barns the raiders were greeted by the hum of a threshing machine at work. Capturing horses was largely a matter of opening a barn door, seizing the animals from the surprised Dutch farmers and riding away.

The local farmers found a Confederate raid on their property to be incomprehensible, many refusing to believe the truth even after being told. Frequently, the raiders left with the locals still thinking they were renegade Union men. Often, as they rode away, they were followed by unconvinced farmers shouting to them that they were as good Union men as any and threatening to bring the full fury of the authorities down on them for their criminal actions.

Despite the strict prohibition against it, the troopers found all sorts of reasons and excuses to engage in some individual plundering. The sleek draft horses they seized were soon joined by all manner of foodstuff. Throughout the column, men were seen loaded down with hams, turkeys, fresh bread, fresh milk, cheese, and other food of every description. The well-stocked larders of the farmers proved to be an enticement the hungry graybacks simply could not ignore.

As the day wore on, intermittent rains showers began to fall, soaking the gray riders. They pressed on, arresting as a matter of course any traveler they met who might spread the alarm. Stuart, in keeping with his well-known gallantry, exempted women from this inconvenience, instructing his men not to seize the horses of female travelers.

At noon, the men of the Second South Carolina entered Mercersburg. The townspeople, unaware of their approach, refused to believe their town had been invested by Confederates. One storekeeper was flabbergasted after outfitting the South Carolinians with shoes to find himself paid with Confederate money.

While in Mercersburg, Captain W. W. Blackford, Stuart's engineer, discovered that one of the town's families possessed a detailed map of the region. Knowing such a map would prove invaluable, he sought out the house of the owner. When he arrived, he was greeted by a group of women, all the men having taken the precaution of leaving before his arrival. He demanded the ladies turn the map over to him. Not only was his demand refused, the women declared no such map existed. Not to be deterred, Blackford dismounted and pushed his way into the house past the furious women, whom he described as rather rough specimens. Inside, he found the map hanging on a wall and proceeded to cut it from its rollers and place it in his haversack. This all took place under the watchful eyes of the women who subjected him to looks and language he called fearful.

While the troops waited in Mercersburg, Stuart mulled over his next step. He considered attacking Hagerstown, Maryland in the hope of destroying the large Federal stores maintained there. Despite the temptation, he reluctantly abandoned that idea when he became convinced the enemy would be ready for him and possessed sufficient force to deny him his objective. That decision made, he quickly chose an alternative and headed the column north again in a steady downpour toward Chambersburg, Pennsylvania.

Shortly after dark, the Rebel column halted on top of a low hill and looked at the lights of Chambersburg about three-quarters of a mile in front of them. Word of their coming had preceded them. From the town, they heard the rolling of drums as the inhabitants were alerted to their arrival. The patrician Hampton, uncertain what military force might be in the town, was reluctant to enter until this could be determined. Exercising caution, he brought cannon forward and placed them in position to bombard the town if necessary. Then, he dispatched Lieutenant T. C. Lee with twenty-five men under a flag of truce to demand the town's surrender.

The dripping raiders were met by three of the local citizens headed by A. K. McClure. Lee declined to answer McClure's anxious questions as to the terms of the surrender or who their leaders were, simply telling him the town had thirty minutes to give up or be bombarded. At McClure's request, Lee escorted him to Hampton who identified the command and told McClure the terms were unconditional surrender. Continuing in what McClure described as a respectful and soldierlike manner, the Rebel general assured him that private persons and property would be unmolested, except as necessary for the use of the Confederate Army, but officials of the state and federal governments would be detained until a decision was made as to their parole. This last statement caused McClure some concern since he was a militia colonel. He decided to conceal that fact, however, and agreed to the terms. The surrender accomplished, the gray column entered the city through the driving rain.

Behind them, the Union Army had regained its composure after some confusion following the initial notification of the raid. Brigadier General W. W. Averell, a veteran of frontier fighting and only recently recovered from wounds suffered at the hands of the Navajos, who had moved westward to counter the feint by Colonel Imboden, was ordered to move rapidly down the Potomac and take up Stuart's trail. Orders went out sending a division under Brig. Gen. William B. Franklin, a topographical engineer and veteran of First Bull Run, toward Chambersburg via the Hagerstown Road; Maj. Gen. John E. Wool, a veteran of both the War of 1812 and the Mexican War, was ordered to supply troops to Harrisburg and to send troops to Frederick where Brig. Gen. George Stoneman, who always seemed to fall a bit shy of what was expected of him, waited; Brooks was ordered to place his brigade and Brig. Gen. Hasbrouck Davis's cavalry regiment in pursuit of Stuart; and Col. John H. Kelly was ordered to picket the upper Potomac between Cumberland and Hancock. Cox's Kanawha Division that had barely missed Stuart at McCoy's Ford was halted and loaded aboard a train with steam up, ready to move at a moment's notice to assist in the capture or destruction of the Rebels. Pleasonton was instructed to add his cavalry to the pursuit but did not get the message until the next day. An order was also given to establish a network of signal stations that would be capable of observing all routes Stuart could reasonably be expected to take and to have the stations in operation no later than the next morning.

Civilian authorities were active also. Governor A. G. Curtin of Pennsylvania kept the telegraph lines hot with a series of somewhat panicky messages to Secretary of War Edwin Stanton, Halleck, McClellan, and Wool requesting troops, providing uncertain intelligence, and giving advice. Early on the evening of the tenth, Curtin informed Stanton he had received a message from Chambersburg that Rebels were in town under a flag of truce demanding the town's surrender. Shortly after receipt of this message, the line to Chambersburg went dead.

McClellan had operated through the day certain only of Stuart's general direction of march but unaware of his exact location. His lack of information was the result of the raiding column passing through a section of the country that had only limited telegraph service. However, based on the meager information he did possess, McClellan had succeeded in throwing a line of troops across the Confederate rear and was rapidly spreading an envelope of blue troops around them. The uncertainty that plagued the Federal commander was resolved at about eight o'clock when Stanton received a message from Curtin stating simply, "The people have surrendered Chambersburg."

In response to this message, Halleck wired McClellan, "A Rebel raid has been made into Pennsylvania today, and Chambersburg captured. Not a man should be permitted to return to Virginia. Use any troops in Maryland or Pennsylvania against them."

McClellan assured Halleck by return message that, "Every disposition has been made to cut off the retreat of the enemy's cavalry, that today made a raid into Maryland and Pennsylvania." He believed he had Stuart trapped. All he had to do was wait patiently for the Rebel leader to ensnare himself.

In Chambersburg, Stuart, in a rather extravagant gesture, appointed Hampton military governor of the city. The provost marshal was placed in control of the town; the quartermaster dispatched to survey the government stores in the area; a detail was sent to destroy the Conococheague Bridge; raiding parties ordered out to collect all the horses they could find; and 275 sick or wounded Union soldiers found in the town were placed on parole. The troops of Hampton and Jones were moved through the town to positions just beyond its limits. Lee was left behind to cover the rear.

Butler was ordered to occupy the bank building and to seize any funds he found. He immediately took over the building and instructed the cashier to turn over the bank's money. Protesting that no money was there, the cashier showed Butler that all containers that could hold cash were empty. It had been spirited away just ahead of the Rebels' arrival. Butler, convinced the man was telling the truth, gave up the search. The cashier was so impressed by Butler's courtesy that he had the ladies of his family prepare food for the Rebel's troops even though they had not requested it.

After surrendering to Hampton, McClure gave some thought to trying to escape because of his official status, but a desire to protect his property caused him to discard the idea. Instead, he hurried home hoping to deny the raiders his whiskey and horses. He succeeded in destroying the whiskey supply but had to watch as Rebel horsemen galloped off on his prize horses.

Later, a group of raiders returned to the road in front of McClure's residence and made camp. He watched as they fed their animals from full shocks of corn stacked in his fields and otherwise prepared for the night. Finally, one of the troopers approached McClure and, after bowing to him, respectfully asked for a few coals of fire. The colonel supplied them and even suggested a place where they could obtain wood in the hope of saving his picket fence. His efforts were to no avail. After receiving profuse thanks from the trooper, he watched as the "mild-mannered villain" stripped the fence for firewood. The ice had now been broken and squads came, one at a time, to ask for water. In every instance, they called and asked permission to enter the yard and promptly departed with thanks after obtaining their water.

At about one o'clock in the morning, a group of officers, spotting the fire in McClure's home, asked him for some coffee, offering to pay him well in Confederate money. Their request was granted and soon his living room was filled with Rebels who engaged in conversation about every conceivable subject except their destination. During their conversations, the Rebels spotted some Killickinick tobacco on the mantle. After asking McClure's permission to smoke, they filled their pipes and continued visiting.

Meanwhile, a subordinate officer had approached the kitchen and requested some bread for his men. His request was filled and soon he was followed by others until about a hundred were fed. The evening cost McClure his entire supply of coffee, tea, Killickinick, and considerable food. He noted that throughout all of this the raiders acted with utmost propriety and courtesy and that not one rude or profane remark was made, even to the servants.

According to McClure, this exemplary behavior prevailed throughout the town. He observed that several who misbehaved in some manner were promptly arrested and he knew of only one instance in which the raiders forced entry into a business. He did have one anxious moment, however, when Hugh Logan, a former resident of the area who had gone over to the Confederates, warned him against letting his identity become known. When McClure assured Logan that he had Hampton's word, Logan told him, "Hampton gave it to you. And, if you are arrested and can reach Hampton, he will parole you, for he's a gentleman. But Jeb Stuart wants you and I'm not sure he would let you go on parole."

For Stuart, the night offered neither peace nor rest. The detail that had been sent to destroy the bridge reported back with the news that it had defied their best efforts. Besides the problems caused by the rain, they discovered the bridge was made of steel and it refused to bow to their attempts to destroy it. The rain had become a nagging problem to Stuart for other reasons. He feared heavy rainfall in the mountains would cause the Potomac to flood and would leave him stranded on the enemy side. Three times during the night he roused Captain B. S. White, who had been designated to lead the command back, and sought reassurance from him. White, reasoning that the cavalry column could move faster than the water would rise, assured Stuart he would have no problems crossing the river on their return.

At four o'clock in the morning, Stuart had the bugler sound "Assembly" and waited with his staff in the center of town as the command gathered. During the process, the ill-dressed raiders took advantage of Federal stores to equip themselves with new clothing. One newspaper reported that the entire town became a dressing room as the Confederates shed their tattered clothing. Channing Price, in a confession that could have been typical for most of the men, wrote to his mother that he supplied himself with an overcoat, pants, boots, socks, and other items to the limit he could carry. While this was going on, several men at Stuart's direction were casually dropping the word to watching townspeople that their next stop would be Gettysburg.

At daybreak the column rode out in the direction of Gettysburg with Rooney Lee's men leading the way. Butler was left in charge of the rear guard with orders to destroy all Federal property. As soon as the column had cleared the town, local citizens were warned away and Butler's men set to work. The air was soon filled with smoke and the sound of explosions as depots, machine shops, and warehouses were destroyed. Large stores of clothing, ammunition, and supplies went up in flames as did several railway cars; the track was obstructed; and about six thousand rifles were destroyed. Price estimated the damage to be in excess of one million dollars.

Stuart, in a despondent mood, riding at the head of the column called for Blackford to join him and they rode well ahead of the lead elements. There was a long pause after they were out of earshot before Stuart spoke. "Blackford," he said, "I want to explain my motives to you for taking this lower route and, if I should fall before reaching Virginia, I want you to vindicate my memory."

Stuart then pulled out a map and explained to Blackford how Cox's command would be waiting behind him and that the hilly country would be easy to defend. He went on to say the enemy would not expect him to follow the route he was taking and the lower fords would be difficult to defend. Besides, the flat and open country through which they would pass would give an advantage to them. The only disadvantages Stuart could see were that the distance they must travel would be longer and they would pass close to the enemy.

Blackford assured his chief he understood perfectly and, if necessary, would make certain Stuart's actions were understood by others. The conversation, which had been laden with emotion, seemed to relieve Stuart's anxieties and restored him to his usual cheerful confidence.

The rain of the previous night had ended. The command pushed forward rapidly beneath clearing skies. The rain-soaked ground kept the cloud of dust that normally hovered above a moving cavalry column from developing. No sign of bluecoats was seen as the column trotted along north of the screen of Federal troops McClellan had deployed. As they rode, part of the force again fanned out on either side to sweep the country clean of horses.

Again, many troopers satisfied their hunger at the expense of farmers along the route. This led to one incident that was later recounted with great amusement. At one home, deserted except for some women and small babies, a hard-eyed veteran of the Ninth Virginia asked the ladies to prepare him some food. His request was rejected out of hand. At this, the Virginian eyed the young babies hungrily and observed that, while he had never eaten human flesh, the babies looked mighty tempting. He then mused aloud that, if there was no other food, he would just eat one of the pink youngsters. This comment caused a dramatic change in the attitude of the women and a bountiful meal was prepared with alacrity.

The miles fell swiftly behind the hurrying column as it moved ever closer to Gettysburg. They crossed Catoctin Mountain and halted just outside of Cashtown for thirty minutes. While the troops fed the animals, Stuart dropped to the ground and, propped against a tree, got a few minutes of sleep. After this short break, the column moved to Cashtown, about six miles from Gettysburg, and swung sharply south. They held a course along the Hagerstown Road for about six miles, then swung southeasterly toward Emmittsburg. Blackford was now riding far in front, using a pair of powerful glasses to survey the country ahead for signs of the enemy. Troopers frequently changed horses, making full use of captured mounts to maintain the killing pace.

By the time the column reached the Maryland line, it was stretched out over a distance of five miles. At this point, the advance was halted long enough for the formation to close up and orders were given to stop collecting livestock. Then, the column plunged on toward Emmittsburg.

Federal troops were on the move early on the morning of the eleventh, attempting to pull the noose tight around Stuart. In response to the order sent the day before, Pleasonton left Knoxville and marched to Hagerstown. There, he received erroneous information that the Rebels had doubled back and were in the Mercersburg area. He immediately headed in that direction, moving about four miles before being halted. Then, he was ordered to turn around and proceed to Mechanicstown. He arrived there at eight-thirty at night and threw out scouts toward Emmittsburg, Taneytown, Middleburg, and Graceham.

At six-thirty the next morning, Colonel Rush was ordered to send cavalry north from Frederick to scout toward Gettysburg. Four companies were immediately dispatched in that direction. They arrived at Emmittsburg near four o'clock and pushed on toward Gettysburg.

At Poolesville, Stoneman was notified to take precautions against the raiders attempting to cross the Potomac opposite Leesburg. He moved troops to the mouth of the Monocacy River, White's Ford, Edward's Ferry, and the mouth of Seneca Creek, retaining a reserve of seven hundred infantry, a section of artillery, and two hundred fifty cavalry at Poolesville. Cavalry was also deployed along all roads leading into this area.

These actions resulted in a band of enemy troops being deployed completely across Stuart's line of march. In addition, cavalry was proceeding toward him in strength on his right and heavy patrols were moving from the south in his direction. McClellan was certain no way had been left open for the Rebel command to slip through and cross back into Virginia.

Rebel cavalry jogged into Emmittsburg just after Rush's men had passed through. They quickly swept up the Union pickets left in the area and closed all the roads. Rush was cut off from his scouting squadrons and the raiders turned back or captured all couriers he sent out in an attempt to contact his troops. Stuart reported that he regretted exceedingly that time and the direction of his march did not permit him to pursue and overtake Rush.

The people of Emmittsburg greeted the Rebel raiders with great enthusiasm. Southern sympathy was strong in this area and they were delighted to see the gray force, although they could not have been more surprised, according to Blackford, if the Rebels had dropped from the sky. Food and drink were pressed on the gray horsemen; but they had to satisfy themselves with eating and drinking in the saddle since Stuart would permit no delay.

The column headed south from Emmittsburg at a trot, with Stuart riding at the front to set the pace. Finally, satisfied with the pace, he ordered it maintained and directed no gunfire under any circumstance. The advance was told to draw sabers and ride over anything that appeared in front of them. Stuart then moved back down the column giving instructions that any threat from the flank was to be dealt with in the same manner as soon as detected without waiting for orders from him.

Shortly, there was a commotion at the head of the column and Stuart galloped back to the front to find a Union officer courier had been captured. The dispatches he carried provided key information. Stuart learned that Pleasonton was only five miles to his right with a strong force, that Frederick was too heavily defended for him to attempt to pass that way, and that the Federal forces were still uncertain of his location. Having learned this, he ordered the column to swing in an easterly direction, cross the Monocacy River, and proceed to Woodsborough. The nearness of danger was emphasized a little later when the column drove off a Union patrol in the darkness.

Before reaching Woodsborough, the column rode head-on into the enemy in the form of a Union officer driving a buggy. Relying on his rank to overawe the riders, he drove into the column yelling for them to make way for him. When he found his way blocked, he shouted, "I'm an officer of the Seventy-ninth Pennsylvania on recruiting service, and I must get on!"

The Rebels simply crowded around him and waited for Stuart to appear. When he arrived, the man asked him, "Are you the officer in command?"

"I am," Stuart replied.

"Then be good enough to order your men to make way. I'm a Pennsylvania officer on recruiting duty and it is important for me to get ahead," the Federal officer told him.

Stuart spoke quietly to a young trooper who dismounted and climbed into the buggy, taking the reins.

"What do you mean, sir?" the indignant officer demanded.

"Nothing," the trooper told him.

"Who are you?" the Federal wanted to know.

"Nobody."

Thoroughly unhappy with this turn of events, the officer asked, "Who is that officer?"

"General Stuart," was the reply.

Not satisfied, the officer persisted, "What General Stuart?"

"Jeb Stuart, major general of cavalry, Confederate States of America," the trooper told him.

"By god, I'm procured!" the officer said in astonishment.

"I rather think you are," the gray trooper agreed as he turned the buggy and drove away.

At seven o'clock, Rush was ordered to send out more scouting parties. He sent two companies to the east, one toward Johnsville and one toward Woodsborough. The second company arrived at its destination just in time to run into the head of the Confederate column. Except for one man, they immediately fell back to report the enemy force. The remaining man, Cpl. John Anders, in a display of conspicuous bravery entered the town in disguise. He was able to move about and gain valuable information before he became suspect and was arrested. But, he kept his head after his capture and was able to escape under cover of darkness during some confusion, and he returned to his unit with the intelligence he had obtained.

At twelve-thirty, Pleasonton received word the raiders had passed in front of him at a trot about an hour before, going in the direction of Woodsborough. He was also told indications were that the Rebels would attempt to cross the Potomac at the mouth of the Monocacy. He immediately turned his tired command south and pushed it hard; aware that he had the shortest route to the river. Now, the issue was between Stuart, Pleasonton, and Stoneman. The Union men had the advantage. Stoneman had the fords covered with a strong force and Pleasonton was certain to arrive in the area ahead of Stuart. McClellan could still feel confident he had the raiders trapped.

Leaving Woodsborough, the Rebel command swung east to Liberty and then south through New Loundon to New Market. There they took the time to obstruct the railroad and cut the telegraph. All this time, scouts were steadily reporting with information that indicated the enemy was closing on them.

As the Rebel troops jogged through the dim moonlight, fatigue began to take its toll. In the darkness, the steady thump of hoofbeats and jingle of equipment beat out a rhythm that lulled men to sleep. Occasionally, some would dismount and walk in an effort to stay awake. Up and down the line snores could be heard above other noises as exhausted men slept in the saddle. Blackford noted that weariness caused the mind to play tricks. He repeatedly saw large houses in great detail only to discover a moment later they were only clumps of trees. He compared the experience to the agony of thirst.

The monotony of the night was broken once for Blackford by a bit of hand-to-hand combat. As they were passing a lonely farmhouse, Stuart asked him to speak to the farmer in an effort to obtain information. Stuart waited at the gate while Blackford dismounted and walked toward the house. He had covered about half the fifty-yard distance when he was attacked by a large, very determined bulldog. Since the use of a gun was impossible, Blackford received the assault with his saber. He managed to stick the dog in the shoulder with its point and divert the initial rush. Far from being intimidated by the blade, the dog became wary and more furious. He circled Blackford, looking for an opening, while the latter held his saber in front of himself, awaiting another charge. Stuart found this vastly amusing and kept shouting, "Give it to him, Blackford," between roars of laughter. The duel was resolved when the farmer called off the dog. Relief from the attack was all that was obtained from the farmer, however, for he was unable to answer Blackford's questions.

Just after midnight, Stuart decided on a diversion that was incredible under the circumstances, but typical of his style. Earlier in the year while operating in Maryland, he had established his headquarters in Urbana near the home of a Mr. Cocky whose house was occupied by a number of lovely young ladies. One of these had been christened the "New York Rebel" by Stuart and was a particular favorite of Blackford's. The cavalier had promised the women when he left that he would call on them if he were ever in the area. Now, he rode up to his engineer and asked, "Blackford, how would you like to see the New York Rebel tonight?"

Blackford needed little encouragement. He assured his commander that would suit him fine.

"Come on then," Stuart said and swung off on the road to Urbana accompanied by about a dozen staff members and couriers.

The group, who were thoroughly familiar with the roads, traveled rapidly and without incident to Mr. Cocky's house. They dismounted in the yard and knocked on the door. An obviously frightened female voice from upstairs called, "Who's there?"

Stuart laughed and said, "General Stuart and staff."

A head appeared at an upstairs window, gave a soft scream and disappeared. Her disappearance was quickly followed by the sounds of people scurrying about inside the house. Nonbelievers inside were heard asking again who it was in voices that betrayed fear. In a few moments, another female head covered with curling papers looked out the window and asked, "Who did you say it was?"

Again, Stuart let out a ringing laugh and replied, "General Stuart and staff. Come down and open the door."

The window was quickly closed. There were sounds of hurried dressing followed by a rush of feet down the stairs. Bars were lifted, bolts drawn, locks opened, and the ladies of the house spilled out into the moonlight to greet the raiders. The urgency of the situation allowed for only a brief, frenzied visit. After thirty minutes, Stuart reminded the ladies he had kept his promise and the men rode out.

They rejoined the column at daylight just as it was passing through Hyattstown. They were still twelve miles from safety. So, despite the weariness of his troops, Stuart maintained the hard pace they had kept throughout the night. They pounded into Barnesville just after it had been cleared by Federal cavalry under the command of Col. Alfred Duffie, a Parisian graduate of St. Cyr who had cast his lot with the Union. The veteran of service in Senegal, against the Austrians, in the Crimea, and in Algiers was trying hard but could not make solid contact. Stuart now knew that both Stoneman and Pleasonton would be in front of him and he was certain that the Yankees had a signal station on Sugar Loaf Mountain that was observing him. It was apparent his route of escape was slowly being choked off.

Pleasonton arrived at the mouth of the Monocacy at eight o'clock in the morning on the twelfth. He found four hundred to five hundred infantry guarding that point who reported they had seen no sign of the enemy. The hard night's ride had badly depleted Pleasonton's command, leaving him only about four hundred men. Despite this, he took them, with two of Lt. Alfred Pennington's guns, and crossed the Monocacy heading toward Poolesville. One company was detached from this group and ordered to scout in the direction of Barnesville.

As soon as the morning mist had burned off, the signal station on Sugar Loaf spotted the Rebel force. They wired headquarters, "It is reported that the Rebels have crossed. We can see heavy bodies of troops near Hyattstown."

As they pressed south, Stuart consulted his guide concerning the best route to follow. Captain White, a native who knew every foot of the land they were crossing, told him about an old, unused road branching off the Poolesville road that would lead them to White's Ford. Stuart decided to take this route but hoped to mislead his pursuers. Positive they were being observed from Sugar Loaf, Stuart kept the column in plain sight in an attempt to make the Federals believe he was heading for Poolesville.

Before they came to the old road, the column entered a thickly wooded area that concealed them from observation. Here they found someone had blocked their path by stacking rails across the road. It was the work of only a few moments to remove the rails; and the column pushed steadily on toward the river. After a short distance, they saw the company Pleasonton had sent north approaching them. Since most of Stuart's men were wearing the blue coats they had acquired in Chambersburg, the approaching Union commander was uncertain of their identity. He continued to move slowly forward but his uncertainty showed.

Stuart, who was riding at the head of the column, noticed the hesitation in the enemy ranks. He ordered his men to hold their pace and make no threatening move. They continued forward normally for some distance; then Stuart ordered the charge and the Rebels broke into a gallop. The startled bluecoats took time to fire a ragged volley then broke and ran.

The raiders pursued them to the top of the ridge overlooking the Little Monocacy where they spied Pleasonton's force gathered in front of them on the opposite side of the river. Stuart spread his men out along the ridge and brought up one of Pelham's guns which opened fire on the Union force. Stuart was determined to hold the ridge because it gave him the room he needed to reach the Potomac. If he could keep Pleasonton pinned down, the ridge would shield the Rebels as they made their escape.

Stoneman had received word the previous evening indicating Stuart intended to cross at the mouth of the Monocacy. He did not believe it definite enough to justify his repositioning his forces, however, and held his position. At nine o'clock in the morning, he received word that removed all doubt from his mind. He immediately ordered additional forces in Stuart's direction and heard firing commence at about the same time. He had waited too long. The issue would be decided now on the basis of what Pleasonton could do and Stoneman's ability to reposition his forces.

Pleasonton held his position waiting for his artillery to come up. It proved to be a fateful wait. The artillery horses, totally exhausted from a day and night of marching, were unable to pull the artillery up the steep hills. While time passed swiftly, the horses struggled with a burden that had become impossible to carry. At last, in desperation, men were ordered to help and the guns finally got into position. But the two hours that Stuart so urgently needed had passed.

With Pelham and a small force positioned to hold the ridge, Stuart ordered Rooney Lee to take the remainder of the command and cross the river. Lee, followed by Jones and Hampton, pushed toward the river two miles away. When they arrived, they found an enemy force positioned on a steep quarry bluff overlooking the crossing. Lee recognized he was in a tight situation and that it would be risky attempting to dislodge the enemy troops. Not wanting to make the crucial decision, he sent word back to Stuart asking him to come forward. Stuart answered that he was fully occupied and Lee would have to solve the problem himself.

Lee decided his only choice was to mount a two-pronged attack on the bluff from the front and left flank: As he attacked, he intended to send some cavalry and one gun in a dash for the river. If they could cross, he could then bring the enemy rear under fire. Still, the situation appeared so desperate to Lee that he hesitated to attack. Instead, he decided to try a ruse on the enemy commander. Under a flag of truce, he advised his opponent that Stuart's entire command was facing him. He suggested resistance in the face of this force was obviously useless and the Federal commander would be wise to surrender to avoid needless bloodshed. Lee offered the Union officer fifteen minutes to make up his mind, saying that at the end of that time he would charge.

The fifteen minutes passed without a response or any movement from the enemy. Believing his ruse had failed, Lee ordered his guns to open fire and his troops started forward. To their complete astonishment, the Federal force, flags flying and drums beating, began to withdraw in good order without making any attempt to defend the ford. The raiders were only too happy to let them depart unmolested.

Their way now clear, the Confederates dashed across the river, whipping their thirsty horses to keep them from stopping to drink. A gun was quickly set up to cover the ford from the Virginia side and another to cover the tow path leading along a canal that followed the river. Behind them, Pelham started to withdraw, moving slowly from position to position. As he withdrew, he alternated his fire upriver at Pleasonton and downriver at another force moving up to threaten them. Finally, all was ready for a complete withdrawal except for the rear guard which had not arrived. Several couriers had been sent to hurry them but no word had been received.

Blackford was stationed at the ford to make sure Stuart's instructions concerning the crossing were carried out. Now, his commander approached him with tears in his eyes and said, "Blackford, we are going to lose our rear guard."

"How is that, General?" Blackford asked.

"Why," Stuart told him, "I have sent four couriers to Butler to call him in, and he is not here, and you see the enemy is closing upon us from above and below."

"Let me try it, General," Blackford said.

Stuart paused, then offered his hand and said, somewhat melodramatically, "All right. If we don't meet again, good-bye old fellow."

As Blackford dashed away, he heard Stuart call to him, "Tell Butler, if he can't get through, to strike back into Pennsylvania and try to get back through West Virginia. Tell him to come in at a gallop."

Blackford pushed his tired horse as hard as he dared along the route the column had followed. As he rode, he met the couriers, one after the other, who told him they could not find Butler. He pressed on for over three miles and was about to give up when he rounded a turn and ran into the rear guard; halted, facing to the rear, and surrounding an artillery piece mired in a patch of soggy ground.

He hurriedly searched Butler out and told him, "General Stuart says withdraw at a gallop or you will be cut off!"

Butler was not to be rushed. He told Blackford coolly, "I don't think I can bring off that gun. The horses can't move it."

"Leave the gun," Blackford demanded, "and save your men."

"We'll see what we can do," Butler replied.

His troopers whipped the weary horses one last time and to everyone's surprise the gun popped free. Wasting no time, the cannon's crew led a mad dash to the ford with Butler's troopers following close behind. As they galloped, they were subjected to ineffective fire from both flanks. Ignoring the Union attempt to stop them, they plunged into the river and in moments the last man was safe in Virginia.

Pleasonton finally got into position and directed some ineffective fire across the river. At that moment, he was joined by Brigadier General Ward with three regiments of the Second Brigade.

Ward asked, "Is there anything I can do?"

"You're too late," Pleasonton roared. "You should have been here three hours ago!"

Ward, determined to retrieve something, elicited Stoneman's help and attempted to get permission to follow Stuart into Virginia. But, Stoneman had had enough. He flatly refused Ward's request.

From the Southern point of view, the raid was a great success. The party had ridden 130 miles in three days, covering the last 80 in about twenty-four hours, circling the entire Army of the Potomac in the process. Their losses to enemy action had been minimal—one wounded and two missing. In addition, Stuart's servant, Bob, imbibing too heavily on applejack, fell out, went to sleep, and was captured along with two of Stuart's horses. They had also been forced to abandon sixty horses worn out from the hectic pace.

The gain to the South was not limited to improved morale, however. The raiders had done a great deal of physical damage to the Union effort. Equipment and supplies worth at least a quarter of a million dollars were destroyed; about twelve hundred horses were brought back to Virginia; some thirty civilian and a like number of military prisoners were taken as hostages; 275 soldiers were paroled; railway and telegraph lines were disrupted; and considerable amounts of clothing, revolvers, and other equipment were appropriated by individual raiders. And they had gained the desired intelligence for Lee.

In terms of Union morale, the damage may have been even greater. In addition to having ridden the Union horse soldiers into the ground, the raiders had greatly undermined what little confidence the North still had in its cavalry and the ability of the army's commanders. Lieutenant Price felt that this raid, in conjunction with the earlier one on the peninsula, had established that Stuart could ride around McClellan at will. Stuart felt the morale and political value of the raid could hardly be estimated, noting that the ". . . consternation of property holders in Pennsylvania beggars description."

Feats such as this one were always enthusiastically received by the South and its army. There can be no question that Stuart's success had a positive influence on both. Price commented, "General Lee is excessively gratified at the result of the expedition and expressed warmly his thanks to the cavalry, and their gallant and noble leader."

Stuart believed the credit belonged elsewhere. He said, "Believing that the hand of God was clearly manifested in the signal deliverance of my command from danger, and the crowning success attending it, I ascribe to Him the praise, the honor, and the glory." Perhaps Stuart was right, but daring, skill, determination, and good judgment did not hinder the Almighty's hand in accomplishing His work!

For the losers it was a matter of trying to explain the unexplainable. McClellan put the blame on a failure of some of his commanders to follow his orders properly and on the poor condition of his cavalry due to the remount situation. The former caused Stoneman to demand a court of inquiry to establish the truth and the latter infuriated the Union quartermaster general. Neither sufficed to explain McClellan's failure.

McClellan, in his report on the operations of the Army of the Potomac, said, "I did not think it possible for Stuart to recross, and I believed that the capture or destruction of his entire force was perfectly certain; but, owing to the fact that my orders were not in all cases carried out as I expected, he effected his escape into Virginia without much loss."

He had some justification for holding this view. Stoneman's judgment and speed of reaction is questionable even after making allowances for the wide area for which he was responsible. It seems clear that with greater effort he could have brought additional forces up in time to block Stuart at White's Ford. The actions of Lt. Col. Edwin Biles, who commanded the forces that blocked Rooney Lee at the ford, in retreating without offering any resistance, were inexcusable. There is no question that Pleasonton's command was badly exhausted and depleted when he finally made contact with Stuart. Still, he does not seem to have pressed the issue within the limits of his capability. But, perhaps nothing they could have done would have helped. Blackford was probably correct in saying, "It would have been a cold day for any force of their cavalry which they could bring into action then to have placed themselves in the way of men such as ours, fighting toward home."

McClellan's complaints regarding his cavalry got little sympathy from his superiors. Their view was clearly indicated by the president as he continued to press McClellan to get on with the war. To his complaint following the raid that his horses were fatigued, Lincoln asked sarcastically, "Will you pardon me for asking what the horses of your army have done since the battle of Antietam that fatigues anything?"

When McClellan objected to this, Lincoln replied, "Of course, you know the facts better than I; still, two considerations remain. Stuart's cavalry outmarched ours, having certainly done more marked service on the Peninsula and everywhere since. Secondly, will not a movement of our army be a relief to the cavalry, compelling the enemy to concentrate, instead of foraying in squads everywhere?"

The degree to which McClellan had exhausted the patience of his commander in chief is probably best illustrated by this story: Shortly after the raid, Lincoln was returning by boat from a review near Alexandria when a member of his party asked, "Mr. President, what about McClellan?"

Lincoln did not reply for a moment. He just sat with his head down and slowly traced a circle on the deck. Then, without looking at the questioner, he said, "When I was a boy, we used to play a game, three times 'round and out. Stuart has been 'round him twice; if he goes 'round him once more, gentlemen, McClellan will be out!"

Perhaps in this instance, and on this single subject, Lincoln was too harsh in his judgment. It is difficult to fault McClellan's actions in retrospect. Given the information he possessed, it is hard to see how he could have deployed his forces much better. Although the blame for failure must always rest with the commander, there were some factors in this case to mitigate the blame. The truth is McClellan simply did not have commanders available at the crucial point that could match Stuart in skill and daring. And, even if he had, with success in their grasp and home in sight, it is extremely doubtful his troops could have matched the wild-riding raiders who followed the Cavalier's plume.

CHAPTER V

Fightin' Means Killin'

apitulation of the Confederate stronghold at Vicksburg, Mississippi was the principal objective of Union forces in the West in the autumn of 1862. Major General U. S. Grant's army, joined later by Maj. Gen. William T. Sherman's forces, applied the major pressure. Moving through west central Mississippi, Grant, applying force with the methodical determination that became his hallmark, was steadily pressing Lt. Gen. John C. Pemberton's back against Vicksburg and the Mississippi River. By 20 November 1862, the pressure became so great that the Confederate commander, a veteran of the Seminole and Mexican Wars and the Utah expedition against the Mormons, was forced to call on Gen. Braxton Bragg for help.

Positioned east of the Tennessee River in relative safety, Bragg refused Pemberton's request for reinforcements but told him he would use cavalry to create a diversion behind Grant to relieve the pressure. The controversial Bragg felt the best way to achieve his goal was to strike the Union communications and supply lines that paralleled the Mississippi Central Railroad across western Tennessee. To lead this operation, he selected the man who earlier in the year had successfully led a raid that resulted in the capture of Murfreesboro, Brig. Gen. Nathan Bedford Forrest.

71

Forrest, a daring leader and furious fighter, had in that raid and earlier at Fort Donelson, Nashville, Shiloh, and Corinth proven to be an effective and tenacious leader. His complete lack of formal military training was offset by an innate ability to grasp a military problem and quickly divine its solution. He had little but contempt for textbook fighters and expressed it by saying, "Whenever I met one of them fellers who fit by note, I gen'ally whupped hell out of him before he pitched the tune." He coupled the fear and devotion he inspired in his troops with audacity and unorthodox methodology to wreak havoc with Union commanders sent against him.

Unfortunately for the South, these traits had led Bragg, a strict disciplinarian and believer in literal adherence to regulations, to conclude that Forrest had little potential other than as a raider. Consequently, he had been shifted about and consistently given raw, poorly trained and equipped troops to command. This was the case with his current cavalry brigade that consisted of Colonel A. A. Russell's Fourth Alabama, Col. James W. Starnes's Fourth Tennessee, Col. George G. Dibrell's Eighth Tennessee, Colonel J. B. Biffle's Ninth Tennessee, and Freeman's Battery of Artillery. All, except the Alabamians and the artillery, were green troops armed primarily with shotguns and flintlock muskets and critically short of percussion caps for the weapons that used them.

When Bragg ordered this force into West Tennessee in early December, Forrest objected on the basis that his troops were raw and had not been provided adequate arms and equipment. Bragg was unmoved. Ignoring Forrest's objection, Bragg sent him a peremptory order to move without delay. Forrest accepted the order but thought it was mad. He was convinced his being required to cross a wide river heavily patrolled by gunboats in midwinter to engage a vastly superior enemy force was a deliberate attempt to sacrifice his command.

Forrest was neither a fool nor a martyr, however. Anticipating Bragg's action, he had already dispatched men into West Tennessee. Some were ordered to determine Union strength and disposition; others were instructed to build two ferries to be used to cross the Tennessee River; and one "citizen" was instructed to "liberate" the needed percussion caps from Union stores in Memphis. On the eleventh of December, Forrest moved toward the river.

The Union command was aware that Forrest was up to something. On the tenth, Maj. Gen. William S. Rosecrans, commanding XIV Corps, Army of the Cumberland, had wired Grant, "Tell the authorities along the road to look out for Forrest." This word was quickly passed to Brig. Gens. Grenville M. Dodge at Corinth, Thomas A. Davies at Columbus, and Jeremiah C. Sullivan at Jackson. In addition, Forts Donelson and Henry and forces in Kentucky were alerted.

Rain and low-lying fog obscured the Tennessee River Valley when Forrest arrived at Clifton on the fifteenth of December. Immediately on arrival at the river, groups of scouts were dispatched up- and downstream to huddle in the freezing rain while keeping a lookout for gunboats. The remaining troops promptly started boarding the two ferries the advance had constructed. These boats were able to carry only twenty-five horses and men at a time, which, compounded with the inclement weather, made the river crossing an agonizing operation. To cope with the strong current, these clumsy craft had to be taken upstream each trip and crossed at an angle, pioneer style, a source of further delay and aggravation. Cold and miserable, the command worked steadily without benefit of fires for warmth. Finally, on the seventeenth, all twenty-one hundred Rebels were on the western bank and the boats were sunk for concealment and future use. The troops then moved about eight miles inland where, for the first time in two days, they could build fires and dry out. Here, the "citizen" who had gone to Memphis, showed up with fifty thousand percussion caps, resolving one of the most serious shortages the command faced.

Despite their heroic efforts at concealment, the gray force's activity had been observed. On the day the crossing started, Sullivan, who commanded the District of Jackson, wired Grant, "Forrest's cavalry . . . are crossing the Tennessee River at Clifton today."

Grant promptly ordered reinforcements to Jackson to support Sullivan and asked for additional troops from Corinth and Forts Henry, Donelson, and Heiman. Sullivan dispatched a column of cavalry, infantry, and artillery under Col. Robert G. Ingersoll, a lawyer in civilian life, to meet the invaders. Cut off by the river to his rear and surrounded by superior forces, Forrest should have been easy prey; but the Union Army was to quickly discover he was not.

The next morning the Rebels made their first contact when they bumped into the leading elements of Ingersoll's column. The Union force quickly fell back and took up a strong position in some woods behind Beech Creek, which crossed a road leading into the town of Lexington. The creek could be crossed only by a single bridge that was rapidly rendered impassable by the removal of its flooring.

The Alabamians, led by Capt. Frank B. Gurley, arrived at the creek first to find the Second Tennessee (Union) drawn up on the opposite shore waiting for them. Without hesitation, Gurley ordered his troops to attack. They spread out along the creek and concentrated heavy fire on the Union force, driving it back into the woods. Working hurriedly, they replaced the bridge floor using fence rails and moved across the creek pressing their attack. Their movement forward soon ground to a halt, however, when they met heavy fire from the blue artillery. Forrest arrived at this point and took charge. Deciding against a direct assault, he put Freeman's Battery into action against the Federal cannon, sent the Alabamians to the right, and made a demonstration of attacking from the front.

Using the cover of a ravine, the Alabamians were able to move to the immediate rear of the Union artillery, now protected by the Second Tennessee, unseen. As soon as they could form up, the Rebels charged, completely routing the Tennessee troops. Gurley was on top of the Union battery almost before they saw him. Yelling Alabamians immediately rode the gunners down even though the blue artillery-men died by their weapons. Gurley described the end saying, "The gunners stood by their guns and died like soldiers. The last shot was fired just as we reached the battery, and my first sergeant, J. L. P. Kelly, and his horse were blown to atoms by the explosion. With the taking of the guns the cavalry gave way in a stampede, and many of them were captured in the chase from there to Jackson." About 150 Union soldiers (including Colonel Ingersoll) surrendered, giving up, in addition, seventy horses and the two pieces of artillery.

The defeated Federal commander was overwhelmed at his misfortune. He told Forrest, "I thought I was a soldier, but you surrounded and captured me before I knew what it was all about. I'm not a soldier, and I'm not going to try to be."

One of the raiders, describing the fight, put it this way, "Ingersoll made a good fight but if he really believed that there is no hell we convinced him that there was something mightily like it."

Reports now pouring into Grant grossly overestimated the size of the Confederate force. Sullivan wired him, "My cavalry was whipped at Lexington today. Colonel Ingersoll taken prisoner. The enemy reported to be from ten thousand to twenty thousand." Other reports suggested that Forrest had been joined by both Maj. Gen. Benjamin F. Cheatham's brigade and Lieutenant Colonel T. A. Napier's command. Forrest's troops did all in their power to reinforce the exaggerated Union estimates of their strength. Most of the locals were friendly and the troops took full advantage of them.

Pvt. Tom Jones of the Fourth Tennessee was asked by a local lady, "How many soldiers have you got?"

He responded, "Madam, I would tell you if I could. Do you know how many trees there are standing in west Tennessee? Well, we've got enough men to put one behind each tree, and two or three behind the biggest ones."

Unimpressed by the reports and acutely aware of the danger Forrest posed, Grant was determined to stop him. He ordered Dodge north from Corinth and directed Col. William W. Lowe to take fifteen hundred men from Forts Heiman and Henry and attack the Rebels. Brig. Gen. Mason Brayman, a former journalist and lawyer, arrived in Jackson to bolster Sullivan who wired Grant that he could hold against ten thousand and go out and whip five thousand. Grant responded by telling him, "Don't fail to get up a force and attack the enemy. Never wait to have them attack you." Sage advice that the former naval officer failed to heed.

The Rebels pushed on rapidly from Lexington, sweeping up stragglers as they went, arriving in the vicinity of Jackson just before dark. Forrest knew he was in great danger and was determined to hold Sullivan in the city. He had no intention of attacking Jackson but wanted Sullivan to believe otherwise. To accomplish this, Forrest immediately set about convincing the Union general he was faced by an overwhelming force of Rebels. Troops marched back and forth in the enemy's sight, kettle drums were beaten at various locations to suggest infantry movements, hundreds of extra campfires were lit, and no opportunity was overlooked to exaggerate the size of the attacking force to local civilians or to prisoners deliberately allowed to escape. Sullivan was convinced, held his position, and braced for an attack. At about eight that evening, satisfied that Sullivan was frozen in position, Forrest struck in two directions.

Biffle and Colonel N. N. Cox, racing south to destroy the railroads leading to Corinth and Bolivar, reached their objectives in a few hours. Encountering practically no resistance, they tore up large sections of track, destroyed bridges and culverts, and repeatedly cut telegraph lines. The only incident that marred the trip in their view was that they broke the railroad to Bolivar too late to prevent Col. John W. Fuller's brigade from joining Sullivan.

Meanwhile, Dibrell charged north in the covering darkness to hit Carroll Station at a gallop just at daybreak. The hard-riding Tennesseans chose a moving train as their first target but could not stop it even by pelting it with heavy fire from engine to caboose. The train lost, the raiders swung back toward the station and charged its stockade on foot. It took only a few minutes for the defenders to decide the graybacks were too much for them. The 101 troops staffing the stockade made only a brief show of resistance before surrendering to the attackers. The Rebels quickly converted all the supplies they could carry to their use, set fire to the stockade, and tore up the railroad and telegraph lines for some distance in each direction. Within thirty-six hours, Dibrell, Biffle, and Cox's forces had rejoined Forrest.

Reinforced by Fuller, Sullivan now decided to probe the surrounding area with six regiments under the command of Col. Adolph Englemann. Upon leaving the confines of the city, this force instantly found itself in deep trouble. Forrest, lying in wait, caught them in an artillery cross fire. Unable to stand up to the barrage, the Union force quickly fell back, although Englemann rather petulantly observed they did so ". . . without having first obtained any orders from me to that effect." They soon received such orders, however, as Forrest, keeping up the pretense of a general assault, drove them back into Jackson. Once again, Sullivan girded for an attack that never came. Finally, on the morning of the twentieth of December, confused and tired of waiting, Sullivan decided to mount a full-scale attack against the Rebel force. Leaving two thousand men to guard Jackson, he reached eastward but Forrest had vanished.

While Sullivan had waited for the expected attack the previous night, Forrest was on the move. Using the Fourth Alabama as a rear guard, he marched north to Spring Creek, halting there and waiting through the rest of the night for his separated force to regroup. All had arrived at daybreak. Now, Forrest split his force again. Dibrell was ordered to destroy the stockade on Forked Deer Creek, Starnes to take Humboldt, Biffle to get in the rear of Trenton while Forrest attacked the front, and Russell to again cover the rear.

As Sullivan groped futilely to the east, the ill wind that was cooling Union fortunes in the West rose in intensity to hurricane force. As Forrest's men fanned out to the north, Maj. Gen. Earl Van Dorn struck a body blow to the south. Charging out of the predawn darkness, his cavalrymen rode over the huge Northern supply depot at Holly Springs, Mississippi. By nightfall, they had destroyed it and tied down a strong Union force that could have been used against Forrest in other circumstances. Meanwhile, Bedford was steadily obliterating the Union lines of communication through Tennessee.

Dibrell, a Tennessee farmer and converted Unionist, moved quickly to Forked Deer Creek intent on destroying its bridge and stockade. Again he met a train, but this time it was filled with Union soldiers who were disposed to fight. Dibrell's troopers managed to fire one volley into it before it moved across a bridge and unloaded the troops. They took cover in a wooded area and laid down such effective fire that the Rebels had to leave the bridge. Turning to the stockade, they found it also a tough nut to crack. Boggy ground kept Morton from bringing his guns into action and a spirited defense prevented a successful assault without artillery. Recognizing the hopelessness of this effort, Dibrell retreated to rejoin the column.

At one o'clock, Starnes, a physician who had decided to soldier, hit Humboldt like a summer thunderstorm. His charge into the town was so sudden and overwhelming, the Union forces surrendered with hardly a shot fired. Starnes's bag consisted of one hundred prisoners, four cassions, five hundred arms, 300,000 rounds of ammunition, and large stores of supplies. In keeping with their pattern, the Rebels took what they could carry and burned the remainder. The materiel burned included a magazine that provided a short but splendid display of fireworks. Again, the railroad, culverts, and telegraph lines were destroyed. Starnes then sped off north to rejoin his leader.

Forrest arrived at Trenton at three o'clock and charged without preamble. The Union force under Col. Jacob Fry was waiting this time, barricaded behind cotton bales and hogsheads of tobacco with sharpshooters posted on top of several buildings. They let fly such a hail of lead into the charging Rebels that Forrest immediately broke off the attack. Not one to risk men unnecessarily, he started redeploying his force to surround the town and ordered up artillery. Before it got into position, Biffle arrived and completed the linkup to surround Fry. All the while, Rebel sharpshooters kept the bluecoats occupied, allowing Freeman to position his weapons. Once the artillery was set, he chose a depot in the center of the barricaded area as his initial target. Three rapid rounds from the field pieces smashing through this area convinced Fry it wasn't his day and the white flag ran up. With Trenton, Forrest took 250 prisoners, thirteen wagons, seven cassions, twenty thousand rounds of artillery ammunition, 400,000 rounds of small-arms ammunition, a large number of horses and mules, and a considerable store of supplies.

As his world crumbled around him, Fry offered his sword to Forrest, commenting that it had been in his family for forty years. Forrest examined it, then handed it back saying, "Take back your sword, Colonel, as it is a family relic; but I hope, sir, the next time you wear it, it will not be against your own people."

North of Spring Creek, Russell's rear guard waited like a spider on its web for any pursuing force. Late in the afternoon, their prey, in the form of an infantry column, cautiously crossed the stream. Without warning, Russell's troops, half as infantry and half as cavalry, pounced on the enemy foot soldiers. The swarm of yelling Rebels led by a sheet of deadly fire was too much for the startled pursuers. They panicked and fell back across the creek, burning the single bridge behind them. The Alabamians waited on the opposite shore until darkness, then slipped north to join their leader. Sullivan promptly upped his estimate of Forrest's strength to twenty thousand.

While his lieutenants joined one by one through the night, Forrest held Trenton. As he waited, he reequipped the remainder of his force and continued to practice the fine art of deception. He now had almost twelve hundred prisoners that he decided to parole. As this process was going on, he loudly instructed "couriers" to tell various "generals" to bring up their "commands." Again, extra campfires were built and detachments of troops were marched about with the result that all the parolees were convinced Forrest had an extremely large force at his command. Before the night ended, his commanders had rejoined him and Lieutenant Colonel T. A. Napier had arrived with an additional 430 troops.

With Sullivan minimized as a threat because of his timidity, indecisiveness, and inflated estimate of his opposition, Forrest developed a keen interest in intimidating Davies and his five thousand troops at Columbus. Davies, a civil engineer who had left a mercantile business to return to the army, accommodated him by being as gullible as Sullivan, swallowing any bait Forrest chose to offer. Davies was convinced it was really Bragg who was approaching and had no intention of leaving Columbus. In fact, as time passed, he became so nervous that he started loading thirteen million dollars' worth of supplies on boats, dug a network of trenches, and ordered the commander of Island Ten to spike his guns and destroy the ammunition.

Daybreak on the twenty-first of December saw the Confederates in action again. The stores at Trenton, after having been systematically looted to equip the raiders, were destroyed and the Rebels again moved north. It was a greatly changed force now. Every man was completely equipped, courtesy of the Union Army, and their numbers had actually increased since crossing the river.

The Rebel march followed the line of the Mobile and Ohio Railroad. In turn, Rutherford Station, Kenton, Union City, and, finally, Moscow, Kentucky fell before the gray tide. As they marched, the Rebels methodically and thoroughly destroyed the railroad. A common statement heard during the war was that railroads destroyed by cavalry were back in operation almost before the sound of the hoofbeats died away. No such accusation could be leveled at Forrest's men. When they left a railroad, it took new rails, ties, bridges, culverts, and a lot of work to put it back into use.

On the twenty-fourth, the Rebels arrived at the Obion River bottoms. Here the Mobile and Ohio had some fifteen miles of bridges and trestles snaking their way through the swampy bottomland. Arming his men with impressed axes, Starnes assaulted the railroad. It proved a formidable opponent. The raiders sloshed about in hip-deep mud and slimy water in the freezing cold while they hacked away at timbers "as hard as horn with axes dull as froes." To aid their efforts, they split wood and built fires around supporting timbers and on trestles caked with ice and sleet. Before night fell, the cold, muddy troopers had the satisfaction of seeing the trestles topple over into the frigid swamp. That same evening Forrest received word that ten thousand troops were moving to cut off his retreat and that a sizable force under Brig. Gen. Isham N. Haynie, a former judge, was nearing Union City.

Although troubled by this disquieting news, Forrest decided to give his men a day of rest on Christmas. They spent it in quiet relaxation. The troops loafed through the day, lounging around fires, idling away the hours smoking, drinking coffee, and swapping stories. Their commander wandered about among them telling jokes, praising their efforts, and making certain they knew he had seen and appreciated all they had done. When darkness fell on the Christmas day, it blanketed a proud Rebel force, filled with confidence, ready to tackle anything in its way. The next day they would have to get out of west Tennessee—if they could.

On the twenty-sixth, Forrest turned southeast to avoid Haynie. A bone-chilling rain fell throughout the day, turning already miserable roads into almost impassable quagmires. Nevertheless, the raiders made twenty-six miles and destroyed an important bridge on the Paducah branch of the railroad. At dark they were in Dresden where they halted for the night, awaiting word from scouts that had swept the countryside during the day.

Forrest's intelligence clearly showed that the stumbling Union jug-
gernaut had finally gained purposeful motion. Colonel Lowe was
waiting for him to the north; gunboats were covering the Tennessee
River up as far as Clifton; all ferries had been destroyed; the bridges
from Paris south to Jackson had been destroyed and strong forces
were on guard at all crossings; Dodge was moving north from
Corinth to block Forrest if he moved south; and Sullivan had Col.
Cyrus L. Dunham and Colonel Fuller underway from Trenton to hit
the Rebel flank. A blue noose had been spread around the raiders. All
that remained was for the Union Army to jerk it tight.

At eleven o'clock at night on 27 December, Dunham pulled out of
Trenton with eighteen hundred men. He was followed at daybreak by
Fuller, accompanied by Sullivan and Haynie, with two thousand men.
The Union commanders, certain that Forrest would attempt to cross
the Tennessee at Reynoldsburg, were intent on striking a paralyzing
blow to his flank. Forrest crossed them up, however, by moving
southeast instead of east. At dark on the twenty-seventh, he went into
camp above a branch of the Obion near McKenzie, just above the
Union line of march. The raiders held this position through the night
while Dunham passed by on the other side of the Obion, headed east.

Forrest moved early the twenty-eighth, pulling up at sundown on
the bank of the Obion that separated him from the Union forces.
Here an old bridge, so decrepit no one had bothered to destroy it,
offered the only unguarded crossing in the area. In addition to the
appalling condition of the bridge, it had quarter-mile-long causeways
leading up to it on each end that had the appearance of impassable
bogs. To the weary riders, it offered little hope as a way to escape.

Night came as it can only in the South in the dead of winter.
Gloomy and foreboding, the gathering darkness was filled with mist
punctured by a light drizzle of freezing rain. Slipping and sliding in
the muck, Forrest carefully examined the bridge, then dismounted his
men and started them repairing it. He led the way, swinging an axe
alongside some of his troopers to provide timbers, while others struggled on the slick structure, repairing it in the fitful light of torches
and candles. Within an hour, the first of the cavalry was crossing the
shaky structure.

Once the cavalry was across, Forrest ordered the wagons to follow
but found the drivers reluctant to commit their charges to the dilapi-
dated bridge. Losing his patience, Forrest climbed up onto the lead
wagon, grabbed the lines, and urged the team forward. Lunging and

slipping on the muddy causeway, they scrambled onto and over the bridge. This example encouraged the other drivers and the wagon train started to move. Unfortunately, the next two wagons over-turned and the operation stopped as the Rebels looked on in disap-pointment. Forrest completely lost his temper and waded through the troops, shouting and swearing to jar them out of their despondency. Under the lashing tongue of their leader, they plunged into the icy water, righted the two wagons and got them across.

Now Forrest put the men to repairing the causeways by filling holes with sacks of captured sugar and coffee. This done, he had every vehicle surrounded by men and set the train in motion again. Men pulled on vehicles, pushed on teams, fell into the cold mud and water but, with much cursing, sweating, and straining, the last of the force got over the river at three o'clock in the morning. The raiders now lay in the bottoms between Fuller, who was camped at Shady Grove, and Dunham who was several miles to the east.

At daybreak on the twenty-ninth, Fuller moved out toward Huntington, arriving there in the afternoon. Sullivan wired Grant that Fuller had arrived in Huntington before Forrest knew that he had left Trenton, adding that the Union troops had Forrest's men in a tight place and were closing from three directions. Sullivan would have been astonished to know that Forrest knew exactly what the blue troops were doing and was at that time bivouacked sixteen miles from Lexington at Flakes Store in the rear of the Union force.

Forrest now decided to change his objective and destroy Grant's last large store of supplies located at Bethel Station. Grant had already recognized the danger of this and had wired Sullivan that the road south of Jackson had to be protected "peradventure." It was no longer within the capability of the outmaneuvered Sullivan to pro-vide the desired protection, however, if Forrest chose to strike.

Forrest was aware that a strike at Bethel Station under existing conditions would force him to run grave risks. He knew he could destroy his objective; but he would be left with an exhausted force to use in breaking through to the Tennessee River. The time it would take him to destroy Bethel Station would also probably provide enough time for Dodge to join Sullivan. If that happened, he would then face a force too strong for him when he broke for the river. After thinking it over, Forrest decided that he would first destroy Sullivan. He would rest his force on the thirtieth, split Sullivan's brigades and crush them piecemeal on the thirty-first, and destroy

Bethel Station on the second of January. He was so positive he could do this that he sent a company to destroy the telegraph lines and bridges and prepare forage twelve miles south of Jackson.

With Dibrell guarding the flank toward Trenton, Forrest made his first move on the night of the thirtieth. He sent his brother, Bill, and his company, christened "The Forty Thieves," to draw Dunham out. He wanted him at a place called Parker's Cross Roads about seven miles below Clarksburg where the Clarksburg and McLemoresville roads intersected. Bill hit Dunham and immediately fell back in the desired direction. Dunham started a forced march to cut off Bill's retreat and wired Sullivan for immediate reinforcement. Sullivan was stunned when he heard Forrest was in his rear and delayed making any move for fear that he was being duped again by the Rebel commander.

With Sullivan reacting as he had anticipated, Forrest sent four companies to watch him and closed on Dunham. The two forces were about equal in manpower but Forrest had eight pieces of artillery to Dunham's three. Never willing to risk men unnecessarily, Forrest decided to defeat Dunham with artillery.

At Forrest's order the gray artillery pulled up on the crest of a hill to find the Union force drawn up in line of battle about four hundred yards in front of them. They swung the field pieces into position and sent a round winging toward the Yankee positions. It was immediately answered by the blue artillery and the duel was on. After about half an hour, the Rebels had destroyed one Union gun and forced Dunham back to the top of a nearby ridge. Forrest now ordered the attack and the raiding troops advanced in good order. The two forces met with a shout and after a very short skirmish the blue force gave up the ridge. They regrouped quickly, however, and charged back up the ridge but could not stand the cloud of musket balls, grapeshot, and canister that enveloped them.

Forced steadily back, Dunham took refuge in a wooded area enclosed by a rail fence and surrounded by open fields. Forrest moved up more artillery and sent Russell to the right rear and Starnes to the left rear of the opposing force. Dunham, observing this move, immediately charged the weakened Rebel front. Again, a hail of grape and canister broke the charge, forcing the Union troops to fall back. Giving them no time to regroup, Russell hit their right rear, capturing their wagon train. Simultaneously, Starnes crashed into the blue left rear but could not break it. Forrest now increased the pressure on the front and broke the Thirty-ninth Iowa momentarily, but they quickly rallied and regrouped at the edge of the woods.

Napier had been holding on top of a nearby knoll. Forrest now ordered him to crush the Union right flank that had moved out into the open. At a word, Napier's troopers swung into the saddle, raised the yipping Rebel yell, and galloped into the blue force. The Union broke under the charge and dashed back into the woods, losing their wagon train. Here and there among the Federals, white flags began to wave and Forrest ordered the firing stopped. He sent an orderly forward to take the surrender and, in his words, "save further effusion of blood." At the same time, he advised Dunham that, if he did not surrender, "I will put every man to the sword."

Dunham knew he was whipped but still hoped reinforcements in the form of Fuller's brigade would arrive in response to a wire he had sent Sullivan. Playing for time, he sent Forrest word that he could pass on unmolested if he wished. Forrest had no interest in passing on and was about to tell Dunham so in unmistakable terms when the sound of heavy firing came from his rear.

According to a story, probably apocryphal, this sudden firing caused Col. Charles Carroll of Forrest's staff to dash up to the general and excitedly tell him, "General, a heavy line of infantry is in our rear. We're between two lines of battle. What'll we do?"

The unruffled Forrest is alleged to have promptly replied, "Charge both ways!"

Whether or not the story is true, Forrest did rush to his rear to find Fuller's troops already among the Rebel horse holders. Boxed between the Union forces, the raiders were looking disaster squarely in the eye. Had Dunham moved quickly as soon as Fuller struck, he might well have tipped the scales. However, Russell and Starnes were too quick for him. Guessing the meaning of the firing to the rear, they charged Dunham from two sides, nailing him in position. Meanwhile, Fuller pressed his advantage. He swept over part of the Confederate force, capturing three hundred of Napier's troops and their horses, two Rebel artillery pieces, and recapturing the three pieces Dunham had lost. He also got a section of his artillery in position and poured heavy fire into the fleeing Rebels.

Dibrell's men, exhausted after a killing march from Trenton, took the full force of the Union cannon fire. Bodies flew through the air as the rounds from the heavy weapons crashed down among them. Seeing the heavy casualties his troops were taking, the enraged Forrest managed to get about fifty of the scattering troopers to join his escort. As soon as he could get them under control, he urged them forward, leading a headlong charge straight into the Union guns. This act was so totally unexpected that the surprised gunners and their infantry support were scattered in just a few hectic minutes. Quickly, the Rebels grabbed two of the Union cassions and rode free. Forrest, now clear of Fuller and behind Dunham, regrouped his scattered force and dashed toward Lexington.

Behind him, Sullivan wired Grant that "Forrest's army is completely broken up" and that all he needed was "a good cavalry regiment to go through the country and pick them up." Grant immediately dispatched the cavalry regiment. How much Sullivan believed what he told his commander is indicated by the fact that he held his position at Parker's Cross Roads for twenty-four hours expecting a counterattack at any moment.

The Rebels arrived in Lexington in the early evening and went into bivouac. At two o'clock in the morning, Forrest ordered "To Horse" sounded, and they moved out toward the Tennessee River. Forrest was deeply troubled about being surprised by Fuller. Unaware that his patrol had misunderstood his order and passed parallel to Fuller rather than meeting him head on, he rode along deep in thought, trying to unravel the puzzle.

Capt. John W. Morton, riding beside his general, felt the hot breath of a musket ball as it whispered by him and saw Forrest's head drop. "General, are you hurt?" Morton asked anxiously.

Forrest reached up, pulled his hat off, and stared at the hole drilled in it. After a moment, he shook his head and said, "No, but didn't it come damn close to me?"

With men ahead to raise the ferries, the column moved easily almost to Clifton. Here they met the "good regiment" of cavalry Grant had sent to pick them up. The "good regiment" hardly knew what hit it. Dibrell stormed through its center, while Starnes and Biffle rolled up the flanks. In minutes it was over—the end of Union efforts to stop the raiders.

Determined not to be surprised again, Forrest deployed a regiment as rear guard and ordered Lt. Edwin H. Douglas to support it with artillery. As they moved into position, their commander gave a demonstration of his lack of formal military knowledge. According to Douglas, "When our section was ordered to take position and get ready for action, according to the manual of artillery drill we galloped up to the position, unlimbered, and the horses were moved obliquely to take their place in the rear of the guns and out of range. The general did not understand the rapid movement of the horses to the rear. Mistaking it for a cowardly runaway by the drivers, he rode up to the man on the lead horse, and, as he struck him over the shoulders with the flat of his sabre, yelled: 'Turn those horses around and get back where you belong, or by God I'll kill you!' The artillery-man answered: 'General, I'm moving in accordance with tactics.' Forrest yelled back at him: 'No you are not; I know how to fight, and you can't run away with the ammunition-chest!'"

Douglas goes on to describe how his commander reacted when corrected. "A few days after I took my book of tactics to the general's tent and showed him that it was necessary for the horses to move off out of range, and offered to give him an exhibition-drill, so that he could see the reasons for such a manoeuvre. This was accepted, and he became greatly interested. In less than a week he had mastered the manual and become an expert among experts in placing a battery and in the use of the guns. I may also add that he was just as prompt and earnest in his apology to the soldier he had wronged as he was in the infliction of what he then believed to be a merited rebuke." Perhaps, this incident demonstrates one of the basic reasons that Forrest quick-ly overcame his training deficiencies to become a great commander.

At noon New Year's Day, the return river crossing started. Vehicles and equipment crossed by ferry; the horses were forced to swim the river in groups led by a trooper in a skiff holding the bridle of a lead animal; the men rode the ferries, made rafts, or swam the wide stream. At eight o'clock that evening, the last trooper hit the eastern shore and the raid was over.

At last Sullivan, who one of his officers described as a "genius at tardiness," moved again to the complete disgust of everyone in his command. They knew Forrest was gone and pursuit useless. Nevertheless, they stumbled through the cold, rain, and mud in a last futile effort. Late on the second, they arrived at the river to find only rain, silence, and a long grueling walk back home.

The South was jubilant over Forrest's success and his reputation as a winner was clearly established. He had taken a green, ill-equipped brigade across the river and, although he lost five hundred men, he added more than he lost and returned with a brigade in which every man was fully equipped and battle hardened. He had captured, wounded, or killed fifteen hundred Union troops, including the colonels of four regiments; captured five pieces of artillery, eleven cassions, thirty-eight wagons, and destroyed immense stores of sup-plies; utterly disrupted communications; and severely damaged the railroad. Most important, he had played a major role in causing the Union plan for Vicksburg to fail completely. This raid, coupled with

Van Dorn's on Holly Springs, forced the Union Army to rely on an extremely long rail line for logistics support. This was too risky for Grant and he fell back out of central Mississippi.

The untutored general had outwitted the best the Union could throw against him and succeeded beyond the wildest dreams of his own commanders. Completely fearless, possessed of boundless confidence in his own ability, and absolutely realistic in his approach to war, Forrest had proved himself a master at his newly acquired trade. Those who marveled at such ability in an untrained general could have learned much of the secret of his success from this story: After returning to camp, Forrest was examining a saber he had taken at Trenton. He noticed that, in keeping with time-honored custom, it was sharpened only at the point. He called an orderly and put him to turning a grindstone while he sharpened the blade to razor keenness along its entire length.

An officer with years of service in the Regular Army was appalled at this. Screwing up his courage, he protested to Forrest that what he was doing was in violation of all military precedent. Forrest transfixed the officer with a cold stare for a few moments, then said, "War means fightin' and fightin' means killin'." Then, he faced back to the slowly turning grindstone.

CHAPTER VI

A Visit to Holly Springs

The Union battle plan set in motion in late 1862 was designed to partially dismember the Confederacy by amputating those states west of the Mississippi River. The key to successful surgery was crushing the Rebel stronghold at Vicksburg, Mississippi. A modified pincer movement was selected as the instrument to be used. Major General U. S. Grant's army formed one jaw of the pincer as it moved down the Mississippi Central Railroad east of the Yazoo River bottoms, to lure Lt. Gen. John C. Pemberton out of the city. Once it had engaged the Confederate Army, the other jaw, Maj. Gen. William T. Sherman's army, would close by landing at Chickasaw Bayou to invest the city from the north. The plan had an Achilles' heel, however. It was the long, vulnerable supply line stretching from Bolivar, Tennessee through Holly Springs to Oxford, Mississippi.

Rebel Col. John Griffith spotted this weak link and called it to Pemberton's attention. He suggested that a well-executed cavalry raid could destroy the huge Union depot at Holly Springs and relieve the pressure Grant was bringing to bear on Vicksburg. After some long, rather agonizing discussions with Griffith, Pemberton agreed to give it a try. Keeping the mission a secret, he ordered Griffith's Texas Brigade, Col. William H. "Red" Jackson's Tennessee Brigade, and

Brig. Gen. Robert "Black Bob" McCullouch's Missouri and Mississippi Brigade, some thirty-five hundred troopers, to assemble at Grenada. To command, he chose the impetuous, red-haired Maj. Gen. Earl Van Dorn, the much maligned loser at Pea Ridge and Corinth.

A veteran of the Mexican War and of fighting in Indian Territory (now Oklahoma), the South had expected great things of Van Dorn. Grant's classmate had thus far proven to be a huge disappointment. He simply did not have the perspective and patience to control a large army. A swift-moving, highly flexible cavalry group was another matter altogether as the fiery little ladies' man, destined to die at the hand of a jealous husband, would soon demonstrate.

Van Dorn would have some additional help in his forthcoming effort to emasculate Grant. In response to a request from Pemberton, Gen. Braxton Bragg had already dispatched Brig. Gen. Nathan Bedford Forrest to raid into central Tennessee. So, just as Van Dorn began his play, the fierce Tennessean struck savagely into that state. Between them, they would teach Grant a never to be forgotten lesson about the hazards of relying on a long, tenuous line of supply.

The first of Van Dorn's troops arrived at Grenada, Mississippi on 12 December 1862. They were followed closely by the remainder and all were in place by the fifteenth. On that date, the command, fully formed, moved out, and crossed the Yalabusha River. Here they went into camp to finish their preparations and to await Van Dorn's arrival. Each man was directed to cook three-days' rations and draw sixty rounds of ammunition, a box of matches, and a container of turpentine. When they completed these actions, the troopers were told to be ready to move at the sound of the bugle.

Early the next morning, Van Dorn arrived and waved the command forward. With a cheer, the column moved out. All day and into the night it plodded through driving winter rain that hampered its progress while chilling the miserable riders to the marrow. Late that night, they pitched camp to spend the remaining few hours of darkness in a futile effort to get comfortable enough to rest a bit. At daybreak, they swung wearily into the saddle and moved again, reaching Houston, Mississippi about noon. Van Dorn kept them moving through the town and for another fifteen miles before allowing them to stop for the night. The rain had continued to pound them all day, sapping their enthusiasm and impeding their progress by flooding streams and turning the earth to a sea of mud.

Again at dawn the troopers were on the move. By noon, they were passing through Pontotoc, Mississippi, their leader permitting them to accept offerings of food from local citizens only if they remained in the saddle. Here, the Union got its first warning that something was up when the Rebels were spotted by cavalry forces under Colonel T. L. Dickey.

Dickey was operating about ten miles from Pontotoc when refugees fleeing the Confederate force told him a body of troops estimated to have between six thousand and fifteen thousand men was in front of him. Concerned about the size of the force, he moved forward very cautiously, arriving at Pontotoc just in time to observe Van Dorn's rear guard pass. The gray troopers spotted the blue cavalry and turned in their saddles but made no move to fight—they had bigger fish to fry. Dickey also elected not to fight, losing the opportunity to slow Van Dorn down enough for Grant to counteract his move. Instead, he dispatched messengers to Grant, made a weak demonstration, and moved on rapidly toward Oxford.

Although the rear guard had elected to ignore the Federals, their commander played it safe and sent a messenger at a gallop to warn Van Dorn. Pulling up in a flurry of mud, the excited courier saluted and announced, "General, the Colonel sent me to inform you that the Yankees have fired on his rear!"

"Are they in the rear?" Van Dorn wanted to know.

"Yes, sir," the messenger replied.

"Well," Van Dorn said, "you go back and tell the Colonel that is exactly where I want them."

Unfortunately for the Union, Dickey's couriers got lost. Grant did not receive the reports until Dickey arrived in Oxford on the afternoon of the nineteenth. The Federal commander received the announcement of the Rebel movement in his usual stoic manner even though he instantly recognized the danger Van Dorn posed to Union operations. When Dickey finished his report, Grant quickly walked the quarter mile to the telegraph station and began to write out orders to his commanders. He ordered Colonel J. K. Mizner to assemble all available cavalry and immediately take up the pursuit. The commanding officers at Holly Springs, Davis' Mill, Grand Junction, La Grange, and Bolivar were advised, ". . . cavalry has gone north with the intention of striking the railroad . . . and cutting off our communications. Keep a sharp lookout and defend the road . . . at all hazards. . . ." In addition, Grant ordered Colonel R. C. Murphy at Holly Springs to send out all the cavalry he could afford to watch Rebel movements.

Moving north, Van Dorn deliberately crossed all routes to Holly Springs hoping to cause the Yankees to think Bolivar was his objective. Late in the evening of the eighteenth, they crossed the Tallahatchie River and went into bivouac. Already drenched and miserable, they got a double dose of the miseries when a terrific storm hit the area forcing them to move to avoid the rapidly rising river.

Morning came with biting cold. The shivering graybacks simply humped up against it and hurried northward again toward the main Ripley Road. Late in the afternoon, they turned off on an obscure road that was little more than a trail and struggled through a swampy area toward Holly Springs. About midnight, they captured Murphy's outposts, made a cold camp, ate, and tried to find ways to ward off the bitter chill while waiting for word to attack.

In the gray morning hours, the men were formed into a column of fours. The Texans were ordered to approach from the east and to attack anything in front of them; the Mississippians were to charge through the infantry from the northeast and grapple with the blue cavalry; the Missourians, dismounted, were to engage the infantry behind the Mississippians; and the Tennesseans were to screen the city to the north. Dispositions complete, the shivering troopers were ordered to draw sabers and charge. The first streaks of light were just breaking the darkness of the eastern sky as the Rebels swept out of the night to fall on the sleeping city.

A Mrs. Mason, one of the local citizens, was awakened by a sound she described as akin to the singing of a log on a fire underscored by a dull rumble. As she listened, the noise rapidly swelled into the sound of the hair-raising Rebel yell overlaying the drumming beat of galloping hooves. At a long run, the Mississippians poured over the sleeping infantry before it could move and smashed into the hastily aroused Union cavalry.

On the other side of town, a Mr. Wing and a Mr. Lough, who were sharing a bed in a rented room, were rudely awakened by the sound of cheering. Lough, feeling perfectly secure in the arms of the Union Army, commented, "There is a regiment going up."

Before Wing could reply, the morning was shattered by a burst of gunfire. He ran to the window to see the street filled with wild-riding Texans yelling at the top of their lungs. "Get up, the town is full of Secesh!" he yelled.

Lough ran to the window, glanced out, and in a disbelieving tone of voice said, "Wing, we're gobbled, by Judas!"

The unwarned and poorly positioned Federal infantry hardly knew what had hit them. The gray troopers' horses had torn through their midst, uprooting tents and bowling people over like tenpins. In addition to their confusion, their predicament was further complicated because they had been divided into small detachments and many of their officers, disregarding Grant's instructions, were snugly tucked away in Rebel homes. In isolated pockets, the infantry tried to resist, but to no avail. For the most part, the disoriented, shaken foot soldiers simply gave up with, at best, a token struggle.

The Federal cavalry was a different matter. Although they too had been surprised, they quickly rallied and formed to meet the Confederate attack. Completely encircled, they fought viciously, briefly pushing the Rebel line backward. Finally, a heavy force of Texans advancing from the east tipped the scales. Escape was now the only thing remaining for the Union horsemen. Perfectly formed up, sabers drawn, the bluebirds charged across the square into the Mississippians and Missourians who had formed to take the blow. The two lines met with a crash and swayed back and forth for a bit, hacking away at each other. Then, the Federals fell back, paused, regrouped, and charged again. This time the gray line burst and six companies of the Second Illinois tore free, the only Union unit to distinguish itself that day.

The fighting represented the wildest confusion—guns firing, men yelling, people running into the streets, horses plunging, and officers screaming orders in an effort to control the boiling cauldron of battle. A Southern reporter on the scene described the activity with great exuberance, but probably lacking something in accuracy and objectivity:

> The rapidity with which the tents of the enemy were vacated was marvelous; and, impelled by burning torches and rapid discharge of sidearms, the Yankees took no time to prepare their toilets, but rushed out into the cool atmosphere of a December morning, clothed very similarly to Joseph when the lady Potiphar attempted to detain him. The scene was wild, exciting, tumultuous. Yankees running, tents burning, torches flaming, Confederates shouting, guns popping, sabres clanking, Abolitionists begging for mercy, "Rebels" shouting exultingly, women *en dishabille* clapping their hands, frantic with joy, crying, "Kill them! Kill them!"—a heterogeneous mass of excited, frantic, frightened human beings—presented an indescribable picture, more adapted for the pencil of Hogarth than the pen of a newspaper correspondent.

By 8:00 A.M. it was over. The Rebels had full possession of the town and over fifteen hundred Union officers and men. Among those captured was the hapless Colonel Murphy, caught either at the telegraph station calling for reinforcements or hiding under a bed, depending on whose story one wanted to believe. And, stories spun out of the blue sky were plentiful. There were even some reports which claimed that Mrs. U. S. Grant was captured, with the reporters assuring readers she was treated with the greatest respect and courtesy throughout the Rebel stay.

The depot at Holly Springs was stuffed with all types of supplies and equipment. The poorly fed, clothed, and equipped Rebels fell on this bonanza like a horde of hungry grasshoppers. Utter chaos threatened to take over as the deprived Rebels sought "to set things right" in an orgy of looting Federal stores. High on the list of their favorite items was an immense whiskey supply. Confederate officers, shouting instructions in an attempt to restore some semblance of order, emptied barrels of whiskey to keep their men sober. Their efforts were in vain. The supply was so abundant that what they destroyed was scarcely missed. As one Rebel put it, "We stepped from privation to plenty and many were disposed to inaugurate a jubilee, inspired by the spirit of John Barleycorn, Esq."

Van Dorn was eventually able to restore order out of incipient chaos. He ordered the town searched and had Northern officials, cotton buyers, and sutlers brought together in one area. Here they were questioned and many relieved of their money and other valuables. In several instances, Northerners saved their funds by asking Southern ladies to hold them. Later reports held that, without exception, the full amount was returned after the gray troopers had departed.

The Rebels systematically destroyed the Union depot while the interrogations were going on. Warehouses, the railroad depot, engine house, and a train of forty-three cars and two engines were burned. Great quantities of hay, corn, oats, barrelled beef and pork, rice, whiskey, molasses, clothing, and medical supplies were added to the conflagration. Soldiers rolled bales of cotton together in the square and burned them. As a result, numerous buildings caught fire, including some housing sick and wounded Union soldiers. Union Surgeon Wirtz later filed a report accusing Van Dorn of deliberate brutality and disregard of the sick and wounded. Whether these acts were deliberate or the result of overexuberance and whiskey has never been established.

The Federal force had converted a large brick building on the square into an arsenal. Nearby was a large commissary. Van Dorn ordered the contents of both destroyed. Through a misunderstanding of orders or a lack of obedience, the latter building was fired. The flames quickly spread to other buildings, finally reaching the arsenal. At 3:00 P.M. it exploded with a noise like the crack of doom. Fire, shrapnel, and pieces of building material were scattered over a large area causing some additional casualties. Windows were shattered for blocks around, doors torn from their hinges, and many additional structures set on fire.

His work at Holly Springs finished, Van Dorn sent a message to Pemberton, "I surprised the enemy at this place at daylight this morning; burned up all the quartermaster's stores, cotton, etc.—an immense amount; burned up many trains; took a great many arms and about 1,500 prisoners. I presume the value of the stores would amount to $1,500,000. I move to Davis' Mill at once." At four o'clock, the first elements headed north.

When he heard that Holly Springs was captured, Grant immediately stepped up the effort to stop the raiders. The Twentieth Illinois under Colonel C. C. Marsh was loaded aboard a train with orders to run the train as near Holly Springs as possible, debark the troops, and retake the place. Although Grant was sure this force was sufficient to do the job, he sent other troops to support them and urged his cavalry forward.

Maj. John J. Mudd, who had led the charge of the Second Illinois in their escape at Holly Springs, was furious in his report. He told Grant, "I cannot close this report without expressing the opinion that this disaster is another added to the long list occasioned by the drunkenness or inefficiency of commanding officers. I cannot doubt but that the place could have been successfully defended by even half the force here had suitable precautions been taken and the infantry been concentrated, their officers in camp with them and prepared to fight. This was not done; but on the contrary they were scattered in four or five different sections of the place, their officers quietly sleeping at the houses of Rebel citizens, who were no doubt unusually agreeable and polite and lavish with their wines and brandies."

Mudd's anger was mild compared to Grant's. In Special Field Order No. 30, issued at Holly Springs on 23 December 1862, he said, "It is with pain and mortification that the general commanding reflects upon the disgraceful surrender of this place, with all the valuable stores it contained, on the 20th instant, and that without any resistance except by a few men, who form an honorable exception, and this too after warning had been given of the advance of the enemy northward the evening previous."

His full wrath was reserved for Colonel Murphy. Ironically, Grant, despite a denunciation by Maj. Gen. William S. Rosecrans, had saved the colonel from a court-martial only two months before. In this instance, Murphy had evacuated Iuka, Mississippi at the enemy's approach, leaving a large amount of supplies undestroyed. Now, despite Murphy's plea that his fate was already mortifying, that he had done his duty, and that he had wished a hundred times he had been killed, Grant was determined to rectify his earlier error in judgment. Foregoing a court-martial, he dismissed Murphy from ". . . the service of the United States, to take effect from the 20th day of December, 1862, the date of his cowardly and disgraceful conduct."

On 21 December, Van Dorn, flushed with victory and supremely confident, arrived at Davis' Mill. In this quiet little Mississippi hamlet there were two hundred infantry and fifty cavalry commanded by Colonel W. H. Morgan. He too had been warned of the possibility of a Rebel attack and had made good use of his time. An old sawmill had been converted into a blockhouse and an earthwork had been constructed about 350 yards from the bridge over Wolf Creek leading into town. These fortification efforts were still underway when the gray troopers arrived.

Van Dorn, disdaining an easier approach, dismounted part of his men and formed them up as infantry. With a loud cheer, this group charged across the uneven, swampy ground onto the Wolf Creek Bridge. They were met by such a swarm of bullets that the charge immediately stalled and they fled to safety.

Meanwhile, their force had been steadily growing until a front extended for about four hundred yards up and down the creek. From this front, a hail of lead was directed at the defenders and several unsuccessful attempts were made to cross the creek at points other than the bridge. Now, greatly reinforced, the Rebels mounted a second attack. Urged on by their officers, with banners flying they again charged out onto the bridge. Again, a curtain of accurate fire ripped their ranks and, again, they faltered and fell back.

Now, the attacking force concentrated a withering fire on the earthworks and blockhouse. The defenders had tasted victory, however, and were not intimidated by this effort. A third assault suffered the same fate as the first two, although a few Confederates succeeded in crossing the bridge and taking cover under it. All they gained, though, was the opportunity to surrender to Morgan's men shortly thereafter.

Apparently satisfied that the earthworks and blockhouse could not be taken except at prohibitive cost, and maybe not at all, Van Dorn ordered the bridge burned. Using balls of cotton soaked in turpentine, several of the raiders rushed forward in an attempt to fire the structure. Their efforts failed as extremely accurate fire from the defenders drove them to cover each time they approached. Giving up the bridge as a hopeless cause, the attackers retreated to an area of complete safety out of sight and range of the defenders. After a short pause in activity, the raiders sent a flag of truce forward. The bearer approached Morgan with a verbal message from Van Dorn wanting to know if he contemplated surrender. To this query, Morgan gave a respectful but unmistakably negative reply. With this, the Rebel force left the area.

Van Dorn again headed north. He passed to the west of Grand Junction, then swung east across the Mississippi Central Railroad below Middleburg. Passing east of that community, he again turned north leading his saddle-weary troopers toward Bolivar, Tennessee.

Up to this point, the Federal pursuit of Van Dorn had been extraordinarily inept. Marsh and his trainload of the Twentieth Illinois failed to arrive in Holly Springs until 21 December. Marsh, who had previously distinguished himself in combat, had been eagerly seeking an opportunity to win his star. Now, with it in his grasp, he faltered and for some inexplicable reason was overcome by an almost terminal case of extreme caution. Seven miles from his objective, without seeing a single enemy soldier, hearing the sound of a single shot, or finding one obstruction in front of him, he halted the train, dismounted his troops, and formed up in battle array. Then, he proceeded to lead them virtually "tiptoe" into Holly Springs, arriving there long after Van Dorn had vanished to the north.

The cavalry pursuit was no better. Mizner, though ordered to join Marsh as rapidly as possible, made little effort to do so. Grant, completely exasperated with Mizner's performance, removed him from command and gave the pursuit to Col. Benjamin H. Grierson, who would one day show his metal as a premier cavalry leader. He gladly accepted the challenge and pressed northward hard. He had little useful information to go on, however, since every Union post in the area was reporting the Rebel force nearby. Still, he pushed doggedly on, arriving at Grand Junction early the twenty-third. He rested for three hours then moved on to Bolivar, arriving there at about eleven o'clock at night. He was certain his quarry was close.

Bolivar was too much for Van Dorn and he knew it. He had to be satisfied with no more than a feint at the city. He made this by approaching from the east then dashing across just below the limits of the city before circling back from the west. He rushed near enough to capture the pickets on that approach and came within easy range of the town's fortifications before breaking off the attack.

Grierson had some fuzzy information about this and moved out to meet the Rebels. He was able to make only tentative contact, however, before they disappeared to the north. Uncertain of Van Dorn's intentions, Grierson pulled his main force back into the city while sending two companies in pursuit of the Rebels.

The raiders now plunged south, arriving at Middleburg by mid-morning. A garrison of 115 men of the Twelfth Michigan Infantry, commanded by Colonel W. H. Graves, held this small village. Graves watched from a blockhouse through a field glass as the Rebels approached. Some distance away, they halted and sent a flag of truce forward. He met the bearer of the flag a short distance from the blockhouse. The Confederate officer bearing the flag, who Graves found pompous and overbearing, demanded the immediate, unconditional surrender of the blockhouse in the name of Colonel Griffith, commanding Texas Brigade.

Graves was made of sterner stuff than Murphy. Irritated by the manner of the flag bearer, he later reported, "I sent my compliments to Colonel Griffith, with the answer that I would surrender when whipped, and that while he was getting a meal we would try to get a mouthful."

This response greatly irritated the Rebel officer, who wheeled his horse without comment and spurred it back toward the Confederate line. Graves knew what was coming and raced for the blockhouse entrance. He had hardly flung himself through the door before Rebel bullets splattered against the building.

The raiders pressed the attack for over two hours but made no headway against the well-entrenched Union infantry. At last, realizing that he was not going to subdue the blockhouse without artillery, Van Dorn broke off the attack. Again turning south, the gray command proceeded through Van Buren en route to Saulsbury.

Escape now became the paramount issue for the raiders. They were bone weary from nine days of riding and fighting and were feeling the pressure of hot pursuit by the Federal forces. Grant had found the trail and Grierson was on it with a vengeance. Van Dorn, who had accomplished his purpose, now pushed his worn men and horses to the limit in a determined effort to escape the Yankee forces bearing down on them.

Grierson left Bolivar as soon as he was certain of Van Dorn's direction of march. Moving rapidly south, the leading elements of his command contacted the rear of the Confederate column just after it left Middleburg. Throughout the remainder of the twenty-fourth, Grierson kept up the pursuit, occasionally skirmishing with small segments of the Confederate force, until darkness halted pursuit just beyond Saulsbury. Here Grierson camped, waiting for part of his lagging force to catch up. Scouts were sent forward to keep an eye on the Rebel camp.

At two o'clock in the morning on Christmas Day, the scouts reported the Rebel force had broken camp and was on the move. Grierson had his force on the road at four o'clock. He met Mizner, unfortunately for the Union restored to grace in Grant's eyes, about eight miles out of Saulsbury and relinquished command to him. The Federal force moved on rapidly to Ripley where it was joined by part of Mudd's Second Illinois. Just out of Ripley, contact was made again and a running fight ensued for about seven miles. Finally, the Rebel troopers turned, formed up, and charged. The lines hit with a crash and the gray troopers fell back. Twice more they formed and twice more they charged. Each time the blue troopers repulsed them. Then, to the Union's surprise, the Confederate force suddenly broke up and vanished.

Unknown to Mizner and Grierson, they had been fighting a small rear guard, detached for the express purpose of delaying them. While this unequal contest was in progress, the main Confederate force had dashed free.

It was almost dark when the last Rebel charge had been broken. Undeterred by the hour, Grierson wanted to press on and make a night attack. He was vetoed by Mizner who wanted no part of it. As a result, the Union force camped for the night, letting pursuit wait until early the next morning. Once underway, they galloped south to New Albany, crossed the Tallahatchie, and continued another six miles toward Pontotoc. Here, it became obvious their game had slipped the net. The frustrated Federals turned back toward Holly Springs empty-handed.

In Mississippi, as other Confederate commanders had done elsewhere, Van Dorn had forcibly demonstrated that a properly

employed cavalry force could be a devastating weapon. His capture of Holly Springs was the greatest victory the South enjoyed
in that area of operations in 1862. His five-hundred-mile ride
was a great lift to sagging Southern morale in the west and did
much to restore the tarnished reputation of the cocky little general. Coupled with the depredations of Forrest to the north, this
raid totally relieved the pressure on Vicksburg for the time being
and assured the Confederacy a few more months of survival in
the West.

Grant, his communications to the north completely cut off for over
a week and his supply line destroyed, gave up his movement on
Vicksburg. Instead, he recoiled slowly northward toward Memphis,
sweeping the Mississippi countryside clean to provide forage for his
troops. In the process, he resolved to never again rely on a long,
lightly defended line of supply.

Cut off from Grant, Maj. Gen. William T. Sherman, proceeded to
execute his part of the grand design to subdue Vicksburg. On sched-
ule, he came ashore at Chickasaw Bayou on the twenty-ninth to find
an unoccupied Pemberton waiting for him. As the Union forces struggled through the rugged, swampy ground separating the bayou from
the bluffs overlooking the Yazoo River bottoms, they found every
approach covered by Rebel rifle and artillery fire. After taking over
two thousand casualties, they gave up the effort. Sherman grimly
reported, "I reached Vicksburg at the time appointed, landed, assaulted, and failed."

While the loss to the Union was heavy, it was not fatal. After a few
months respite, the Federals would again move south and, after a
grueling siege, Vicksburg would fall. And, while Grant learned to distrust supply lines, he learned another lesson that was to have disastrous consequences for the Confederacy.

By his admission, Grant took a little time to realize the significance
of his successful foraging in northern Mississippi. But, realize it he
did. Supply lines were not necessary in the South! An army could
effectively survive for long periods off the land. The true importance
of this discovery became apparent later in the war when Sherman was
unleashed on his "march to the sea." Once the states west of the
Mississippi River had been successfully amputated, Sherman would
turn east, ripping the soft underbelly of the South open, living off the
land as he did so. While that transpired, to the north, Grant would
methodically beat the remaining life out of the Confederacy with a
series of sledgehammer blows to the head.

CHAPTER VII

Lay Your Wires
to Kill Him

As 1862 ground slowly through autumn toward winter, which promised to be miserable, a pall of gloom settled over the Union. Federal armies had been unable to achieve a decisive victory over their Southern opponents in any theater. In the East, Maj. Gen. Ambrose Burnside, a man later charged with the ability to snatch defeat from the jaws of victory, had just been soundly drubbed by Gen. Robert E. Lee at Fredericksburg. In the West, Major General U. S. Grant was pressing inexorably on Vicksburg but progress was slow and painful. In Middle Tennessee, Maj. Gen. William S. Rosecrans was struggling to rebuild the disorganized army he had inherited from Maj. Gen. Don Carlos Buell. As Pres. Abraham Lincoln surveyed this murky panorama from Washington, he was acutely aware of the strains tugging at the foundation of the country. Somehow, a compelling success had to be fashioned or the Union might succumb to the combined forces of the internal and external pressures being exerted on it. The East was hopeless for the time being; therefore, circumstances forced the president to look to his western commanders for the victory so desperately needed.

Winning would be no easy matter for either of the western generals, for both faced formidable obstacles. Grant was uncertain as to the extent of his authority and control over large segments of the force ostensibly committed to him. Rosecrans had taken an army that had almost one-third of its troops hospitalized or absent without leave and the remainder poorly drilled and equipped. Both armies dangled at the end of a very long supply line that was extremely vulnerable to the cut and slash tactics of the Confederate cavalry. Even the weather seemed to be conspiring against them. Torrential rains had swollen streams and turned roads into quagmires, making movement difficult and uncertain. And, when the rain stopped, smothering fog, impregnated with bone-aching cold, blanketed the countryside.

Despite the obstacles facing them, these tough-minded leaders were making an effort to rise to the challenge. By mid-December, Grant had Lt. Gen. John C. Pemberton's back firmly against the wall and was slowly strangling Vicksburg. Desperate to relieve the pressure, Pemberton called on Gen. Braxton Bragg for help. Together, they played the trump cards they were holding in their hands. In what was at best a loosely coordinated action, they slipped the leashes on two of their war dogs, sending them ranging far behind enemy lines. On 15 December, Brig. Gen. Nathan Bedford Forrest slipped across the fog-shrouded Tennessee River and slashed north along the Mobile and Ohio Railroad breaking the Union supply and communications lines that stretched through Middle Tennessee. Five days later Maj. Gen. Earl Van Dorn streaked out of the predawn darkness to obliterate the giant Union supply depot at Holly Springs, Mississippi. From there, he proceeded almost to the Tennessee border, cutting the Central Mississippi Railroad and with it Grant's line of supply. By New Year's Day, that Union leader was temporarily out of action and was preparing to withdraw toward Memphis, Tennessee.

All the while he was dealing with the Grant problem, Bragg kept a part of his mind on Rosecrans. In fact, earlier in the month he had told Brig. Gen. John H. Morgan to prepare to attack into Kentucky. Fully aware of the condition of Rosecrans's army, Bragg had not been overly concerned about it. Now, he decided prudence dictated it be checked out and dispatched scouts for that purpose. Believing he had good intelligence about the condition of that army, he confidently expected to find it withdrawing to safety. Instead, the returning scouts reported the Union force preparing to assault the Confederate

Army in the vicinity of Murfreesboro, Tennessee. This unexpected development did not especially concern Bragg. Since Rosecrans was afflicted with the same tenuous supply line vulnerability as Grant, Bragg decided to give him identical treatment. John Morgan would be the attending physician. Bragg would dispatch him into the Bluegrass country in an attempt to snip the umbilical attaching Rosecrans to Louisville.

The general target was the meandering Louisville and Nashville Railroad. This line of track had the same vulnerabilities as all railroads with an added attraction. Essential to the continuity of the entire network of iron that comprised the railroad were two huge trestles in eastern Kentucky near Muldraugh's Hill. If these towering structures could be destroyed, Rosecrans's line of supply would collapse. These giants were the prize Morgan sought; the touchstone for the ultimate success or failure of his planned raid. If he were successful, he could well complete the checkmate of the Union's western generals and, perhaps, unchain the demon of defeat that was beginning to haunt the president.

The last thing in the universe Rosecrans needed at this time was John Morgan hacking away at his supply line. The prickly, hard-drinking, profane general, nicknamed "Old Rosey" by the troops, had solved staggering problems in whipping his army into condition in the face of heavy, unwarranted pressure from Washington. In fact, the pressure had become so intense by early December that the Union's chief soldier, Maj. Gen. Henry Halleck, had bluntly told him, "If you remain one more week in Nashville, I cannot prevent your removal."

Not even the commander in chief of the Army intimidated the crusty Rosecrans. He promptly wired back with his reasons for delay, terminating his message by caustically telling Halleck, "To threats of removal or the like I must be permitted to say that I am insensible."

Now that he had withstood Washington, solved his army's problems, and was ready to move on Bragg, Morgan popped up and began threatening his lifeline.

Morgan had started his preparations earlier when Bragg ordered him to ready his brigade for a thrust into Kentucky to break the railroads behind Rosecrans and destroy his communications with Louisville. Morgan had reorganized his forces into a division of two brigades. The first of these, under Col. Basil Duke, consisted of Lt. Col. John Hutcheson's Second Kentucky, Maj. Richard Gano's Third Kentucky, Colonel R. S. Cluke's Eighth Kentucky, and Capt. Baylor

Palmer's Battery of two twelve-pounders and two six-pounders. The Second Brigade, commanded by Col. William Breckinridge, consisted of Lieutenant Colonel R. G. Stoner's Ninth Kentucky, Col. Samuel Johnson's Tenth Kentucky, Lieutenant Colonel D. W. Chenault's Eleventh Kentucky, Col. James Bennett's Fourteenth Kentucky, Captain B. F. White's three-inch Parrott, and Captain C. C. Corbett's two mountain howitzers. The total strength of the division exceeded four thousand, but, after eliminating the sick or disabled and some of the unarmed, an effective strength of about thirty-one hundred remained available for the raid. This group assembled on 21 December in a heavy grove of evergreens near Alexandria, Tennessee.

Before dawn on the twenty-second, "Reveille" sounded and the order passed to move out at nine o'clock. The weather had relented and the day broke crisp and clear, the early morning sunshine bathing the countryside. At the appointed hour, the gray troopers began emerging from the green cedars, a regiment at a time, and formed into a long column moving at a trot. After about two hours, a cheer started at the rear of the column and rolled up its length in a swelling tide of sound. The cheer marked Morgan's progress as he galloped down the column, plumed hat waving in his hand, while he smiled and bowed, acknowledging the accolade from his troopers.

Like his counterpart in the east, Maj. Gen. Jeb Stuart, Morgan was the epitome of a cavalry leader. He stood over six feet tall, was always impeccably dressed and finely mounted, and presented the air and manner of a polished gentleman. He successfully hid his limited military background behind an innate talent which offset his lack of formal military training. His attention-grabbing successes had firmly established his reputation as a winner and earned him the total devotion and dedication of his men. To them, he was invincible and their attachment to him was barely short of idolatry.

Late in the afternoon of the twenty-second, the column arrived at Sand Shoals Ford on the Cumberland River. Without delay, Duke's brigade pushed forward, scrambling to get across the river ahead of the swiftly falling winter darkness. Breckinridge halted and pitched camp between Caney Fork and the main channel of the Cumberland to await daylight before crossing the river. The men were unaware as they settled in for the night that Union forces were already searching for them. Although uncertain as to exactly what was happening and ignorant as to the location of the Rebel force, Federal troops had been on the hunt for them for seven days.

Rosecrans had received intelligence on 15 December indicating that Morgan was raiding in Kentucky. Reacting promptly to this information, although it had not been confirmed by any of his subordinate commanders, the Union general sent warnings in all directions. Forces throughout the state stirred into motion. During the next several days confusion mounted as local commanders girded to meet this phantom attack. Gallatin appeared to be a very likely target. Major General J. J. Reynolds, commanding Fifth Division, XIV Corps, Army of the Cumberland, and Brig. Gen. Speed Fry, commanding Third Division, Center, Army of the Cumberland, rallied to protect it and to watch all crossings and roads in that vicinity. Meanwhile, Maj. Gen. Gordon Granger, commanding District of Central Kentucky, Army of the Ohio, moved rapidly in the direction of Bowling Green hoping to surprise the raiders. Maj. Gen. Thomas L. Crittenden, commanding Left Wing, XIV Corps, Army of the Cumberland, dispatched a hurried reconnaissance to check out reports that Morgan was supported by Confederate Lt. Gen. E. Kirby Smith, commanding the major Southern forces in that area.

Despite all this frantic activity and numerous reports of Rebel movements, no contact was made. By the end of the day on 19 December, senior Union commanders were entertaining serious doubts regarding Confederate activity. Maj. Gen. Horatio Wright, commanding Department of the Ohio, expressed the general feeling in a wire to Brig. Gen. Jeremiah T. Boyle, commanding District of Western Kentucky, Department of the Ohio, who had previously experienced the effects of a Morgan raid, at Louisville, ". . . if he really comes (which I do not believe) . . . Our troops must understand that they are expected to fight, and if they do half their duty they can whip Morgan's rascals. . . ." At last, by nightfall on the twenty-second Union commanders had convinced themselves they were only threatened by the possibility of a raid. Across the state they let their guard down in relief. The next morning, Morgan struck.

The raiders moved early on the twenty-third, pushing swiftly toward Glasgow, stopping just short of that point at dark. Once in camp, three companies were detached with orders to scout ahead and determine Union strength. These troops arrived in Glasgow well after nightfall and probed gingerly through the feebly lighted streets of the sleeping town. Groping forward near the town's center, they bumped into a Michigan battalion that had not given up the search and were scouting from the opposite direction. A panicky fight broke out immediately, guns flashing sporadically in the blackness as both sides hunted cover.

It was a quick, indistinct, and dirty fight as indicated by Lt. Samuel Peyton's experience. Moving through the flickering gunfire, he suddenly doubled under a crushing blow and stabbing pain as a Yankee slug found its mark. Disoriented from shock and pain as he stumbled through the darkness, he became separated from his company. Slowly regaining his senses, he found himself hard-pressed by two Michigan men who were determined to take him prisoner. Dodging through the deeper shadows, he snapped off his one remaining round, dropping one pursuer in his tracks. Now out of ammunition, Peyton charged the remaining enemy bare-handed and grappled with him. The two strained, swaying back and forth, then toppled to the ground. Groveling desperately in the darkness and dirt, Peyton managed to free his pocketknife and with a single quick motion slit his adversary's throat. As he struggled to his feet, he heard the firing stop. The Federal cavalry had had enough of Glasgow and was retreating rapidly up the Louisville Pike.

Rebel activity on the twenty-third rejuvenated Union interest in Morgan and his whereabouts. Rosecrans started receiving a deluge of messages reporting the raider at widely scattered points and, for the most part, grossly overestimating his strength. Again the Union forces began to stir. Scouts were sent to pinpoint the location of the Confederates while troops were shifted to cover weak points. Rosecrans, almost ready to move on Murfreesboro and determined not to be distracted, gave Wright the primary task of pursuing Morgan. Still, apparently concerned about his commanders' ability and his troops' willingness to stand and fight, "Old Rosey" exhorted them to find the raiders, concentrate their forces, and fight like the devil.

The sober dawn of Christmas Eve day broke over the gray riders hurrying down the Louisville Pike. Out in front, an advance of fifty men under a Captain Quirk spotted an unsuspecting unit of blue cavalry. Without breaking their pace, the advance rode them down, routing the group before the main column could even slow the march. Holding steady at their mile-eating pace, the raiders pressed through the day with no opposition until well into the afternoon. Then, rounding a bend in the road, Quirk confronted a battalion of troops that was dismounted and formed in line across the Rebel route of march. Again, his yelling graybacks charged, crashing through the thin blue line. Before the Federals could regroup, Quirk whirled his command and charged back into them. In the lead, bent low over his horse, Quirk took two rifle balls across the top of his head. Miraculously, the wounds he received were superficial, although one observer noted that the slugs did mark out a neat angle in his hair. The enemy scattered.

Now, Johnson sloughed off and rushed toward Munfordville in a successful effort to convince the enemy of an attack in that direction. The main column pressed steadily on, capturing what Duke called the most enormous wagon, perhaps, ever seen in the state of Kentucky, filled with a variety of items including whiskey. The hapless wagon owner was forced to watch the marauders quickly empty the giant transport of its load of Christmas goodies and ride away. They crossed the Green River that night and, just before daybreak, went into camp near Hammondsville.

On the twenty-fourth, Rosecrans's army was moving on an unwavering course to Murfreesboro, ignoring the gadfly hovering about it. As Wright's forces struggled to locate and neutralize Morgan, reports streamed in placing him in the vicinity of Gallatin, Glasgow, and Bowling Green. His strength was estimated to be as much as twelve thousand, and one report credited him with twenty guns. Another report advised that Kirby Smith was immediately behind Morgan with an even larger force. Colonel S. D. Bruce was directed to make a forced march to Bowling Green; Reynolds told to move up the Scottsville Road; and Granger ordered forward from Lexington. "Old Rosey" now cautioned his commanders that Morgan would attempt to stampede everyone by stories of magnitude of force and concluded by assuring them, "We will catch and kill those rascals yet."

By Christmas Day, Wright was certain that Morgan's strength was no more than about three thousand men and eight guns. He now ordered Col. John Harlan to Cave City; told Reynolds to cut Morgan's line of retreat; and sent Fry to Bowling Green to support Bruce. He ordered Boyle to mass the cavalry and get on Morgan's trail at Munfordville, warning him that infantry could not catch the raider. Rosecrans joined in urging Boyle not to believe the stories of Rebel strength and assuring him that he could whip Morgan to death. He closed by commanding Boyle to, "Lay your wires to kill him."

The weather changed drastically on the twenty-sixth, a driving rain turning the world to seemingly endless mud. Hutcheson, with parts of the Second and Third Kentucky, plodded forward through the downpour, aiming for the Louisville and Nashville Railroad bridge at

Bacon Creek. This important span was protected by a small, one-hundred-man detachment posted in a stockade. However, in a stroke of bad luck for the Rebels, this unit was joined by a battalion from Munfordville just as the Rebels arrived. The Second Kentucky quickly drove the newcomers off but found the troops in the stockade made of sterner stuff. Heavy artillery fire rapidly breached the stockade in several places and flattened an old barn in its center. But, to the disgust of the attackers, the defenders not only held, but returned a hot and heavy fire.

Losing his patience, Hutcheson ordered the bridge destroyed regardless of cost. As the Rebels scrambled to carry out the order, the Union force laid down a withering sheet of fire wounding several of them. It was not enough, however. Pressing on, despite the heavy fire, the raiders finally made the bridge and set it on fire. They soon discovered to their chagrin that the flames had to be constantly fueled or the rain would put them out. In an almost futile effort, a few attackers crouched behind an abutment and pushed burning wood onto the bridge only to have most of it knocked off by the hail of bullets that continued to envelope the structure.

The situation was beginning to look hopeless for the raiders when Morgan arrived on the scene. He took charge, sending a flag of truce to the stockade and demanding its surrender while offering generous terms to the defenders. Once convinced that it was really Morgan before them, the gallant Yankee troops gave up. In minutes the bridge was fired completely.

Meanwhile, Duke arrived at the Nolin Stockade and demanded its surrender. Playing for time, the commander told Duke he would capitulate provided he could be shown a certain number of artillery pieces. Duke promptly put them on display. The Federal commander then said he wanted to consult with his officers. Suspecting his opponent's motives, Duke moved the artillery forward and trained it on the Union defense. Then, he positioned men where they could cover every loophole in the stockade. After this maneuvering was complete, he released the Federal commander to conduct the desired consultation. The Yankee was back in a very few minutes to throw in the towel. Duke's men then destroyed the bridge, several culverts, and some cattle guards. By nightfall, the division had regrouped and had gone into camp near Elizabethtown which was held by six hundred troops under Lieutenant Colonel H. S. Smith.

Early on the twenty-seventh, as the raiders approached the town, they were met by a Federal corporal who handed Morgan a note

from Smith scrawled on the back of an envelope. The Rebel chief
could hardly believe what he read. Smith demanded his unconditional surrender, announcing he had the raiders surrounded and would
open his batteries on them in twenty minutes if they failed to comply
with his demand.

Duke thought this to be the "most sublimely audacious" demand
ever to ". . . emanate from a Federal officer, who, as a class rarely
trusted to audacity and bluff, but to odds and the *concours* of force."

Morgan elected to respond in kind. He formally replied to the
Union commander that, in fact, the situation was exactly reversed
and concluded by giving Smith the same option he had offered—
unconditional surrender. The Yankee was allowed ten minutes in
which to decide.

The spunky Smith wasted no time. He bluntly told the raider that,
". . . it is the duty of United States soldiers to fight, and not surrender."

While this exchange of messages transpired, the raiders were getting into position. Cluke's regiment moved to the right of the road
and dismounted while several additional companies spread out further in that direction to encircle half the town. Stoner duplicated this
move on the left and the Parrott gun was set up in the center of the
road leading into the village. Palmer's four guns were then positioned
on top of a hill to the left, some six hundred yards from the town's
outskirts.

Smith's final note got him a coughing reply from the Parrott followed instantly by the crash of Palmer's battery. Cluke moved forward slowly, wary of two stockades in front of him which turned out
to be empty. Stoner's Ninth Kentucky charged at a run and were
soon in the houses at the edge of town forcing their defenders to surrender. Cluke now entered the town, meeting only light resistance on
his right. With the raiders in the edge of town, Palmer moved his
guns forward concentrating their fire on a large building flying the
Stars and Stripes. Corbett, with one howitzer and a company to
guard it, moved rapidly forward to a position on top of a railroad
embankment and began hammering away at the same building.

Corbett's artillery was so situated that the defenders had difficulty
firing at it from inside the building. Consequently, after each barrage,
the Union troops would rush into the street and fire a volley at the
cannoneers. The riflemen assigned to protect Corbett soon put a stop
to this practice by sweeping the street with a hail of fire each time the
bluebirds flocked out. A staff officer watching this action decided the
Rebel company protecting Corbett was not effective and ordered

them to charge. They did so without question, running forward into full view of the defenders. Instantly, they were engulfed by Yankee bullets. Their officers, frantically trying to correct this mistake, hastily directed a confused return. Quickly taking advantage of the disorder, the Federals poured out into the street and concentrated heavy fire on Corbett's gunners, driving them away from the field piece. In a few moments, however, the gray company regained its composure and regrouped. In seconds, they had forced the Union defenders back inside the building. And, again, Corbett's gun went into action.

After a few more minutes of cannonading, a white flag waved from one of the building's windows. Smith had not authorized this action and tried to stop it. The troops had had enough, however, and, despite their commander's displeasure, tumbled from cover and laid down their arms. Smith escaped but the remainder of the garrison was captured. With them, Morgan netted six hundred rifles to better arm some of his troopers and to equip the remainder who still had no weapons.

The Union Army was continuing to scramble frantically to close with the raiders. Misinformation, confusion as to Morgan's strength and location, and a growing feeling of unease for the safety of Louisville were combining to render these efforts largely ineffective. To bolster the spirits of the pursuers, Rosecrans announced, "Morgan is in the toils and being rapidly hemmed in." Wishful thinking that fell far short of reality.

The next day, the Rebel division moved slowly up the railroad toward Muldraugh's Hill, methodically destroying it as they went. Finally, they caught sight of their main objective. The two great trestles, each eighty to ninety feet high and over five hundred feet long, loomed against the clear blue sky. Both structures were protected by garrisons, one of six hundred and one of two hundred men. When the Rebels neared them, Morgan split the division and attacked the defending units simultaneously. After only token resistance, both surrendered. The main body of raiders then went to work on the two wooden bridges. After hours of back-breaking labor, their efforts were rewarded by the sight of these monsters crashing into the gorge in a fiery display of sparks, smoke, and flames.

While the major part of the Confederate force was occupied with the destruction of the trestles, smaller units had destroyed the Cave Run Bridge and two smaller bridges on the Lebanon branch of the railroad. That night, regrouped, the division camped near two fords on the southern branch of the Rolling Fork River.

The next morning a regiment with two guns went south to destroy a bridge over the Rolling Fork; a court-martial convened to try Lieutenant Colonel J. M. Huffman for allegedly violating Morgan's surrender terms at Bacon Creek; and the remainder of the force started slowly fording the swollen, treacherous stream. At eleven o'clock, just as the court acquitted Huffman, the command was jarred by the rumble of artillery rounds dropping among their outlying vedettes. To the consternation of the Rebels, Harlan had caught up with them. Morgan was now in a quandary. If he continued the crossing, it would mean the certain loss of the force sent downstream. On the other hand, if he stopped the crossing, he ran the risk of losing an even larger force. Reluctance to sacrifice the troops that had gone downriver was the deciding factor. He ordered Duke to assemble a force and prepare to fight.

A meadow about three hundred yards wide and eight hundred yards long ran back from the river to a heavily wooded area. This open field was bounded on both sides by extremely rough ground covered with a thick growth of trees and matted underbrush. Some two hundred yards from the river, a sharp depression ran across the meadow providing a natural earthworks. Duke placed his troops in this depression, giving excellent protection to the men but not the horses.

The force advancing on them consisted of five thousand infantry, two thousand cavalry, and several artillery pieces. Had Harlan charged with speed and determination, he could have handily swept the raiders into the boiling river. Instead, he advanced with extreme caution, fitfully sparring with small groups of Confederates harassing him from the wooded areas as they slowly fell back. At last he reached the meadow's edge where he halted and opened up with four or five Parrott guns.

This fire had hardly begun when the troops returned from downriver at a gallop, the two guns in the lead. Knowing these sixpounders were no match for the Union Parrotts and hoping not to start a hot fight, Duke ordered the artillery and all but five companies of this force across the river at the upper ford. The remainder were thrown into his defensive line. Morgan now ordered Duke to retreat but, although he devoutly wished to do so, he could not. The enemy Parrotts were wreaking havoc among his horses and artillery rounds were falling into the ford with disconcerting regularity. The gray force could do nothing but huddle in the depression and wait for the inevitable charge.

Finally it came. The Union artillery redoubled its efforts and a long line of blue infantry, covered on the right by cavalry, moved out of the woods, bayonets gleaming. The blue line moved with majestic slowness across the brown meadow, the defiant cheers of the gray defenders providing music for their march. As soon as the attacking line came within range, a Rebel volley crashed out and, unaccountably, the Federals reversed their march and withdrew to the woods. Duke could hardly believe his eyes for he was certain the Federals had not lost a man.

Leaping at this opportunity, Duke ordered a diversionary charge at the Union center and instructed Captain V. M. Pendleton to silence the Union Parrotts. Pendleton led a reckless charge across the meadow, overrunning the guns, killing several gunners, and silencing this threat for about fifteen minutes. Now, Dame Fortune took a hand in the game and gave the beleaguered Rebels her brightest smile. A third, sheltered ford was discovered and the raiders dashed across the river leaving their tormentors empty-handed. No pursuit was attempted. Again, timidity and delay had frustrated Union efforts.

The raiders left the area at a gallop, Chenault breaking off to destroy the stockade at Boston. At nightfall, the division, completely reformed, camped at Bardstown.

Despite the ineptness displayed by the Union Army to this point and Harlan's failure to press with determination, the Federal forces were slowly closing around Morgan. Heavy effort effectively executed could still result in the capture of the elusive raider. But, Rosecrans, about to close with Bragg, was ready to wash his hands of the whole affair. To requests for more troops, "Old Rosey" replied, "If General Wright, with twenty thousand men, cannot take care of Morgan, I shall not send anymore troops up. I have already sent three brigades." The number of troops was not the problem; their employment was.

On the morning of 30 December, Johnson moved out well in front and swept down on the pickets in front of Lebanon. The attack was so vicious that Col. Edward Hoskins, the Union commander in Lebanon, became convinced he was Morgan's next objective. In preparation, he recalled a cavalry regiment from New Market to strengthen his force and, by so doing, opened an avenue for Morgan to slip away without a fight.

At three o'clock that afternoon, Morgan cantered into Springfield to find himself still in serious trouble. At Lebanon, eight miles ahead, eight thousand troops with artillery waited for him; scouts informed him that a large force was en route from Glasgow to Columbia to intercept him if he evaded the force at Lebanon; and Harlan was again pressing him from the rear. Morgan mulled this information over for a time before deciding on his next move. He later described his decision saying, "In this emergency I determined to make a detour to the right of Lebanon, and by a night march to conceal my movements from the enemy, outstrip the column moving from Glasgow to Columbia, and cross the Cumberland before it came within striking distance."

When darkness fell, Morgan's men built hundreds of fires in front of Lebanon hoping this ruse would make Hoskins hold to his belief that he was about to come under attack. The Yankee took the bait, bracing himself for an assault he was confident he could crush. At midnight, the Confederate division moved. They plunged into a stygian night that was bitterly cold. Struggling and stumbling in the pitch blackness, they blindly forced themselves and their animals forward, both man and beast suffering terribly in the relentless grip of the numbing cold. Years later, men who followed Morgan through his entire wartime career remembered this night as their most difficult experience. At daylight, they had traveled only eight miserable, suffering miles. Daylight speeded them up, however, and by one o'clock they were on the Lebanon and Columbia Road trotting toward Campbellsville.

As the column jogged along through the leaden winter day, Capt. Alexander Tribble and Lt. George Eastin fell behind. Suddenly, they found themselves hotly pursued by Col. Dennis Halisy's blue-clad cavalry. The Rebels were well-mounted and easily outdistanced the main body of pursuit. But, looking back while traveling a straight stretch of road, they saw four Union men out in front, rapidly closing the gap between them. On rounding a sharp bend in the road, Tribble and Eastin decided to wait for the four pursuers. They felt they could take them by shooting two with rifles and then disposing of the remaining two hand-to-hand.

For some unknown reason, two of the pursuers stopped and only Halisy and a lieutenant galloped around the corner toward the waiting Rebels. The graybacks, both crack shots, squeezed off a round and missed! The foes then rushed at each other, meeting with a thump of horseflesh, and struggled in the saddle momentarily before falling to the ground. Wrestling, slugging each other when they could, the four rolled along the ground in a tangle of arms and legs. Finally, Tribble forced his man's head into a pool of water, making him surrender to avoid drowning. In a few more seconds, Eastin pressed his pistol against Halisy's temple and demanded his surrender. The Union colonel agreed, but then, as he got to his feet, jerked out his pistol and fired at Eastin. The shot grazed the raider's face leaving a streak of blood. Eastin promptly killed the Yankee colonel where he stood. The Union called it murder. Morgan had a different point of view, observing that Eastin and Tribble ". . . deserve the thanks of the civilized community for putting to rest such an exponent of the Butler and Turchin school as Colonel Halisy."

At Campbellsville, the raiders found a large store of commissary supplies that were quickly distributed to the tired and hungry men. Rested and fed, on the morning of New Year's Day, they moved out, arriving at Columbia at three o'clock. Here they waited until dark before moving again. Then, once more they stumbled through inky darkness and gripping cold en route to Burkesville. On 2 January, they crossed the Cumberland and the raid was over.

The raid was eminently successful in attaining its immediate objectives. Rosecrans's railway artery was decisively severed with the destruction of the trestles at Muldraugh's Hill. Including these trestles, the raiders had destroyed twenty-two hundred feet of bridges, three depots, three water stations, a large number of culverts and cattle guards, long sections of railroad track, and, by Morgan's estimate, two million dollars in supplies and equipment. He had captured 1,877 prisoners, killed or wounded a large number, and pulled more than twenty thousand troops that Rosecrans needed away from him. Morgan's loss was two killed, twenty-four wounded, and sixty-four missing. As with all successful raids, this one bolstered Southern spirits and resolve, an intangible but immensely valuable return.

Yet, while Morgan had disabled Rosecrans's land line of supply for weeks and caused Union Brig. Gen. Robert B. Mitchell, commanding Fourth Division, Center, XIV Corps, Army of the Cumberland, to tell "Old Rosey," "Everything looks blue in Kentucky," he could not close the Cumberland. The river became an able substitute for the railroad and provided the Union Army its sustaining lifeline. Perhaps of even more serious consequence, he did not return in time to help Bragg at Murfreesboro. When the Union and Confederate Armies met at Stone's River just before the end of Morgan's raid, they almost hammered each other to bits. Fairly well-matched, Bragg's forty thousand men and Rosecrans's forty-four thousand men relentlessly pummeled each other, by coincidence, under identical battle plans. The struggle ended indecisively with both armies exhausted, but it was the gray one that finally had to fall back. It had been a near brush for the Union Army. Had they failed at this point, the defeat would have been one that, according to Lincoln, ". . . the nation could have scarcely lived over." And, had Morgan returned in time to bolster Bragg at Stone's River, it might well have spelled defeat for the Union Army and altered the outcome of the war.

CHAPTER VIII

The "War Child" Rides

Christmas season of 1862 was a harsh and bitter time in middle Tennessee. Ominous clouds of destruction hovered in the grim winter sky as the fratricidal civil war threatening to dismember the nation ground through another holiday season. From northern Mississippi through central Tennessee, far into the Blue Grass of Kentucky, ferocious bands of Rebel horsemen led by Gens. Earl Van Dorn, Nathan Bedford Forrest, and John Hunt Morgan left a wake of desolation as they raced through the countryside severing supply arteries carrying the lifeblood of the Federal armies in the west. But, even as these vital lines slowly collapsed, the Union Army in Nashville under Maj. Gen. William S. Rosecrans, ignoring the devastation behind it, gathered its strength to attack. The adversary lay scattered along meandering Stone's River near the sleepy hamlet of Murfreesboro, Tennessee—forty thousand battle-hardened Confederates under the veteran Gen. Braxton Bragg.

The Confederate commander, winner of three brevets in the Mexican War, was a talented organizer and strategist, but something less than a military genius. Currently, short a division of infantry he had sent to Vicksburg and the cavalry of Forrest and Morgan that was raiding in Tennessee and Kentucky, he grudgingly held the defensive. As he settled into position, having convinced himself that

114

Rosecrans was too weak to attack, he ordered feisty Brig. Gen. Joseph Wheeler, his commander of cavalry, to keep a close watch on the Union force. Wheeler, who had commanded an infantry regiment at Shiloh and around Corinth prior to his current assignment, took up his charge with determination. Making himself as pesky as a "nit fly" in summer, he "watched" so hard that Federal commanders often had to fight the Rebel cavalry to obtain forage. As the gray troopers probed the enemy lines and hovered about the periphery of the blue army, they came to the stunning realization that, instead of retreat, Rosecrans was thinking attack. Undisturbed, and confident he could crush the Federal force, Bragg imperturbably watched and waited.

The twenty-sixth of December dawned reluctantly, daylight straining feebly through sheets of rain that saturated the cold winter air. Peering through this watery curtain, advance elements of the Confederate cavalry watched as three massive columns of blue soldiers slowly moved out of their bivouacs around Nashville. The Union force had barely started to move forward before couriers were galloping toward Murfreesboro to inform Wheeler of the coming attack.

As soon as he received the news, Wheeler set out in search of his commander. He found him in conference with two of his senior commanders, Lt. Gens. William J. Hardee and Leonidas Polk. Interrupting their meeting, he reported the Union movement and stepped aside. Bragg wasted no time in issuing orders for his army to form a line in front of Murfreesboro. This action completed, the commanding general turned to his cavalry leader and asked, "How long can you hold them on the road?"

"About four days, General," Wheeler quietly replied.

Polk shook his head in disbelief and Hardee snorted, "They will run right over you!"

These skeptical officers would soon learn they had grossly underestimated the ability of this diminutive horse soldier. Only twenty-six years old and less than five years out of West Point, Wheeler had justly earned a reputation as a sound, resourceful commander. Although barely five feet five inches tall and weighing only 120 pounds, his dignified bearing and intense earnestness about everything made his presence commanding. Possessed of boundless energy, he was restless as a caged panther. Bounding, rather than walking, he seemed to be everywhere, all the time. His burning eagerness to close with the enemy and tenacious fighting qualities caused his troops to tag him with the sobriquets the "War Child" and "Fightin' Joe." Years later, one of his old troopers would sum him up by saying, "I'll tell you, Joe Wheeler was the gamest little banty I ever seen. He warn't afeered of nuthin' or nobody!"

Wheeler's cavalry was divided into two commands, one under the Texas lawyer, Brig. Gen. John A. Wharton, and the other under the Virginia-born West Pointer, Brig. Gen. John Pegram. On the right, Pegram's command consisted of the First Alabama, Third Alabama, Fifty-first Alabama, Eighth Confederate, two battalions of Tennesseans, and an Arkansas Battery. On the left, Wharton had Terry's Texas Rangers, Harrison's Georgia Regiment, Cox's Regiment, Davis's Battalion, Malone's Battalion, and White's Battery. This force, totaling 4,237 horsemen, backed by Maj. Gen. Benjamin F. Cheatham's division of infantry, stubbornly steeled itself to hold up an army ten times its numerical strength. The tactic they had chosen to accomplish this Herculean task was to hit the front, force it to form in line of battle, then strike a flank and the rear, and fall back when the pressure became too great.

As the blue soldiers plodded forward in the driving rain, struggling through thick cedar brakes, and fighting the clinging mud, the gray horsemen struck. Using the rugged, rolling country and thickly wooded hills to their maximum advantage, the Rebel troopers chipped away at the blue mass rolling down on them. This incessant pecking away had its effect, however, slowing the Union advance down to a crawl. Maj. Gen. Alexander McCook's command, forced to skirmish its way slowly down the Nolensville Pike and across Mill Creek, finally came to a halt as it confronted a strong Confederate force barricaded in the town of Nolensville. The Union commander, who had been a first lieutenant teaching at West Point when the war started, had little choice. He formed eight regiments into line of battle and moved forward. He found the defenders tough to deal with and succeeded in moving them only when he supported the infantry attack with two batteries using grape and canister. After a vicious fight, he finally took the town but immediately found his progress blocked by a force entrenched on top of a nearby line of rocky hills. Again, he had to form his troops in line. Silhouetted against the somber evening sky, they charged with fixed bayonets and carried the hills. With this final effort, the Rebel soldiers retreated into the shadows of early evening.

Some distance to the north, Maj. Gen. George H. Thomas, who would later become known as "The Rock of Chickamauga" for his stubborn defense of his position in that battle, and Maj. Gen. Thomas

L. Crittenden, who would lose his career in the same battle when his corps was overrun, were also finding the going tough. Skirmishing constantly as they crawled forward, Union forces took Franklin and spilled onto the Wilson's Creek Pike. As Crittenden approached Stoney Creek, he found the enemy in force at a church house and had to use a bayonet charge to drive them off. This completed, his troops swarmed across the creek and, as night fell, halted before the town of La Vergne. The obstinate Rebel cavalry had held the day's Union advance to a bare three miles.

After a miserable night spent in cold, soaking rain outside of La Vergne, the Union force slogged out of camp and headed toward the town. The leading elements were immediately pinned to the earth by a pelting shower of Rebel rifle balls. The Confederates had used the night to post themselves in buildings and the surrounding woods so they could bring the Federal advance under a heavy cross fire. Despite the galling fire sweeping over them, the Yankees gradually formed into line, fixed their bayonets, and charged through the sucking mud of an open field. Gaps appeared in their ranks as accurate Rebel fire exacted a toll on the straining, mud-caked blue troops. Still, they surged forward until, at last, the pressure became too great and the defenders fell back.

To the south, morning added a dense mantle of fog to the driving rain. With visibility less than three hundred yards and any movement attracting Rebel fire from the cloaking mist, McCook and Thomas were forced to hold their positions until almost midday. When the fog lifted, the blue army moved toward Triune, again constantly skirmishing with the gray cavalry. As the leading elements of the advance arrived at the village, Wharton, supported by Wood's Alabama Brigade of infantry, crashed into them. Enfiladed by Rebel artillery and cringing under the stinging small-arms fire of the cavalry, the blue advance suffered near chaos until a heavier force could get into position. Again, the Yankees fixed bayonets and charged doggedly through mud and brush to dislodge the blocking Confederates.

As evening wore into night, the Rebel cavalry fell back across Stewart's Creek, a narrow stream rushing between high, steep banks, and fired its single bridge. Desperate to save this structure, the Third Kentucky Volunteer Cavalry (U.S.) charged through exploding artillery rounds and heavy musket fire to engage the Rebel rear guard. After a few minutes of savage combat, the Confederates retreated. Their departure allowed the blue horse soldiers to heave the stack of burning rails into the creek and secure the undamaged structure. Chagrined at their loss, the Fifty-first Alabama mounted a counterattack but lacked the strength to retake the bridge.

As darkness closed in, the Federals went into camp along Stewart's Creek under the vigilant eyes of gray pickets on the opposite bank. Behind the pickets, Wharton and the supporting infantry, on orders from Bragg, fell back to Murfreesboro.

Sunday, 28 December broke bright and clear, the sun taking the nip out of the crisp winter morning. As the hours of daylight crept by with no Union movement, Confederate Pvt. John Duncan started his own personal war with a Yankee he had singled out across the creek. In a desultory fashion the two exchanged an occasional shot and, between rounds, occupied themselves by shouting insults back and forth. Finally tiring of the game, Duncan suggested to his opponent that they cease fire and exchange newspapers. The Yank agreed, and soon there was a general parley all along the line, ending in an informal armistice. The opposing forces gathered along the creek and chatted amicably until sundown, a symbol of the impersonal nature of war—battlefield antagonists briefly stranded in time idly gossiping as friends. When each side had returned to camp in the swiftly falling darkness, the clouds, which had gradually obscured the sky while the enemies talked, opened and a drizzling rain started to fall.

The next morning, the Yankee Army moved ponderously forward again. As it moved, Wheeler's riders again hammered away at the leading elements; slowing but not stopping the overwhelming blue force grinding inexorably ahead. As this day slipped away and evening approached, a rider handed Wheeler a note from Bragg directing him to fall back without further resistance and telling him, "Your command has already done more than their duty most nobly." Bragg had the promised four days.

At nightfall, Wheeler led his mud-spattered, exhausted troopers through friendly lines with the Federals in such close pursuit that he lost a man just as the gray lines enveloped his command. Leaving his men to feed themselves and their animals, he rode off to find Bragg. After a bit, he located his commander, along with Hardee and Polk, sitting on their horses beside the road in the gathering dusk. As Wheeler approached, these stern veterans lifted their hats in a silent salute to the "boy brigadier." Then, with a nod to the embarrassed young officer, Bragg said, "General Wheeler, you have not only accomplished what Generals Polk and Hardee said was impossible, but very much more. . . . we will now take the enemy in hand and see by the grace of God what we can do with him."

As Wheeler turned to leave, Bragg told him to be ready to depart on a raid by midnight. He gave the "War Child" directions to sweep around the Union flank and destroy the enormous supply trains moving up to support the attacking army. Despite their extreme exhaustion following four days of almost incessant fighting, the Rebel riders were calmly being ordered to undertake a mission that would have taxed a rested force to the limits of its capacity. Wheeler accepted the order without a murmur.

"To Horse" sounded at the stroke of midnight, the strident notes of the bugle driving bone-weary troopers from their blankets to grope in the rain and darkness for equipment and horses. In a very short time, the force was mounted and ready to go. Sinking spurs to their horses, they plunged into the utter darkness of the wild winter night at a full gallop. As they thundered along, unable to see the man beside them, they maintained direction by the sound of the horses' hooves drumming on the macadamized roadway. They knew they crossed Stone's River only because the water splashing around them was heavier than the rain and they could hear the sound of the rushing river as it swept against their booted legs. Ahead of them thousands of Union campfires flickered in the falling rain, a horde of will-o'-the-wisps in the deep darkness. One private remembered thinking, if they were going to charge the enemy line in the darkness, it sure would be a mess. His fears were unfounded, for shortly the group left the main road and headed toward Jefferson. Near that village, at daylight, they stopped at last to feed their horses.

Back in the saddle and moving forward again after a brief rest, the Rebels spotted a wagon train moving into a park outside of town. Dismounting his force again, Wheeler formed them into line and charged the train guard, Col. John Starkweather's Twenty-eighth Brigade, on foot. Taken by surprise, the initial response of the Federals was poor. The gray troopers rapidly overran the portion of the guard facing them and moved among the wagons. Starkweather rallied his men before the Rebels could secure the entire train, however, and a hot fight broke out. For two hours, the soggy morning air was filled with the popping of small-arms fire as the two groups struggled among the wagons and in the adjoining cedar brakes. Deciding he was not going to prevail totally, Wheeler saw to the destruction of twenty wagons, broke off the engagement, remounted his force, and dashed off.

Racing toward La Vergne, Wheeler swept up stray troops foraging and captured and destroyed a small wagon train. At La Vergne, he found a large concentration of wagons guarded by several hundred blue troops. Quickly dividing his force into three columns, he ordered them to charge the unsuspecting guard. Without delay, they rushed wildly forward, firing and yelling as they galloped down on the startled Union soldiers. The defenders jerked off a few rounds in panic, then surrendered.

While Rebel officers paroled the prisoners, their men released their destructive energies on the heavily laden wagons. The scene was one of chaos as the gray troopers set to their work with a will. One Confederate officer reported, "Around La Vergne the turnpike as far as the eye could reach was filled with burning wagons. The country was overspread with disarmed men and broken-down horses and mules. The streets were covered with empty valises and trunks, knapsacks, broken guns, and all the indescribable debris of a captured and rifled army train." Wheeler's final bag at La Vergne was seven hundred troops captured and about three hundred wagons containing almost one million dollars' worth of supplies destroyed. "It was," one Rebel smugly stated, "a sight to make all Rebeldom glad."

Many Rebel riders took the opportunity to pick out fresh horses from the captured train to replace their jaded mounts. One private complained that their furious pace wore out horseflesh at a terrific rate, remarking wryly, "Wheeler's 'critter company' didn't know much about walking horses those days, a gallop being our natural gait."

In scurrying to obtain new mounts, a Rebel sergeant garnered a large mule. The beautifully proportioned, iron-gray animal, standing sixteen hands high, was paraded before the troops by his proud new owner. As mule and master strutted along, a bystander shouted, "Tom, look at your mule's eyes." To the vast amusement of the watchers, the sergeant stared at the mule's eyes momentarily, then dropped the reins as if they had turned white hot. The unfortunate animal was totally blind.

Their work of destruction done, the raiders hit the saddle and, again at a gallop, sped off toward Rock Springs. They fell on this little village, which contained a wagon train, like a summer thunderstorm. Again, a group of luckless, unprepared wagon guards were overwhelmed and forced to watch as flames converted their precious wagons and supplies into billowing clouds of smoke.

From Rock Springs, the raiders hurried to Nolensville. Here they found another train of 150 wagons which, with its full complement of guards, was quickly captured. The wagons, except several ambulances converted to Confederate ownership, were put to the torch. As for the captured guards, Rebel Capt. George Miller said, "The Yankees were sent on their way rejoicing, as paroled prisoners of war, back to their New England households."

A short distance from Nolensville, the raiders topped a line of low hills to see a wagon train strung ribbon-like through the small, quiet valley below them. Shattering the early evening air with their Rebel yells, the troopers stormed down on it. There was a brief ripple of gunfire, then silence as the blue guards threw up their hands. A quick investigation revealed the train to be loaded with bedclothes, furniture, corn, poultry, eggs, butter, and other foodstuffs taken from farmers in the area. The raiders liberated all the food they wanted, then freely applied torches to light up the gathering dusk with burning wagons. The captured guards were paroled, placed bareback on mules, and sent toward Nashville with the "glad tidings" of their misfortune. Five miles out of Nolensville, the weary riders went into camp.

Both armies had spent 30 December jockeying for position. Here and there sharp fights broke out on a limited scale; but the major action had been Wheeler's tumultuous raiding behind the blue army. As night slowly fell over the opposing masses, each general established the final details of his plan of battle. By a strange turn of fate, the plans were identical. Hardee, the premier lieutenant general to serve in the Confederate Army of Tennessee, would initiate the Rebel plan by attacking the Federal right. His mission was to strike its extremity, then fold that wing back in the manner one closes a pocket knife. As the "blade" snapped shut, the collapsing right half of the Union Army would pivot about the center and fall on the rear of the left half. Then Polk, the Episcopal bishop of Louisiana who had returned to service only at the personal request of his friend Jefferson Davis, the Confederate president, would attack on that front and the Federal Army would be crushed. Since Rosecrans's plan mirrored this one, the advantage rested with the general who struck first.

Heavy mist clogged the river valley as the rainy night gave way to dim, chilling daylight. Federal commanders and staff officers peered blindly into the undulating cloud enveloping them, talking quietly, nervously wasting the last minutes remaining before the impending cataclysm. Huddling in the fog, their troops cursed wet wood, tried to cook breakfast over smoking fires, stared vacantly into space, or checked equipment one last time in preparation for the coming battle. Then, far on the end of the right wing, a rising wind began to roll up the misty gray cloud blanketing the area. As the foggy curtain

slowly rose, it appeared to sprout thousands of gray legs. To the surprise and horror of the watching Union soldiers, a long line of
massed Confederate infantry materialized, bearing down on them
with awful determination. To the north, the remainder of the Federal
Army suddenly heard a wind-borne crackling as if an enormous forest fire had sprung up in the morning breeze. Then the rushing
breeze brought the deep-throated roar of artillery as a salvo crashed
into their ranks. Frightened men broke under the assault; their panic
spreading like a rampant fever. In minutes, the extreme right wing of
the Union Army dissolved into a terrified mass. Under Hardee's ruthless attack, thousands of men struggled like a hill of blue ants, running mindlessly in all directions in a futile search for safety.

As the infantry attack mounted the scale of violence, the cavalry
Wheeler had left behind under Wharton streaked for the enemy rear.
This group, followed by a bouncing artillery battery, swung in a shal-
low two-and-one-half mile arc that terminated directly behind the
collapsing blue line. The battery hustled into position and opened fire
while the horsemen formed up. At a word from Wharton, Cox's
Regiment charged pell-mell into the blue foot solders while the Texas
Rangers rode down an artillery battery. This reckless charge swamped
the opposition and in minutes the fifteen hundred men of the
Seventy-fifth Regiment, Illinois Infantry were headed toward the
Rebel rear as prisoners.

Now the attacking cavalry spotted a long wagon train under
infantry and cavalry guard heading toward the Nashville Pike. Spurs
hit horseflesh as the gray troopers charged cross-country after the
fleeing wagons. As they approached, the Fourth U.S. Cavalry
(Regulars) swung into line to meet them. The unit had split into two
groups, one well in advance of the other, both parallel to the road,
facing the Confederates. Wharton halted his advance, positioned the
battery, and opened fire. The field pieces scattered the opposition
momentarily, but it quickly regrouped, challenging the gray troopers
to fight. The challenge was promptly accepted as the leading
Confederate elements drew sabers and charged. They were met by a
blue countercharge, the lines crashing together at a full gallop. The
scene was a melee of swinging sabers, colliding horses, and flying
mud with a background of wild yells and snapping six-guns as the
charges dissolved into a confused mass of desperate horsemen hacking away at each other. After a few minutes of this, the Federals
appeared to be gaining the upper hand; then, the remaining
Confederates rushed into the fray, routing the blue horsemen.

Wharton halted again to reform his lines to attack the second group of Union cavalry. This time the entire brigade charged—two thousand straining horsemen determined to have the wagon train. Using revolvers instead of sabers, the galloping graybacks decimated the blue ranks with their initial thrust. Unable to withstand the withering pistol fire, the Federals retired in wild confusion, pursued by the Rebels until they crossed Overall's Creek. At this point, the attackers wheeled and swept over the wagon train.

It took only minutes to secure the train and its one-thousand-man infantry guard and head it toward Murfreesboro. Now, it was the Confederates turn to be surprised. Scattered out along the wagon train, struggling with wagons and prisoners, the Rebels were engulfed by an unexpected Union cavalry attack. A hot, confused, running fight exploded as the graybacks attempted to regroup and protect their booty. They were finally forced to give up all but a small portion of the wagons, five pieces of artillery, four hundred prisoners, 327 head of beef cattle, and some horses and mules that were safely returned to Confederate lines.

Meanwhile, Wheeler had been fighting his way back from the previous day's raid. In the afternoon, he joined up with Wharton's force to spend the remainder of 31 December supporting the efforts of Hardee's foot soldiers with a series of slashing forays into the enemy rear. Finally, darkness brought a halt to the slaughter.

With darkness, the rain started again, a slow, soaking drizzle. The darkness also brought cold that gripped the battlefield in its icy clasp, slowly sucking the last of life's warmth from the mangled bodies of the wounded. As the night wore on, the cries of the injured gradually died away into a ghastly silence. Then, the clouds slowly parted and the lifeless moon, floating in eternal darkness, fixed its emotionless stare on the folly of man. As its harsh light cast the earth in stark relief, the living were struck speechless at the horror it revealed. Torn, broken, lifeless bodies sprawled grotesquely where Death's merciless scythe had dropped them. They lay singly and in heaps; some stretched peacefully in endless sleep; some were ripped into an unrecognizable mass of tissue and clothing; some, their faces contorted by their final agony, gazed with wide, vacant eyes toward the heavens in mute supplication. A Texan later wrote, "The scenes on the battlefield were aufle," adding with what must have been a shudder, "the hogs got a holt of some of the Yankee dead before the night was over." Bragg wired Richmond, "God has granted us a Happy New Year."

To Bragg's dismay, the first light of New Year's Day revealed the Union Army clinging stubbornly in place. Worse still, the previous day's fighting had left his frontline troops too exhausted to attack. And, there was no reserve adequate to replace them. The day passed in an unnatural pause as the armies restricted themselves to pawing each other like drunken fighters.

Rest was a luxury not permitted the cavalry. Their peppery leader had them in the saddle, racing toward the enemy rear before the new day was many hours old. Outside La Vergne, they spied a wagon train winding along the Nashville Pike. Wheeler sent Wharton straight in to strike the rear of the train, which was still anchored in the town, while he swung wide to drop on its head. A wild, chaotic scene immediately ensued. Galloping riders flitted among the wagons as guards swung smoking weapons after them. Teamsters, in panic, rode off mounted on their draft horses, leaving their wagons parked or overturned. Over this microcosm of churning warfare rose a cacophony of yells, screams, and curses mixed with the sounds of thudding hooves, clashing sabers, and the incessant yammering of small-arms fire. Finally, the guards, desperate to save themselves, ran in disarray for the woods. Here, small bands of gray horsemen waited to pounce on them from the concealing thickets. At last it was over and another Union wagon train provided fuel to fill the foreboding winter sky with black, rolling smoke. Late that night, the raiders rejoined the main army.

Bragg's superb army, which had already left almost one-third of its strength strewn in the rubble of battle, was ordered to attack again the following day. Desperate to break the battered army facing him, Bragg sent the elite of his army under Maj. Gen. John C. Breckenridge, former U.S. congressman, senator, and vice president, against the Union left. Their first goal was to take a low-lying hill immediately in front, then halt before resuming the attack.

The blue army promptly recoiled under the pressure of the furious Rebel advance. So rapidly did the opposition give way that the victory flushed Confederates rushed past their objective without slowing their pace and fell headlong into the gaping jaws of disaster. Rosecrans had massed fifty-eight pieces of artillery in a wooded area behind the hill. With an earthshaking, sky-splitting blast of sound it opened up, raining a hundred rounds of destruction a minute on the advancing infantry. Like automatons with no reverse, they staggered forward a few more yards, faltered, and withered away. As the remnants of shattered brigades streamed raggedly back, the flower of

Bragg's army remained behind, broken gray petals blanketing the soggy, churned up earth. Mercifully, the coming night drew an opaque shroud over the desolate scene.

At nine o'clock, the cavalry, which had held its position throughout the day, heaved aching, fatigue-numbed bodies into the saddle. Behind the bundle of raw energy that led them, once again they galloped into pitch blackness headed for the enemy rear. First light found them far behind the lines seeking combat. During the early part of the day they probed, feinted, jabbed, and harassed the blue rear. At two o'clock, they spotted a heavy ordnance train moving slowly inside a screen of cavalry, guarded by an infantry force three times their number. Without hesitation, Wheeler ordered the charge. The blue cavalry was unable to withstand the assault and scattered. The infantry was a different matter entirely. Repeatedly, the waves of Rebel horsemen charged the blue bulwark only to break and slide away, occasionally lapping over briefly to upset a wagon or two. After two hours of this, Wheeler gave it up and headed his jaded horsemen toward friendly lines.

The main Rebel army had spent the day in stunned inaction, shocked into immobility by the catastrophe that had befallen it. Rain had started to fall again and Stone's River was inching its way toward flood stage. Bragg, with no strength left to attack, had to get Hardee's force across the river or risk having it isolated by flood waters. That would mean the sure destruction of over half the remaining army. The dregs of defeat resting bitterly in his mouth, Bragg gave the dreaded order, "Retreat."

The Rebels streamed disconsolately toward Tullahoma on 4 January, stumbling through freezing rain that alternated with stinging sleet, the two combining to drain them of their last remaining fragments of spirit. Behind them, Wheeler's whipcord-tough riders formed a screen to guard the rear. The victors, as prostrate as the vanquished, staggered into Murfreesboro and collapsed. A feeble attempt was made at pursuit by a small force that fell back immediately, its head bloodied by blows from the ubiquitous gray cavalry. With that, the blue soldiers gave up and huddled together in whatever shelter they could find, trying to escape the raging elements. It was over; but, wherever the Federals looked toward the front, through the shifting wind-driven rain and sleet, there sat gray riders watching them through red-rimmed eyes—just to make sure.

Victory has a hollow ring when applied to Stone's River. Mutual destruction is a more apt description. If two armies ever stood in place and hammered each other to death, it was here. True, the gray one fell back; but it was six months before the blue one could regain sufficient strength to move again. There were, in truth, few to whom laurels could be passed out on either side, with one exception—Wheeler's magnificent cavalry.

This human dynamo and his superb horsemen had done it all. They had delayed a full army four days, repeatedly raided far in the enemy rear, provided normal cavalry support to the infantry, and, finally, acted as rear guard to prevent pursuit. For ten days, they fought almost constantly, not once having adequate rest or sleep. Wherever the "War Child" and his troopers rode, they left behind them a wake of burning wagons and supplies, hundreds of paroled prisoners, scores of dead and wounded, confusion, panic, and monumental frustration. Seldom, if ever, has a cavalry leader matched the accomplishments of "Fightin' Joe" Wheeler at Stone's River.

The basis for the astonishing success of the little general stemmed from the love, admiration, and respect his troopers held for him. After the battle, one of his privates said, "General Wheeler never asked his men to go where he would not lead, and for this we loved him, and gladly rode with him into places where we knew all would not come out alive." The writer, to whom these words were spoken, added, "To the Private's youthful eyes men such as Wheeler seemed giants, and manhood's more discriminating gaze sees them undiminished."

CHAPTER IX

To Steal a General

Heavy, wet snow, melting slowly in the near freezing temperature, gave off a splashing sound as a horse plodded slowly through it. Its rider, a small, slender man with flashing eyes, slumped easily in the saddle. The heavy mist that filled the Sunday morning air frosted his short beard and beaded the black plume waving from a soft, gray cavalry hat. Nothing in the rider's appearance or demeanor reflected the restless daring that burned within him. The fire was there though and one day it would make him the most feared and respected guerrilla on the continent. The name of this lawyer with a penchant for violence was John Singleton Mosby and tonight, if fate smiled on him, he would steal a general.

The stage for Mosby's planned escapade was set when command of the Second Brigade, XXII Army Corps, U.S. Army passed to Brig. Gen. Edwin H. Stoughton in December 1862. The general, a West Pointer who had led the Fourth Vermont Infantry at Yorktown and in the Seven Days Campaign, established his headquarters at Fairfax Courthouse. He commandeered the home of Dr. William Presley Gunnell for his use, quartering his staff, aides, couriers, and a guard of about two hundred in houses surrounding it. The remainder of the brigade was stationed in the vicinity of Centreville, Chantilly, and Occoquon. Most of the cavalry under Sir Percy Wyndham, a British soldier of fortune and veteran of service with Garibaldi's forces in Italy, were quartered near Vienna.

Stoughton, scion of a wealthy Vermont family of high social status, had little consideration for his troops or for the hardships of army life. Headquartered well away from his men, he lived elaborately, doing as he pleased without regard for legality or regulations. His conduct went unreported because his provost marshal, L. L. O'Connor, whose love for the fruit of the vine far exceeded his sense of duty, chose to ignore the general's abysmal disregard of accepted standards of conduct for a senior officer and, indeed, of ordinary propriety. In general, Stoughton had earned only enmity and scorn from his subordinates by engaging in such antics as appointing a female friend, a Southerner named Antonia Ford, an aide-de-camp. He bestowed on her the rank of major and directed she be ". . . obeyed, respected and admired by all the lovers of a noble nature." The disdain of the troops and their less than diligent attention to duty apparently caused Stoughton little concern. Firmly ensconced in a routine of parties and soft living, he gave little outward appearance of interest in his responsibilities.

One of his soldiers wrote a letter, probably lacking a bit in accuracy, to a friend that both indicated the feelings of the troops and contained an omen of things to come. He said, "General Stoughton, who commands the Second Vermont Brigade, has his headquarters in the village, although his brigade is five or six miles away. What he could or would do in case of an attack, I don't know, but it seems to me that a general should be with his men. If he is so fancy that he can't put up with them, the government had better put him out. There is a woman living in town by the name of Ford, not married, who has been of great service to General Stuart in giving information, etc.—so much so that Stuart has conferred on her the rank of major in the Rebel army. She belongs to his staff. Why our people do not send her beyond the lines is another question. I understand that she and Stoughton are very intimate. If he gets picked up some night he may thank her for it. Her father lives here, and this in the little hole of Fairfax, under the nose of the provost-marshal, who is always full of bad whiskey. So things go, and it is all right. No wonder we don't get along faster."

The major irritant in Stoughton's life as he partied away the dreary winter months was the activities of Mosby's nondescript group of Rebel partisans. Small bands of these men flitted about the country-side stealing horses, capturing pickets, and creating general havoc while leading Wyndham's troopers on wild chases through the Virginia countryside. So successful were they in these endeavors that Mosby sent the irate Wyndham a message that, unless he armed and equipped his troops better, they would no longer be worth capturing. Then, to add insult to injury, late in February, with twenty-six men, Mosby swept down on a Federal outpost between Chantilly and Centreville and captured forty Yankees and their horses. This act so infuriated the choleric Wyndham that he publicly announced that Mosby was nothing but a horse thief. The partisan captain scathingly replied that every horse he took had a rider armed with a saber and two pistols. Privately, he determined to punish Wyndham by capturing both him and his commanding general.

On the first of March, Stoughton finally became sufficiently attentive to duty to be concerned about his position and to notify his commander, Maj. Gen. Samuel P. Heintzelmann, that he was endangered by a gap in the picket line toward Dranesville and that he was being spied upon. A. H. Bliss, the Union telegrapher at Centreville, followed up by confirming the picket-line gap on 4 March. Heintzelmann, a somewhat reluctant leader of less than superb military skills, referred the matter to Col. R. Butler Pierce for correction. In response, Pierce dispatched a two-hundred-man reconnaissance unit of questionable capability toward Middleburg to determine the exact situation. Riding along through the cold, dark night, this group of worthies started drinking in an attempt to ward off the penetrating chill. In the wee morning hours, well into their cups, they stumbled into another Union group. In an instant, the well-oiled reconnaissance force was in wild retreat toward Centreville.

After some miles of flight, a few regained their wits sufficiently to return to investigate the situation a bit more soberly. Finding friends on the second inspection, they joined them and proceeded toward Aldie. Arriving there, the group, now totalling fifty-nine men, dismounted, unbridled the horses to feed them, and proceeded to rest from their night of exertion. Suddenly, with a whoop Mosby and seventeen men swept over a low prominence west of the village and charged into the startled group, routing them and capturing nineteen men and twenty-three horses.

This exploit increased the tension along an already restless and jumpy picket line. Reports of Rebel cavalry at Manassas, Wolf Run Shoals, and along the Orange and Alexandria Railroad poured into headquarters. Then, at Union Mills, two Michigan cavalrymen were captured and spirited away under the muzzles of their own artillery.

Immediately, a message was flashed to all commanders to increase their alert. Stoughton, who had a grand party scheduled for 8 March and was not about to cancel it, took no meaningful action to implement the order.

All the while, Fate was smiling benignly on the mercurial Mosby. Several days earlier, Sgt. James F. Ames, Fifth New York Cavalry, had strolled into his camp in full uniform and announced his intention of joining the Rebel leader. Mosby, never asking Ames's motivation and despite the suspicions of his men, took him on probation. The deserter accompanied the group on several forays, convincing them by his actions and the information he supplied that his desire to fight with them was genuine. Now, Mosby was ready to make his move to capture both Stoughton and Wyndham. The date he chose for his operation was Sunday, 8 March 1863.

Mosby's slow morning ride on that fateful Sunday took him by the home of Lorman Chancellor who lived near Aldie. There, Mosby stopped for a leisurely lunch and whiled away part of the day. Late in the afternoon, he mounted his horse and started on, telling his host as he departed, "I shall mount the stars tonight or sink lower than plummet ever sounded."

This flamboyant statement reflected Mosby's style. Idolizing Maj. Gen. Jeb Stuart, from whom he had received his first lessons in the fine art of raiding, he emulated the Cavalier in much he did. Like Stuart, he thrived on the spectacular. Thirsting for fame, he sought it restlessly, his burning desire backed by icy courage, cold-blooded determination, and an almost clairvoyant ability to find the enemy's soft spot. So savage and successful would be his quest for glory, that one day a large section of Virginia would be fearfully called "Mosby's Confederacy" by his opponents.

His contempt for Yankees knew few bounds. He made this clear when he told his less than saintly men, "I will tolerate no blasphemy or profanity in my command under any circumstances but one: When summoning an enemy to surrender, I permit you to call, 'Surrender, you Yankee Son-of-a-Bitch!'"

In Aldie, Mosby met the twenty-nine men he had ordered to rendezvous at the village. Without revealing their destination, he motioned them forward through the cloying mist. As the column rode along, the sound of their movement muffled by the soggy ground, darkness closed in and an icy, drizzling rain started to fall.

The band, starting twenty-five miles from their objective, moved down Little River Turnpike to within three miles of Chantilly and

TO STEAL A GENERAL

Centreville. Once through the Federal line, they proceeded to the Warrenton Turnpike, hitting it four miles behind enemy lines and halfway between Centreville and Fairfax Courthouse. They moved down the pike a short distance to within a mile of the enemy cavalry camp before swinging off into the woods to flank Wyndham's troopers. At two o'clock in the morning, they approached Fairfax from the direction of the railroad station.

Stoughton's party was a grand affair attended by a bevy of beautiful Washington belles and most of his officers except Wyndham, who had been summoned to the capital. Laughter filled the evening as champagne flowed freely, wrapping the party in its warm, golden glow. War seemed a vague unreality to the splendidly uniformed officers presenting their most courtly manners to the resplendent ladies fluttering coyly about the house. Glum sentries, shuffling miserably through the soaking rain, listening to the muffled sounds of music and merriment, paid little heed to anything other than their resentment and discomfort.

At midnight, the party slowly began to break up. As the revelers made their way to bed, lights winked out and darkness, broken only here and there by the dim, murky light of a smoking lantern, quietly smothered the town. By two o'clock, the rain-swept night was still except for the few slowly pacing sentries; its silence broken only by the quiet splashing of a few horsemen making their way toward the courtyard. Even though only infantry was stationed at Fairfax, none of the sentries were alarmed, automatically assuming the approaching horsemen to be Union.

Finally, when the horsemen were almost upon him, one sentry stirred out of his lethargy and desultorily challenged them. From the pitch blackness came an immediate response, "Fifth New York Cavalry." The guard dropped back into his semisomnolent state until a rider stopped directly before him. Amazement slowly tightened his slack features as the dim light from a nearby lantern revealed the gaping muzzle of a revolver. Behind the gun a hard-eyed man in a heavy raincoat told him tersely and explicitly what was expected of him. As the guard hastily nodded his understanding and intent to comply, Mosby remarked wryly, "A six-shooter has great persuasive power."

The raiders now broke into small groups. Some hurried to the stables to round up all the available horses while others searched out the officers' quarters. Ames led a group directly to Wyndham's quarters, eagerly seeking the honor of being the captor of the blustering soldier of fortune. Unfortunately, Ames had to be content with taking Sir

Percy's uniforms and horses since the quarry was not at home. The fugitive sergeant did manage to capture two staff officers, one of whom had been his former commander, Capt. Augustus Barker. Later Ames took the greatest pleasure in presenting his former captain to his new one.

A second squad under Joe Nelson rushed to the telegraph office, even though the wires had been cut. Here they captured Robert Weitbrecht, the telegrapher, and a guard who said his duty station was Stoughton's headquarters. After a brief and fruitless interrogation of the telegrapher, Nelson presented the captured guard to Mosby. The unhappy prisoner quickly confirmed the partisan leader's information regarding the location of his commander's quarters. Taking five men with him, Mosby remounted and trotted through the streets to the darkened house.

Dismounting in front, Mosby bounded up the steps and pounded on the door. There was no response. He hammered at the door again, making it rattle in its frame. At this, an upstairs window flew open and a voice demanded, "Who's there?"

"Fifth New York Cavalry with a dispatch for General Stoughton," Mosby replied.

The window closed abruptly and shortly footsteps were heard on the stairs. The door swung open and a young man dressed only in his shirt and drawers asked for the dispatch. Mosby grabbed him by the collar of his shirt, jammed a pistol none too gently in his ribs, and whispered his identification. The man, a Lieutenant Prentiss, was not a bit slow in comprehending his situation and complied meekly when Mosby ordered him to Stoughton's bedroom.

Once in the bedroom where a dim light burned, Mosby looked down on the sleeping general. Snuggled down in the covers, his short hair tousled and his open mouth accentuating his receding chin, Stoughton snored softly in dreamland, completely unaware of the devilish Rebel gazing down at him. Signs of the recent party were abundant in the room, the most prominent of which were several empty champagne bottles, the contents of which were no doubt contributing to the soundness of Stoughton's sleep. Perhaps fortunately for everyone, all the young ladies had gone to another house for the night.

With an impish smile, Mosby pulled the covers off the sleeper exposing his bare posterior below a tucked up nightshirt. It took only a momentary glance for the raider to decide his next move. His hand, covered with a heavy, wet gauntlet, swept through a wide arc terminating with a sharp whack as it struck the white flesh of the exposed backside. The result of this assault on Stoughton's dignity was, according to Mosby, electric. As the startled general, still befuddled by wine and sleep, bolted into an upright position, Mosby said sharply, "Get up, General, and come with me!"

Giving his head a hard shake to clear it, Stoughton stared at the stranger beside him. Anger now replaced astonishment as the general snapped, "What is this? Do you know who I am, Sir?"

"I reckon I do, General," Mosby answered. Then, bending close to Stoughton's ear, he asked softly, "Did you ever hear of Mosby?"

"Yes!" Stoughton eagerly replied. "Have you caught him?"

With a twinkling eye and a shake of his head, the raider said, "No. I am Mosby—he has caught you!"

Now thoroughly confused, the nightshirted captive asked, "What's this all about?"

"It means, General," Mosby told him, "that Stuart's cavalry have taken over Fairfax and General Jackson is at Centreville. Now, be quick and dress!"

With what Mosby described as a look of agony and despair, Stoughton asked, "Is Fitz Lee here?"

Hoping to create a feeling of complete hopelessness in the general, Mosby said, "Yes."

"Then take me to him," Stoughton requested. "I knew him at West Point."

"Certainly," Mosby agreed, "but hurry."

The raiders' position was precarious at best. They were surrounded by several thousand enemy soldiers with several hundred sleeping right in the town. So far, not a shot had been fired and only a few of the enemy, all prisoners, were even aware of their presence. But, at any moment, they were likely to be discovered and literally engulfed in a swarm of angry blue soldiers.

With this nagging worry, Mosby continued to press the general to get dressed. Stoughton, who had a reputation as a brave man but a fop, totally lived up to his billing. He prepared for his departure with the raider as carefully as if he were calling on the president. Mosby later said somewhat grumpily, "He dressed before a looking glass as carefully as Sardanapalus did when he went into battle."

At last, the fastidious prisoner was ready to go and the party started out. Stoughton then remembered his watch and insisted on having it. An exasperated Frank Williams rushed back to the bedroom, snatched the watch from a bureau, and gave it to him. Outside, they were met by the two men who had been left as guards. They had acquired extra horses for the general and his staff and the entire group mounted and trotted back to the courtyard.

When the raiders regrouped at the courtyard, they discovered their prisoners outnumbered them. Undaunted, they gave each prisoner at least one horse to lead. Except for Stoughton, each prisoner was allowed to hold his own reins. Determined not to lose the general, Mosby had his horse led by Sgt. William L. Hunter. Organized at last, the group started out of town with Mosby leading the way. They had been in Fairfax one hour.

Moving down the street in darkness so thick it was almost palpable, the band happened to pass by the house of Col. Robert Johnstone, who was commanding the cavalry in Wyndham's absence. Johnstone, who had slipped into Fairfax to spend the night with his wife, heard the horses. Thinking they were his men, he leaped out of bed in his nightshirt, threw open the window and shouted, "Halt! The horses need rest! I will not allow them to be taken out! What the devil is the matter?"

Mosby, knowing the man had to be an officer, stopped his band and quietly told Joe Nelson and Walt Hatcher to go get him.

Getting no response from the invisible horsemen below, Johnstone shouted, "I am commander of the cavalry here and this must be stopped!"

This time the officious tone of the Yankee's voice brought a snicker from some of the partisans. As Johnstone heard the laughter and the sounds of someone trying to enter the house, a sick realization broke over him that these riders were anything but friendly. In a frenzied effort to avoid capture, he dashed downstairs and out the back door, leaving the defense of his fireside to his wife.

As Johnstone skittered out the back door, Nelson and Hatcher broke in the front. They were greeted by a furious housewife determined to protect her home and husband. For several minutes, the two partisans had their hands full as Mrs. Johnstone fought them like a blood-crazed tigress. At last, they subdued her and made a quick search of the house hoping to flush her husband. Unsuccessful, they contented themselves with taking all his clothes and rejoining the others.

While his wife fought the invaders, Johnstone looked frantically for sanctuary. Spotting the outhouse at the rear of the yard, he dashed to it and crawled down its open hole, tearing off his nightshirt in the process. Standing nude in the privy pit, he shivered through the remainder of the night, refusing even to answer the calls of his frantic wife.

While Johnstone shivered in the outhouse pit, the raiders pushed hard to make good their escape. Hoping to throw off any pursuit that might develop, Mosby headed toward Fairfax Station. After about one-half mile, he swung the group off at a right angle, traveling through the woods until they regained the turnpike halfway between Centreville and Fairfax Courthouse. As they trotted down the pike, Stoughton, who expected momentarily to hear the drum of rescuing hoofbeats, spoke to Mosby, "Captain, you have done a bold thing, but you are sure to be caught." Mosby did not answer. All his energy was devoted to getting back through the lines before daylight.

About four miles from Centreville, Mosby halted the trailing column to allow it to regroup. He had kept several of his men spread out to the sides and rear hoping to prevent any of the prisoners from escaping. In the darkness, this proved an impossible task and a head count revealed that several were missing, including Lieutenant Prentiss. Mosby noted caustically that, "He never even said goodnight."

The cavalry pursuit Mosby feared was nonexistent. Back in Fairfax, panic reigned supreme. Johnstone, hiding in the privy, would not attempt anything before daylight and cavalry pursuit depended upon him. O'Connor, visiting outposts near Vienna, heard of the raid at three-thirty in the morning. He immediately wired Heintzelmann of the event, telling him that Stoughton, his men, many of O'Connor's patrols, and every horse, public or private, that could be found had been captured. He added that Mosby had searched everywhere for him but, since he was visiting outposts, he had made good his escape. Apparently satisfied with this, he was content to let the matter lie. This was a serious error, for Mosby was not yet past Centreville and there lay the real danger to the raiders.

His command regrouped, Mosby rode ahead some distance to scout for any danger that might be awaiting the partisans. Finding nothing, he called the command forward. When they joined him, he placed Hunter in command, telling him to go ahead at a trot and to hold Stoughton's bridle reins no matter what happened. Later, the spunky little captain dryly noted, "Stoughton no doubt appreciated my interest in him."

Mosby and Nelson now dropped behind the column to guard against surprise. They would trot along for a few hundred yards, then stop to listen for pursuit. Sitting silently in the darkness, ears straining for any sound of hoofbeats in the night, they heard only the spooky hooting of distant owls keeping their nocturnal vigils. They kept on in this manner until the campfires around Centreville appeared.

Hunter had been instructed to slip by the flank of Centreville and slide through the gap between it and Chantilly. Suddenly, Hunter stopped. When Mosby spotted the halted column, he galloped up to find out why. Hunter pointed out the flickering of a low fire beside the road about a hundred yards in front of them—obviously a picket.

Mosby slipped forward to investigate the fire just as dawn began to streak the eastern horizon. Approaching cautiously in the rapidly vanishing darkness, Mosby found the fire deserted. Apparently, the officer in charge had decided there was no danger and returned to camp at Centreville. Mosby waved the column forward.

As they rode past the Centreville redoubt within range of a rifle shot, a sentry challenged them. The column just kept to their steady pace, completely ignoring the guard. This reaction must have convinced him it was a Union patrol for he went back to his pacing without sounding an alarm.

This tense moment had hardly passed when Mosby, back in the lead, heard a shot ring out behind him. Swinging in his saddle, he saw Captain Barker riding for the redoubt at a long gallop and one of the raiders about to fire a second shot. Suddenly, Barker and his horse disappeared in a floundering fall. Some quick pursuit discovered the captain and his mount spread out in a deep ditch. The reluctant captain was rapidly extricated and, with him safely back in the fold, the column pressed on.

In Fairfax, daylight saw Johnstone emerging from the privy hole, costumed as on the day of his birth, to greet the lady who had so stoutly defended him during the night. Despite her genuine distress and concern for his safety, one look and one sniff were enough for this courageous lady, who firmly refused an embrace until her colonel bathed. Bathed, and presumably embraced, the now righteously indignant officer formed a troop and set out in pursuit of the long-departed raiders. Appropriately, he led the column in the wrong direction!

Other than for Johnstone's abortive attempt at pursuit, no one at Fairfax seems to have done much of anything other than to advise the young ladies, who had attended the general's party the preceding evening, of his misfortune. It was reported that they greeted the news with long and loud lamentations for the young general caught ingloriously in bed and spirited off without a chance to say good-bye. In retrospect, this may have been the most constructive act of any group at Fairfax.

While still in cannon range of Centreville, the column came to Cub Run. Rain and melting snow had converted that normally placid stream into an absolute maelstrom of debris and rushing muddy water. Mosby had no choice. Without breaking stride, he led the column into the swirling torrent. Men and horses struggled frantically with the surging current, barely keeping afloat as they fought their way across the swollen stream. Finally, one at a time, every man and horse staggered up the opposite bank. As the shivering Stoughton passed Mosby he said, "Captain, this is the first rough treatment I have to complain of."

Mosby, with all his men across safely, was elated. He said, "I knew there was no danger behind us, and that we were as safe as Tam O'Shanter thought he would be if he crossed the Bridge of Doon ahead of the witches."

Certain that pursuit could not catch them from the rear, Mosby turned the command over to Hunter again. He took George Slater with him and left at a gallop to make sure no force had been sent to intercept them by way of the pike. They crossed Bull Run at Sudley Ford and galloped full tilt through the old battlefield on to Groveton. Here Mosby could see the empty road stretching back to Centreville and knew he had won his gamble.

They waited here until Hunter caught up. As the column rejoined, Mosby watched the crestfallen look that spread over Stoughton's features when he too looked back down the empty road. In that emptiness, the foppish general saw his military career vanish into nothingness. Mosby said later that he felt deep pity for the unfortunate man as he observed this. The feeling was short-lived, however, for as they watched, the sun rose, spreading its dazzling brilliance over the countryside. Elation surged up in the raider captain as he turned to Slater and said, "George, that is the sun of Austerlitz!"

Mosby again fell behind the column and followed it to Warrenton where he found the entire citizenry turned out to give them an ovation. They had breakfast there then pushed on south, crossed the Rappahannock, and stopped for the night near Brandy. Early the next morning in a cold, steady rain, they headed for Culpepper Courthouse and Brig. Gen. Fitzhugh Lee's headquarters.

Mosby led the way into the house Lee was using for an office. The general was seated at a table near a crackling fire writing, not at all prepared for callers. His reaction upon being introduced to his old classmate can only be described as thunderstruck. Regaining his composure, he greeted Stoughton and the other captured officers warmly. His reaction to Mosby was one of indifference, indicating that what the partisan had accomplished did not impress him. Stunned by Lee's actions, Mosby said good-bye to his prisoners, bowed curtly to the Confederate general, and stalked from the house.

Fitz Lee's treatment of Mosby should not have been entirely unexpected by the raider. The two had known each other for a long while and had ridden together behind Jeb Stuart. Mosby's cavalier attitude and less than total awe and devotion for all things military had always rankled Lee. And Mosby had done nothing to allay the general's irritation. As a case in point, he always called a bugle a horn when in Lee's presence simply because he knew it irritated the general. Lee's low-key reaction to the kidnapping of a general, even though a fairly obscure one, by Mosby, though petty, was simply in keeping with the way he normally viewed the partisan.

Stuart on the other hand was delighted. He immediately directed the exploit be announced in general orders, lauding Mosby's boldness, skill, success, daring enterprise, and dashing heroism. He specifically expounded on the capture of Stoughton without loss or injury, calling it a feat unparalleled in the war. This lavish praise from the darling of the Confederacy amply soothed Mosby's bruised feelings brought on by Fitzhugh Lee's indifference.

In the greater scheme of things, Mosby's raid had little impact. His final bag, delivered at Culpepper Courthouse, was one brigadier general, two captains, thirty privates, and fifty-eight horses. Stoughton's capture did, of course, create a great deal of excitement in both armies and rocketed the partisan to instant fame. Its effect on others was just the reverse. The ignominious nature of Stoughton's capture could not be overcome. He was exchanged shortly afterward to find his reputation destroyed and he left the army. In the flurry of recriminations following the kidnapping, Sir Percy Wyndham found himself properly held responsible for the gap in the picket line. For this, he was summarily relieved of duty. Johnstone's nude sojourn in the bottom of the outhouse made him the object of such a storm of ridicule that he resigned and disappeared.

As is usually the case, the innocent did not escape unscathed. Belatedly reacting to an earlier statement by Stoughton that he believed he was being spied upon, the Secret Service swung into action. Sweeping through the portion of Virginia controlled by the

Union, they arrested everyone who could even remotely be suspected. Most were quickly released, although one, the lady named Antonia Ford, was held for months despite monumental efforts to secure her release. Ironically, while her conduct in other matters would not have withstood the light of day, no concrete evidence has ever been found to connect her, despite her protestations to the contrary, to Mosby's raid.

Perhaps, in the final analysis, and other than for its impact on a few individuals, Abraham Lincoln summed the matter up best. Told of the raid and Stoughton's capture, the president scratched his beard and with a subtle glint in his eye said, "Well, I'm sorry to hear about that. I don't care so much about the general. I can make another in five minutes." He paused, then added, "I do hate to lose the horses."

CHAPTER X

Too Late to Gettysburg

In the spring of 1863, the new leader of the Army of the Potomac, Maj. Gen. Joseph Hooker, a malcontent nicknamed "Fighting Joe" whose headquarters at one time were described as a combination bar and brothel, announced his readiness and intention to take on the Army of Northern Virginia, crowing, "May God have mercy on General Lee for I will have none." In short order, at Chancellorsville, Gen. Robert E. Lee made a mockery of his hollow boast. After the battle, Hooker said, "What I wanted was Lee's army; with that, Richmond would have been ours, and indeed all of Virginia." He certainly got Lee's army in spades; but, instead of victory, the bloodied Army of the Potomac reeled backward in defeat, the victim, once again, of inept, blundering leadership. Filled with despair, it retreated northward, slowly regrouping and trying to shake off the gloom of defeat that had settled over it.

There was a certain hollowness in the Southern victory, however. At 9:00 P.M. on 2 May, a North Carolina regiment mistakenly sent a hail of lead into what it thought was Federal cavalry and Maj. Gen. Thomas J. "Stonewall" Jackson, Lee's strong lieutenant, slumped in his saddle with three mortal wounds. When Jackson fell, Lee lost a superb and aggressive commander and the South took a long stride toward its closing chapter.

140

In addition to the extreme misfortune Jackson's death represented, far to the west another chapter was about to be closed. As Hooker regrouped and Jackson was buried, Major General U. S. Grant's war machine drove relentlessly through Port Gibson and Grand Gulf, Mississippi on its way to Vicksburg, the western citadel of the Confederacy. Soon, Lt. Gen. John C. Pemberton, the Rebel commander at Vicksburg, would find himself inescapably caught in Grant's tenacious stranglehold.

Lee had little time to savor the thrill of his victory over Hooker. He knew the vast resources of the Union would allow it to rapidly rejuvenate its army and was keenly aware that war-ravaged Virginia could not continue to support the needs of two large armies constantly maneuvering on its soil. With the flicker of hope for British recognition of the Confederacy still dimly burning, Lee decided to move the Confederate Army out of the state and to spend at least some of the summer in the North. At worst, he expected to relieve some of the pressure on Vicksburg, threaten Washington and some of the Union population centers, and win a battle or so. There was also hope that foreign recognition of the Rebel cause might result from a successful campaign; and, surely, the Army of Northern Virginia would return to its home soil better fed and provisioned than when it left. On 3 June 1863 the northward movement began.

Nearly seventy-five thousand strong, the Army of Northern Virginia was divided into three corps under Lt. Gens. Richard Ewell, A. P. Hill, and James Longstreet. By 12 June, Ewell's and Longstreet's corps were heading toward the gaps of the Blue Ridge Mountains where, once through, they would funnel down the Shenandoah Valley to ford the Potomac River in the vicinity of Shepherdstown, West Virginia. Hill's corps remained at Fredericksburg as a rear guard. Maj. Gen. Jeb Stuart's cavalry, charged with screening the movement of the gray army and keeping Lee informed of Hooker's reactions, spread out in front. For the next week, as the cavalry moved forward, it cleared the way in a series of small, hot fights, exploding northward like a string of firecrackers. At daybreak on 22 June, the Shenandoah Valley beyond the Blue Ridge was teeming with mile after mile of gray soldiers inching their way north.

Once the Confederate Army crossed the Potomac, Lee needed Stuart to act as his eyes and ears on the army's front and eastern flank. Perhaps because of his great confidence in Stuart, Lee was less specific in his instructions than he might otherwise have been when he ordered his lieutenant to that position on 23 June. His evident

intent was for Stuart to act as the army's main probing force, maneuvering his cavalry in such a manner that he could provide Lee the
timely, vital information he had so skillfully used against his Federal
opponents in the past. The crucial portion of Lee's order, forwarded
to Stuart through Longstreet, read:

> If General Hooker's Army remains inactive you can leave two
> brigades to watch him, and withdraw the three others, but
> should he not appear to be moving northward, I think you
> had better withdraw this side of the mountains tomorrow
> night, cross at Shepherdstown next day, and move over to
> Fredricktown. You will, however, be able to judge whether
> you can pass around their army without hindrance, doing
> them all the damage you can, and cross the river east of the
> mountains.

Stuart was then to rendezvous with Maj. Gen. Jubal A. Early's division at York, Pennsylvania.

Longstreet was concerned that the orders lacked clarity. According
to his later comments, in his letter of endorsement he removed the
ambiguity from Lee's order and denied Stuart the discretionary
power he was soon to exercise. Stuart's amended instructions,
according to Longstreet, were to ride on the right of Longstreet's column to the Shepherdstown crossing and to be available to the
Confederate Army as needed.

It was pouring rain on the night Lee's order was delivered to Stuart
at Rector's CrosRoads, a little place between Upperville and
Middleburg, Virginia, where he and a part of his command had
pitched camp earlier in the evening. Officers and men, including
Stuart, were bedded down in the deluge under oilcloths. An old
house stood near where Stuart made his bed, but he refused to sleep
inside saying, "My men are out in the rain, and I will not fare better
than they." A lantern sent a fitful light through the darkness as Major
H. B. McClellan, the division adjutant, worked into the late hours on
the porch of the house handling dispatches and messages. When
Lee's letter of instruction was delivered, McClellan took the liberty
of opening it. Understanding its importance, he woke Stuart and,
crouching beside his sleepy commander, read the letter to him by
lantern light. Stuart pondered its contents for a few moments, then
with a mild rebuke to McClellan for opening such an important doc-
ument before awakening him, fell quickly back to sleep.

At daybreak on the twenty-fourth, Stuart sent orders to Brig. Gens. Wade Hampton and Fitzhugh Lee and Col. John Chambless to form up their brigades at Salem by late evening. These crack outfits, numbering about forty-five hundred seasoned veterans, were complemented by a six-gun battery of artillery and regimental ambulances, but no wagons. Consequently, Stuart's force could take only the amount of grain that could be comfortably carried by each horse—enough for one or two days. This meant the graybacks and their mounts would be forced to forage for sustenance as they moved. Brig. Gens. William E. "Grumble" Jones's and Beverly Robertson's brigades, numbering some three thousand cavalry, were ordered to remain behind to guard the Blue Ridge passes. Their specific instructions were to watch the Union Army closely, report as necessary, and rejoin the main Confederate Army if the Yankees began to move.

At 1:00 A.M. 25 June, Stuart gave the order to move out. The horsemen, animated by anticipation of a new adventure, most considering themselves invincible behind their dashing leader, moved forward rapidly leaving Salem behind as they trotted toward Bull Run Mountain. As dawn streaked the summer sky, the gray riders were filtering through Glasscock's Gap near New Baltimore, some ten miles from Salem. With Maj. John Mosby scouting ahead, the Rebel cavalry now turned their mounts toward Haymarket, Virginia.

Stuart intended to swing northward toward the Potomac along the Leesburg Pike. He soon discovered, however, that the Union Army had already begun to recoil north in response to Lee's movement and that Maj. Gen. Winfield Hancock's II Corps had occupied the road he wanted to follow. Contact with them resulted in a brief exchange of artillery fire as the blue and gray forces rubbed edges; but Stuart quickly withdrew, not disclosing the size of his force, to evaluate the situation. It was readily apparent that Hooker's army was not where it was expected to be but, instead, was moving north. Stuart immediately dispatched a courier with this vital information to Lee but, for some reason lost to the past, the messenger never reached him. The Confederate commander continued northward unaware that his opponent had already begun to unwittingly parallel his course.

Having sent the messenger to Lee with information on his situation and the activity of the Federal Army, Stuart now considered his alternatives as his command regrouped from the artillery skirmish with Hancock's troops. He had to figure out a way to reach York as his orders directed. It was obvious he could not continue his present course since Hancock could easily hold the Leesburg Pike. One alternative was to retrace his route, move to Shepherdstown, then dash north to York, a distance of 105 miles. His other option was to swing to the east, cross the Potomac on the Union Army's far side, and move north to York between the river and Washington, a distance of one hundred miles. Never given to indecision, Stuart quickly ordered the detour eastward and, by evening on the twenty-sixth, was camped at Wolf Run Shoals on Occoquan Creek. His force had traveled some forty miles in less than forty-eight hours, fighting an artillery duel en route.

The encampment at Wolf Run Shoals offered a bit of excitement to some of Stuart's staff. Three of them and a courier broke away from the main column and went in search of a blacksmith. They found the needed service close at hand operated by a smithy who was a staunch Confederate partisan. He was soon busy at work while his wife, a no less enthusiastic supporter of the South, bustled about preparing a late meal of fresh butter, cream, sweetmeats, and cherry pie. The hot, fresh pie earned delighted exclamations of pleasure as the hungry Rebels sat down to eat. But, alas, it was not to be. Without warning, a roving Federal patrol rudely curtailed the festivities by unexpectedly riding up to the shop. The Confederates, mouths full of food and with handfuls of cherry pie, were forced to hurriedly mount their partially-shod animals and gallop away to safety.

The first fingers of light the next morning found the Rebel cavalry moving toward Fairfax. As they entered the outskirts of the town, they surprised a squadron of blue cavalry. With a shout, the gray riders swiftly struck and scattered the bluecoats. The scrap over, the Rebels moved leisurely through Fairfax, helping themselves to such items in businesses as pleased them. As the town faded in the distance, the cavalry sauntered along loaded with smoking tobacco, figs, and ginger cakes. Most had attired themselves in white straw hats and snowy cotton gloves, their dress reflecting the high spirits of the veteran troopers.

Night had closed about the tiring Rebel cavalry by the time they drew up on the shores of the Potomac at Rowser's Ford. The river, swollen by recent rains, was a surging torrent stretching nearly a mile across. No markers gave evidence of the ford but Stuart did not hesitate. He gave the order to cross and down the steep, slippery bank into the rolling river went horse after horse. Soon the riders were stretched in a curving line across the broad expanse. The high water swept over the pommels of the riders' saddles and often the strong current bore the line downriver near dangerous waters. Fortunately, each time this occurred, vigilant troopers saw the danger in time to realign the struggling riders and avert disaster. The cassions and limber chests of the artillery were unloaded to lighten them and the shells and powder were carried across in the cavalrymen's arms. The heavy guns were then dragged into the river, sending up plumes of spray as they sank beneath the boiling surface where they remained submerged during the crossing. That same evening, Lee arrived at Chambersburg, Pennsylvania unaware that the Army of the Potomac had crossed the river and was concentrating at Frederick, Maryland.

It was three o'clock in the morning on the twenty-eighth before all of Stuart's soggy riders and guns reached the Maryland shore. The Confederate column now swung in a wide arc to the east, heading toward Rockville. By midday, Stuart was leading his command into this "vile Secesh hole" about fifteen miles northwest of Washington on the Frederick Road. While his men gathered supplies and destroyed the telegraph, Stuart and his staff whiled away the time with a group of young ladies from a nearby academy. This sparkling group, who had swarmed out to welcome the Southerners, offered the tired troopers a much needed diversion. Unknown to Stuart, while he and his men flirted and joked with the ladies, an action was taking place outside the town that would greatly delay his advance and place him at the center of enduring controversy.

As his command entered Rockville, Stuart had ordered Col. Thomas Lee's Second South Carolina to scout in the direction of the capital. They soon encountered and gave chase to a large supply-laden Federal wagon train headed for the Union Army concentrating at Frederick. Captain W. W. Blackford colorfully described the scene:

> [Some of the wagons] . . . took the alarm, turned and fled as fast as their splendid mule teams could go. After them we flew, popping away with our pistols at such drivers as did not pull up, but the more we popped, the faster those in front plied the whip; finally coming to a sharp turn in the road, one upset and a dozen or two others piled on top of it, until you could see nothing but the long ears and kicking legs of the mules sticking above bags of oats emptied from the wagons upon them. All behind this blockade were stopped, but half a dozen wagons had made the turn before this happened and after them two or three of us dashed. It was as exciting as a fox chase for several miles, until when the last was taken, I found myself on a hill in full view of Washington.

Colonel Lee and his men returned to Rockville with 125 wagons loaded with goods and supplies, reluctantly driven by their crestfallen drivers. Stuart, elated at the prospect of turning over such a haul to his commander, decided to take the wagon train with him. With this decision, he unleashed a demon that would plague him for the remainder of his journey, for he quickly discovered that his swiftly moving unit had become a convoy, its pace dictated by obstinate mules and less-than-willing drivers. The escort duty for the wagon train would become exhausting to his command and would keep him away from Lee for two additional days. But, as Jubal Early put it afterward, "One hundred and twenty-five wagon loads of grub would be mighty hard for a lot of hungry Confederates to leave in the road."

While Stuart and his men were preoccupied with the wagon train, the Confederate Army was winding its way unobtrusively among the rolling hills and shallow valleys in the vicinity of the quiet town of Gettysburg. It was stretched in a rough crescent about fifty miles long with Longstreet's corps near Chambersburg, Hill's corps approximately eight miles east, and Ewell's corps strung out in the vicinity of Carlisle and York. Since he had not heard otherwise from Stuart, Lee assumed that the main body of the Union Army was still south of the Potomac River.

On the Union side, an exasperated Abraham Lincoln had again changed commanders of his army. The new man was Maj. Gen. George Gordon Meade. A stranger to the rank and file of the Federal Army, Meade, a veteran of the Seminole and Mexican Wars, was a fearless, capable commander. He assumed command of the army at Frederick on the afternoon of 28 June amid a great commotion caused by the news that Stuart's cavalry had just stolen the wagon train carrying its provisions. Worse yet, word had it that they had taken it from under the guns of Fort Tenallytown in full view of Washington. The presence of Stuart's cavalry between the Union Army and Washington created a small panic and briefly attracted more attention than the fact that the entire Army of Northern Virginia was in Pennsylvania.

Stuart moved his tired command out of Rockville on the morning of 29 June. As the day broke, the heat of the sun began to take effect. Throughout the command, nearly exhausted riders tottered in their saddles as they fought off the sleep fatigue urged on them. Hampton's brigade, charged with managing the captured wagon train, suffered the most as the sun's scorching rays unleashed the devil in Stuart's decision to keep the train. It manifested itself in thirsty, stubborn mules and cursing, unwilling drivers forcing Hampton's men to exhaust themselves by trying to preserve order from incipient chaos. As ugly-tempered mules blocked long stretches of the road, progress slowed to a crawl and Stuart's command and communication problems became almost impossible to resolve. But, despite the obstacles, the sweat-soaked, red-eyed troopers fought off exhaustion and forced the column erratically forward.

Earlier, Fitz Lee's brigade had broken away from the column. They forged ahead of the slow-moving convoy to cut the Baltimore and Ohio Railroad at Hoad's Mill and Sykesville. After a grueling twenty mile ride from Rockville, they accomplished their task near daybreak on the twenty-ninth and moved on to Westminister.

The remainder of the weary column reached Westminster late in the afternoon of the same day and paused long enough to close up and reform before continuing the march. Five miles further along the Gettysburg Road, at Union Mills, Stuart finally agreed to stop and rest the worn-out men and animals. Making the most of the opportunity, Stuart and his staff dined that evening in the home of Mr. William Schriver, remaining as his guests until well after midnight. Very much at ease in any situation, Stuart assisted in providing the evening's entertainment by joining the family in song, accompanied on the piano by one of the Schrivers.

While Stuart whiled away the evening, reality dealt his commander a heavy blow. Lee suddenly became aware that the Army of the Potomac had stolen a march on him and was concentrated at Frederick. This, to his supreme frustration, had occurred with no word from his cavalry chief. Beleaguered by a bout of personal sickness and the unexpected enemy movement, Lee found himself groping for the proper course of action. What he finally decided was to concentrate his army. The location he chose was Gettysburg.

Following the initial confusion and panic caused by Stuart's presence and the capture of the wagon train, Meade ordered two divisions of Federal cavalry under Brigadier Generals D. M. Gregg and H. J. Kilpatrick to intercept the Confederates. While Stuart's frazzled command rested at Union Mills, Kilpatrick raced to intercept them and Gregg's blue suiters pounded in pursuit some distance to their rear.

The faint rays of early dawn were cracking the eastern blackness as Stuart's men attempted to break camp on the thirtieth. What should have been a simple chore became a vexing problem as recalcitrant wagon train drivers, and especially the evil-eyed mules, made it abundantly clear they were less than eager to begin a new day. Bedlam and confusing delay were the order of the morning as the Rebels struggled to get the march underway. Finally, with the sun a sullen red ball high in the sky, they moved forward; but it was past ten o'clock before Hanover came into sight. As the graybacks moved slowly toward the town from the south, Kilpatrick's cavalry was entering it from the west.

That same morning Lee, deeply concerned over the whereabouts of Stuart and his cavalry, paced slowly in front of a field tent pitched east of Chambersburg. Where were they? He had cavalry, but without Stuart to guide them, he was without the eyes and ears he trusted implicitly.

Meanwhile, to the south, Meade started a northward thrust that would carry him to Gettysburg. He too was confused concerning the total perspective of what was happening around him. But, when he received word of Ewell and Early's movements from Carlisle and York toward the vicinity of Gettysburg, he adjusted to them. Had Ewell and Early remained where they were for another day, Meade would have moved to the Susquehanna River and the Battle of Gettysburg would never have occurred. As Bruce Catton described it, "Gettysburg was an act of fate; a three-day explosion of storm and flame and terror, unplanned and uncontrollable. . . ."

Stuart was now about to enter the mainstream of events leading to the Battle of Gettysburg, but the frequent delays caused by the cumbersome wagon train would again exact a price. Without the train, Stuart would have passed through Hanover on the thirtieth before Kilpatrick's cavalry arrived and could have been in communication with Lee by nightfall. But, as fate would have it, this did not happen and Stuart's advance guard, the Second North Carolina Regiment, bumped into Kilpatrick's blue riders in the town. A disorganized fight quickly broke out, but ended just as quickly as the Confederates were driven back. With Fitz Lee away on the left flank and Hampton guarding the wagon train, no help was immediately available to support the outnumbered North Carolinians.

To get a better view of what was happening, Stuart, with some members of his staff and couriers, trotted off the road into a field of tall timothy grass. As soon as they were separated from the column, a squad of blue cavalry spotted them and charged. The Rebels, not inclined to fight, loped off across the field until they came to a huge gully, about fifteen feet wide and as many deep, hidden by the tall grass. Stuart, superbly mounted on his mare, Virginia, was an accomplished horseman and easily cleared the ditch, but some of his unlucky staff landed in its muddy bottom. The blue cavalry chose not to pursue and drew back without attempting to leap the ditch or extract its humiliated occupants.

Sporadic, brisk mounted skirmishes between the opposing cavalry units around Hanover continued throughout the day, each side probing for an opportunity to strike the other a telling blow. Despite the tenseness of the situation, events resulting in less than full attention to combat by all participants occurred. In one instance, a group of Rebel troops were drawn up awaiting orders near some cherry trees fully laden with plump, ripe fruit. Unable to ignore this enticement, the men, more accustomed to riding than climbing, swarmed into the trees, stuffing themselves, their hats, and haversacks with the juicy fruit. While they were preoccupied with picking cherries, a dismounted line of Federal troops inched its way within firing range, intent on a "turkey shoot." Without warning, this group opened fire on the Rebels in the branches, silhouetted against the sky like monkeys in breadfruit trees. As minié bullets slapped leaves and tore through branches, the Confederates frantically tumbled from the trees. Observing the action from nearby, Stuart roared with laughter and shouted to his men, "What's the matter boys? Those cherries sour?"

While the cavalry probed around Hanover, Ewell and Early were at Gettysburg, eleven miles to the west. Had Stuart known this, he could easily have rejoined the Army of Northern Virginia in a matter of hours. But, his orders were for York and there he would go.

As darkness settled over the Pennsylvania countryside, Stuart detoured away from Hanover toward Jefferson. From there, he intended to swing north toward York. His opponent, Kilpatrick, having sustained the loss of 197 men during the day, elected to pursue the Rebels at a respectful distance. Time, fatigue, and incessant riding and fighting again began to exact a toll on the gray riders. The malevolent mules were almost unmanageable from lack of adequate food and water and many of the gray troopers were in a stupor from fatigue and lack of sleep. As the night wore on, many dozed and some fell off their horses as consciousness slipped from them. It took every effort Stuart and his staff could muster to keep the column moving. The march continued on through what seemed an endless night until the first sunlight of 1 July found them moving in a single column into the town of Dover, about six miles from York.

At Dover, Stuart received his first news of the main army since 24 June. Early's division, which he had expected to join at York, had marched west from that city earlier in the day. Reacting to this unexpected information, Stuart sent staff officers galloping south and southwest in search of Lee in an effort to find out what was happening. He then headed his dog-tired column northwest toward Carlisle, the location of an important Federal depot, some twenty-five miles away. The troops found the march through that burning July day equivalent to a slow descent into hell. It seemed as though eternity had passed before Carlisle was sighted late in the afternoon.

Stuart drew up his command in front of the city and demanded the Federal commander's surrender. His demand was flatly refused. With that, Stuart ordered an artillery barrage and directed his worn troopers to prepare to storm the city. Capt. John Esten Cooke recounted that the utterly exhausted Rebel troopers were falling asleep beside the hot, thundering artillery pieces and that one soldier, who started to climb a fence, swung one leg over and fell asleep in that position. Fortunately, before this stumbling-tired group could begin the attack, two of the officers Stuart had sent to find Lee returned. They had found him and his urgent order was simple, "Come to Gettysburg."

It was past midnight, early into the first minutes of 2 July, when Stuart started his worn out command over the thirty-mile stretch southwest to Gettysburg. He was, as were most of the participants on the scene, unaware of the great drama unfolding. As a parting gesture toward Carlisle, Fitz Lee's troops fired the Union cavalry barracks and the depot. Although unplanned, this action was probably the most important of the entire ride because it immobilized a Federal division for four days.

Lee was wrestling with uncertainty as Stuart hurried to join him. The preceding day had been one of wholesale slaughter. Starting slowly, the day soon exploded in unrestrained combat and, by dusk, the Federals were mangled, the XI and I Corps decimated by horrible losses. All they could do was hang on and pray for reinforcement.

Lee now had the opportunity for complete victory if things worked in his favor. He had clearly won round one. Most of his men were on the field and, for the moment, they greatly outnumbered the Union's soldiers. For that army to survive, it had to hold onto the only strong defensive positions available. These were along Cemetery Ridge, running south to two hills, Big and Little Round Tops. To the north, Cemetery Hill marked the end of this string of undulating landscape that angled off to form Culp's Hill.

Lee's military reputation was not the product of hearsay. He saw immediately that he must take one of these hills to secure any hope of final victory. But, Lee's genius was anchored by his subordinate commanders and in this crucial hour he was poorly served by them. In his courteous manner, Lee ordered Ewell to take Cemetery Hill "if possible." Stonewall Jackson would have grasped the importance of this and carried the order out forthwith. But, Jackson lay silent in his grave and the unpredictable Ewell did nothing but give the appearance of being on the verge of nervous collapse. His hesitation was all the Union needed to move a division into position and secure the hill.

Meanwhile, Stuart, the man Lee relied on as his eyes and ears, was still riding hard to rejoin. Had he been available, he might have been able to provide Lee the information about Meade's army he so desperately needed; but he was not. And, when Lee had made his decision in an information vacuum, it was too late. The die had been cast. Tomorrow the battle would resume.

Stuart rejoined near midday on the second, his troops too exhausted to be committed to combat. When he reported to his commander, Lee's quiet words were, "Well, General Stuart, you are here at last." There were no words of criticism about an eight day cavalry movement originally planned for two.

Late in the afternoon heavy fighting began again. From Seminary Ridge, Lee's army moved against the Union left to the west of Cemetery Ridge and the Round Tops. The Devil's Den, Little Round Top, the Wheatfield, and the Peach Orchard went down in history that day. Thousands of men died before the firing finally faded away near midnight. The Confederates had driven the Union forces back to Cemetery Ridge and had gained some success at Culp's Hill. But, there was no victory for either army and more bitter fighting awaited dawn. Once joined, neither commander would move to disengage. Here, at a place chosen as a battleground, not by design but by circumstance, they would stand and fight it out.

The serene beauty of dawn's quietness was shattered by a heavy Union cannonade dropping on the Confederates at Spangler's Spring. Fighting raged here and at Culp's Hill until nearly noon when the Rebels fell back grudgingly from the gains of the previous day. The Union positions were again secure, but an uneasy tenseness now gripped the opposing forces as Lee and Meade pondered their next moves.

Analyzing the outcome of the long hours of struggle at Culp's Hill and Spangler's Springs, and the success of Wright's Brigade in piercing the Union center late on 2 July, Lee concluded that he was facing an opponent with strong flanks and a weak center. An all-out frontal assault on the Union center might break through and permit him to roll the enemy back. Realizing that failure meant certain defeat, Lee made the decision to hit the Union center. Maj. Gen. Henry Heth's and Maj. Gen. William D. Pender's Divisions, spearheaded by Maj. Gen. George E. Pickett's Division were selected to bear the brunt of the South's last great effort at Gettysburg. Unknown to Lee, as he worried through these critical hours, far away to the southwest, Lt. Gen. John C. Pemberton was corresponding with Major General U. S. Grant concerning surrender terms at Vicksburg, Mississippi.

Expecting to break through the Union center, Lee sent Stuart to flank the Federal right. If the cavalry could break through here, they would be in position to wreak havoc all across the defenseless Yankee rear. At midday, Stuart led his cavalry down the York Pike, swung off to his right and moved toward a position from which he could strike across all roads leading to Meade's lines.

The cavalry angled off to the crest of a ridge that fell away to a level valley where a long stand of timber stood less than half a mile to the east. Behind it waited the cavalry of Brig. Gens. D. McM. Gregg, George A. Custer, and H. J. Kilpatrick. In a matter of moments the opposing cavalry forces became aware of each other. Without a second's hesitation, the blue and gray cavalry, mounted and dismounted, dashed madly at each other to clash in a wild melee of mortal combat. The fight swayed to and fro, all about an open field in a choking cloud of dust. The wild uproar deadened the senses of the participants as sabers flashed wickedly and gun smoke filled the air. Among the many casualties, Confederate Brig. Gen. Wade Hampton was shot in the side and nearly cut out of the saddle by a severe saber slash to the skull.

At center stage of this great drama, long lines of gray soldiers were moving steadily toward the Confederacy's high-water mark. Pickett's charge was underway and rank after rank of men marched grimly toward Cemetery Ridge for a face-to-face encounter with the Angel of Death and, after a brief handshake, to pass beyond the veil into the shadowy mists of legend. Federal Lt. Frank Haskell described the scene from Meade's lines:

> All along the crest everything was ready. Gun after gun, along the batteries, in rapid succession leaped where it stood and bellowed its canister upon the enemy. . . . Men were dropping, dead or wounded, on all sides, by scores and by hundreds. Poor mutilated creatures, some with an arm dangling,

some with a leg broken by a bullet, were limping and crawling to the rear. They made no sound of pain. . . . A sublime
heroism seemed to prevail all, and the intuition that to lose
that crest was to lose everything.

Some Confederate soldiers reached the copse of trees standing
then, as now, on a lonely vigil. But their once-massive, well-ordered
ranks were battered and torn beyond all hope. The charge was broken and the gray tide began a slow, permanent ebb toward its origin.

As Pickett charged, Stuart threw his horsemen into combat on the
right. The battle he fought raged for several hours before the fury
subsided, leaving dead men and horses scattered over the trampled
valley floor. Although the Union loss was more than double Stuart's,
it had served notice that, whatever the outcome of the great assault
on the Union center, the blue cavalry had done its job with the
Confederacy's master horse soldier. No gray riders would go
unleashed behind Meade's lines that day.

The Battle of Gettysburg was over by late evening. Rain fell the
next morning, Independence Day, its cleansing coolness washing the
blood from the grass, as Lee's battered army prepared to march
south. Fight was still in them though, one grayback telling an observer, "We'll fight them, sir, till hell freezes over and then, sir, we'll fight
them on the ice!" But, cooler heads prevailed and through mud and
drizzle the gray line plodded toward home with Stuart's cavalry
guarding the left flank and rear of the retreating Rebels. As they traveled the last folds a final, though yet largely unseen, shadow mantled
the Confederacy from west to east. For as this grand army withdrew
in defeat, a flag of surrender fluttered in the breeze on a hill outside
Vicksburg.

Much to Lincoln's chagrin, Meade's pursuit of Lee was slow,
almost tentative. Even though high water prevented Lee from crossing the Potomac before the Union Army reached him, Meade elected
not to attack his enemy in an entrenched position. By 14 July, the
Confederate Army was across the Potomac and the invasion of the
North was defeated.

In Lee's reports on the Gettysburg Campaign, he was openly critical of Stuart for being completely out of contact for those long, crucial days. He gave no credit, and perhaps none was due, for the capture of the wagon train, for capturing and paroling nearly one
thousand prisoners, riding 250 miles, and drawing two Federal cavalry divisions after him, or for, although it happened by chance, immo-

bilizing the forces at Carlisle before rejoining the army. The cold fact in Lee's mind was that Stuart should have been with or near him during the march north. Right or wrong, he had come to rely on him to such an extent that Stuart represented the Confederate cavalry. It was personified in him and it was almost as if reliable information could be obtained only from him. In truth, neither Stuart nor his hard-riding gray horsemen could have balanced the scales at Gettysburg.

The Army of Northern Virginia had made a valiant, magnificent effort. No nation could have asked more from the men who served it. But, when the dust settled in the arena, the arm waving the brass ring was wearing blue.

CHAPTER XI

Long Ride to Oblivion

From the age-worn crest of the Appalachians, across the muddy Mississippi, into the arid plains of the Southwest, the specter of calamity threw a long shadow over the Confederacy as 1863 reached the halfway mark. Vicksburg floundered without hope of reprieve in the stranglehold of Major General U. S. Grant's army, its tenuous hold on life the last frail impediment to dismemberment of the South. At Tullahoma, in an effort to split the Confederacy east of the river, Maj. Gen. William S. Rosecrans was applying almost unbearable pressure on the army of Gen. Braxton Bragg. In east Tennessee, a small Rebel army under Maj. Gen. Simon Bolivar Buckner offered faint hope of relief to the embattled Bragg; but that hope could materialize only if Buckner moved before a Federal force under Maj. Gen. Ambrose E. Burnside formed to neutralize him. And, in the east, Gen. Robert E. Lee was en route to Pennsylvania to keep a date with destiny at Gettysburg. The result of that rendezvous would cause the specter's shade to spread down the eastern side of the mountains to the sparkling shores of the Atlantic.

This gloomy state of affairs convinced Brig. Gen. John H. Morgan, who commanded a portion of Bragg's cavalry, that the only way to relieve the pressure and, perhaps, reverse the course of the war was

155

to strike deep into Union territory. Obtaining an audience with Bragg, Morgan presented his idea and requested authorization to raid beyond the Ohio River. Bragg listened patiently to the fiery raider, then denied the request. Instead, partially as a sop to Morgan, and because of his desperate need for forage and remounts, he authorized a raid into Kentucky on a limited scale. Disenchanted, Morgan apparently acquiesced. In secret, he told his brigade commanders, Cols. Basil Duke and Adam Johnson, that he had carte blanche to raid in Kentucky and, once there, he intended to cross the Ohio and bring the full force of war to Union residents snuggled complacently beyond its northern shores.

Under a fierce sun peering between puffs of cloud, Morgan's raiders gathered on the banks of the Cumberland River on 1 July to find the drift-dotted river a millrace swollen to over one-half mile in width. Undaunted by this obstacle, they set to work behind a concealing curtain of green underbrush, dismantling their vehicles and loading them and their supplies on flatboats. When darkness fell, the raiders shoved these ungainly vessels into the surging water separating them from Kentucky. By first light, all the gear was safely across and hidden in the heavy thickets choking the far shore. As daylight spread, the main body of troops, many of them stripped to the buff, started crossing at Burkesville, Scott's Ferry, and Turkey Neck Bend, the pull of the river's current forcing men to swim alongside their mounts.

The Union cavalry responsible for guarding the river was badly scattered. Unable to concentrate, they were committed piecemeal and cut to rags by the stronger Confederate forces. These isolated fights erupted as quick, explosive encounters amid the tangled underbrush crowding the riverbanks. The raiders, fresh out of the water, often fought in the nude much to the consternation of their opponents. An exception to the generally ineffective Union response was the cavalry under Col. Frank Wolford. Aware he faced Morgan's full division, this tough, resourceful cavalryman gathered his command and launched a full-scale counterattack at Turkey Neck Bend. Charging at a gallop, the blue troopers ran head-on into Morgan's Parrott guns. These heavy weapons literally shredded the charging Yankees, dissipating the force of their attack. Then, as the demoralized horsemen frantically attempted to retreat, the Ninth Tennessee rolled over their flank. By nightfall, the fighting was over and word went out to Union forces, "The Rebel cavalry has crossed the Cumberland. Morgan is in Kentucky."

The next day, Morgan again met Wolford's cavalry and, after a sharp fight, forced it to retreat. By noon, the village of Columbia was in Rebel hands. Here, the invaders spent the remainder of the day and night regrouping the command. On the morning of the fourth, they moved out for Tebb's Bend on the Green River.

Tebb's Bend was a narrow neck of land choked with fallen trees, clinging underbrush, and matted vines. At the end of this peninsula-like projection, Col. Orlando H. Moore and four hundred men of the Twenty-fifth Michigan Infantry were firmly positioned in trenches and rifle pits behind heavy barricades of fallen timber. Although Moore posed no threat to him, and against the advice of his commanders, Morgan decided to fight rather than flank this force. After surveying the situation, he sent the Eighth and Tenth Kentucky across the river to block retreat or reinforcement and Lieutenant J. T. Tucker forward to demand Moore's surrender.

Moore listened to Morgan's demand, then said, "Lieutenant, if it was any other day I might surrender, but on the Fourth of July, I must have a little brush first." Then he handed him a note for Morgan that read, "It is a bad day for surrender, and I would rather not."

A chill trickled down Tucker's spine as he looked at the tight smile on Moore's face and realized this would be a fight to the death. As he turned away, he heard Moore speak to his troops, "Rise up, men, take good aim and pick off those gunners."

Capt. Edward Brynes opened with a Parrott and the Eleventh Kentucky charged forward at the sound of its booming voice. A thick growth of trees covering the defenders rendered the artillery fire virtually useless and left them free to concentrate their attention on the attackers, whose only option was a frontal assault. In a matter of seconds, they were pinned down in the tangled mass of plant life. For thirty minutes they struggled on their bellies trying to move forward but succeeded only in taking heavy losses. Finally, Morgan threw the Fifth Kentucky into the melee only to have it meet the same fate. At midday, having suffered two-to-one losses, Morgan reluctantly acknowledged his blunder and disengaged. He asked and received permission to bury his dead and then trotted north leaving Moore's victorious troops solidly in possession of Tebb's Bend. That night a Rebel officer confided to his diary, "The commencement of this raid is ominous. Many of our best men were killed and wounded. It was a sad, sorrowful day."

Behind Morgan the chase had started in earnest. Cavalry under Brig. Gens. Henry M. Judah, Edward H. Hobson, and James M.

Shackleford were on the move. Wolford had gathered his scattered force, added four howitzers, and was also hot on the trail.

In the last hours of darkness on the morning of the fifth, the raiders quietly captured the pickets in front of Lebanon. Scouts then hurried into town to get the lay of the land and returned just as rapidly to report that it was held by the Twentieth Kentucky Cavalry (Union) and that the Eighth and Ninth Michigan Cavalry and the Eleventh Michigan Battery were in the area. The Twentieth Kentucky was made up of men from the same area as many of Morgan's troops and Morgan was well-acquainted with their commander, Lt. Col. Charles Hanson. Wanting to avoid a fight if possible, the Rebel leader decided to attempt to intimidate Hanson into surrender.

Morgan formed his troops on a broad front to either side of the road leading into town, placing his artillery in the center. At the sound of a bugle, the entire line moved forward to within sight of the defending breastworks where the artillery fired a few rounds. Morgan's adjutant then went forward to demand the town's surrender. To Morgan's disgust, Hanson brusquely declined.

After waiting thirty minutes for the evacuation of noncombatants, the Rebels opened with an artillery barrage. Forced by deadly rifle fire to stay well back, the gunners did little damage. Giving up hope of subduing the garrison with artillery, Morgan moved the Sixth and Ninth Kentucky to the right and the Eighth and Eleventh Kentucky to the left, intending to flank the town. But, before the attack could start, scouts came pounding in to tell Morgan the Michigan troops were moving up. Abandoning his plan, the Rebel commander detached a force to hold up the reinforcements and ordered a frontal assault.

The Second Kentucky led the charge, running headlong into a hail of musket fire. Sweeping across the charging horsemen, Federal bullets dropped men and horses, dotting the dust with Rebel bodies. In seconds, the survivors were beating a hasty retreat out of range of the galling fire. The Eighth Kentucky now attacked, crawling to avoid the deadly small-arms fire whistling overhead. For an hour they wallowed in the dust but were unable to breach the breastworks.

Time began to press Morgan unmercifully. The fight was four hours old and reinforcements were drawing ever closer. Duke suggested they try a modified pincer movement in an effort to break the stalemate. He suggested the Fifth Kentucky charge the town from the side. Then, with the attention of the defenders diverted, the Second

Kentucky could enter the town from the opposite side. Morgan agreed.

The Fifth charged at a gallop, screeching their Rebel yell. As hoped, the defenders swung to meet this new challenge and the Second slipped quietly into town on foot. They found almost all the Union forces concentrated in the railroad station. Hurriedly surrounding the building, riflemen filled the windows with lead while others pounded in the door with gun butts. Shortly, a white flag ran up and 483 prisoners, a twenty-four-pounder, a large number of horses, and a substantial amount of supplies fell into raider hands.

The taste of victory was flat in their commander's mouth, however. Morgan's younger brother, Tom, had died in the last moments of combat. As Hanson formally surrendered to him, the Rebel leader nodded sadly and said in a choked voice, "Charles, when you go home, if it is any source of gratification to you, tell Mother you killed brother Tom." Then, features tightly set, Morgan walked away. That night a Rebel wrote of another day of gloom, fatigue, and death.

Hurriedly leaving Lebanon, the band moved toward Springfield through a heavy thunderstorm that gave them some relief from the crushing summer heat. As they trotted through the night, a detachment was dispatched to Harrodsburg to hold off enemy patrols and another was sent forward to secure Bardstown. The latter group charged into the town at a gallop, seized a train, shot it out with a Union patrol, and drove the local militia into a stable where it surrendered. Here the column stopped for a short rest and Morgan's telegrapher, Lightnin' Elsworth, cut into the Union telegraph lines. It took him only a short while to determine that massive confusion and exaggeration surrounded the raid and that Louisville expected to be attacked.

Capitalizing on this information, Morgan, who had no intention of attacking the city, sent a detachment in that direction. Riding hard, this band cut near the city then veered off, slashing through Shelbyville, Smithfield, and Sligo, leaving a trail of cut telegraph lines, destroyed track, and burning bridges in their wake.

Another light force went forward to secure Brandenburg and the means of crossing the Ohio. Behind them, the main column led by Duke, who was accompanied by the captured militia commander, followed at a slower pace. As they rode along beside a railroad, they spotted a handcar pumped by four men moving along in front of them. One of the occupants was dressed in blue, so the Rebels assumed they were Federals out to spread the word of their activities and location. Duke and a few men galloped ahead firing their hand-guns and shouting for the car to stop. This had an electric effect on the riders who immediately redoubled their efforts. Suddenly, to Duke's amazement, the captured militia commander sank spurs to his horse and charged forward firing at the hand car and cursing its occupants for their failure to stop. This onslaught worked and four terrified civilians tumbled from the car, hands in the air.

Duke took in this unique show and then, slouched in the saddle, his face a picture of puzzlement, said to his prisoner, "It was to be expected that we would try to catch those fellows, thinking they were Federals, but why were you so anxious to catch them?"

The prisoner fidgeted in his saddle briefly, then with a wry smile answered, "Well, Colonel, I wish I may be shot if I did not forget which side I was on."

The column moved on, derailing a train near Lebanon Junction, capturing and rifling a passenger train near Shepherdsville, and into camp at Garnettsville. On the way, Morgan refined his plans for the raid and Elsworth kept busy gathering information from the tele-graph, while inundating the system with bogus traffic.

Confusion was rampant on the Federal side. Rosecrans, who had practically no responsibility for Morgan, was swamped with mes-sages. Burnside, who did have responsibility, worried and studied his maps. Judah sent a flurry of reports and orders to everyone who popped into his mind. Finally, on 6 July, Rosecrans deciphered the puzzle—Morgan had broken completely through Burnside's cavalry screen and was far into northern Kentucky. This caused Burnside to move. He blistered Judah for allowing his organization to be trapped behind Green River and missing Morgan and gave Hobson carte blanche to catch the raider, telling him, "Morgan ought to be broken to pieces before he gets out of the state."

Judah was so enraged at Burnside's message that he temporarily lost his faculties. He fired off a report that was almost unintelligible, but was excused for it because, ". . . he feels dreadfully at his luck." Then, deciding Morgan would swing back to Tennessee in a wide arc, he cut across the postulated route, isolating himself from Burnside and getting totally out of position to threaten the raiders. Hobson, on the other hand, stayed right on Morgan's trail. Of all the Union com-manders, Morgan could not have found a more determined, tena-cious pursuer.

Morgan moved at midnight on the seventh, arriving on the heights above Brandenburg at daylight. Here the raiders looked down on the wide, mist-covered Ohio. Hidden from their view by the mist, they had to be satisfied with visualizing the virgin territory of Indiana that lay before them. At the Brandenburg dock the steamers *John B. Combs* and *Alice Dean* awaited their arrival with steam up, courtesy of the advance party.

The column, described by an onlooker as "a line of dusty, desperate riders," filed down to the landing and began boarding the steamers. Suddenly, a cannonball screamed out of the mist to land among the horsemen with a jarring explosion. Troopers scrambled frantically for cover as officers yelled for the artillery. Brynes's Parrotts rumbled forward just as a breeze whipped the mist away to reveal a battery of Indiana militia firing from the opposite shore. The Rebel guns, supported by rifle fire, went into action and the enemy artillery beat a hasty retreat. The Second Kentucky then finished boarding the steamers and crossed the Ohio, supported by the Ninth Tennessee. These units quickly dug in, establishing a beachhead about five hundred yards deep.

At this point, a Union gunboat appeared, alternating its fire from shore to shore as it slowly chugged down the river. The Confederate artillery immediately engaged it and the two foes dueled for an hour until the gunboat, out of ammunition, thrashed away. The hour had been a tense one for Morgan. His command split by the river and uncertain when or from where he would be attacked, the raider could do nothing but fret and fume while watching the clumsy antagonists paw at each other.

The remainder of the day was spent ferrying the column across the river. While Morgan fretted, the operation dragged on into the long, summer twilight as falling darkness and gathering mist gradually obscured the spreading sycamores lining the riverbank. At last, near midnight, the final trooper landed and the sound of bugles faded away in the muffling darkness.

The *McCombs* was released on her captain's word that he would leave the area. The *Alice Dean* was put to the torch and a rear guard left to assure her destruction. As this group huddled near the water's edge watching the fire, a fusillade of small-arms fire fell around them. Hobson had reached Brandenburg but too late. Had he not stopped to rest, he would have caught Morgan's command split by the river. Union Colonel A. V. Kautz called this the worst blunder made in the pursuit of Morgan.

Morgan, standing on the northern shore of the Ohio, was free for the moment to strike where he pleased. The disadvantages that faced him were staggering, however. Here, in country that was for the most part covered with an undamaged railroad and telegraph network, he could expect every hand to be against him. Behind lay heavy bodies of Union troops and militia were gathering about him from all points of the compass. Most significantly, the Ohio, which could be forded at only a few points, rushed between him and safety.

The raiders moved out early in the direction of Croydon. Near that town, they struck a force of well-fortified militia and had a tough scrap before dislodging them and taking the town. The raiders did very little damage to the village but did liberate $750 from the county treasury and $2,100 from some mill owners as a ransom for not destroying their property. Incensed by this action and the requisitioning of supplies, a group of furious merchants demanded that Morgan tell them on what authority he acted. With a wan smile, the Rebel general waved lazily at the swarming raiders and in a curt voice said, "There is my authority."

While at Croydon, Morgan received the crushing news that Lee had been defeated at Gettysburg. This information was extremely disturbing to him. All along it had been his intention as a last resort to slip into Pennsylvania and join Lee. Now another escape door had slammed irrevocably closed.

Leaving Croydon, the column moved through Palmyra toward Salem. As they rode, they cut the telegraph wires behind them and filled those in front with "orders" and "dispatches." Part of the time the force was split to confuse pursuit; but, wherever they rode, a constant clamor of church bells heralded their approach. At Salem, they scattered the militia, burned the depot, and ransacked all businesses, which permanently destroyed any chance that the Copperheads, Southern sympathizers supposedly infesting the area and waiting for Rebel support, might rise to help them. Scouts went north to Seymour to burn its bridges and destroy a section of track while the main body of troops moved to Vienna. Here Elsworth pieced together the enemy's situation: Hobson was thirty miles behind, Indianapolis was packed with militia, ten thousand home guards were at New Albany, and three thousand troops at Mitchell. All citizens had been instructed to block the roads with fallen trees and barricades. Most ominous of all, unseasonable rains were pouring torrents of water into the Ohio and it was rising steadily.

Indiana Gov. Oliver P. Morton called for all able-bodied men south of the National Road to form into companies and await orders. All locomotives and cars were placed on standby to move troops and the state arsenal put every available man to work producing ammunition. Indianapolis was the focal point of these efforts and the city quickly degenerated into bedlam. Panic swept across the area from the Ohio to Lake Michigan. Fear, doubt, and uncertainty prevailed the length and breadth of the state.

From Vienna, the column moved through Lexington. A detachment was left to demonstrate before Madison and tie down its two thousand troops while the main column abruptly turned, rode through Paris, and camped near Vernon. Panic intensified in Indianapolis as rumor spread that Morgan would sweep down on it and free six thousand prisoners held there. The raiding force was now estimated to be from six thousand to eight thousand men instead of the less than twenty-four hundred it actually was. In desperation, Brig. Gen. Lew Wallace, who would become famous for his book, *Ben Hur: A Tale of the Christ,* was summoned to deal with Morgan.

Vernon was heavily defended and Morgan decided not to attack it but rather to slip by to Dupont. To divert Federal attention, he sent a flag of truce into the town and demanded its surrender. As the demand was presented, a trainload of troops rattled in to help defend the town and the Federals denied Morgan's demand. While the Rebel chief watched his troops slip past the town, he sent a second demand for its capitulation. Again, the Federal commander, Col. John Love declined and returned a stiffly worded note ordering Morgan to surrender forthwith to a stronger force. The Rebel now fussed and dallied about watching the afternoon, like his troops and supply train, slip away. Then at dusk he sent the flag bearer in for the third time, giving Love thirty minutes to remove noncombatants before his artillery opened. The Federal commander immediately started preparing for the assault and Morgan galloped away into the gathering darkness. For over an hour, the Federals crouched waiting for the attack, but the evening breeze brought only night sounds to their straining ears. At last, scouts were ordered out but they found only silence—Morgan was gone.

Wallace raced toward Vernon with thirteen hundred men but stopped several miles short. From that point, he moved forward cautiously, fearing an ambush. By the time he arrived, Morgan was already near Dupont. Now, troops from Missouri and Illinois were rushed east to strengthen the pursuit. Despite all the effort being expended, excessive caution, timidity, and plain stupidity caused troops to consistently be moved too slowly or to the wrong place.

The only exception was the grim Hobson who kept up his persistent pursuit and was gradually narrowing the gap between his force and Morgan's.

At Dupont, the raiders destroyed the water tank, some freight cars, and the railroad track. Moving on, they destroyed railroad equipment as they went and regularly bumped into groups of militia that had to be shown the folly of combat. While, as a rule, the natives were terrified and fled from them, the raiders occasionally met a fighter. At one house, two hungry troopers were confronted by an old lady waving a carving knife. Glaring at the raiders, she told them, "I'll let you know I'm one of the blue hen's chickens from the State of Virginia and if you try to enter I'll cut your heart out."

"I know those Virginians will fight like the devil and I don't doubt you mean what you say," one rider said and the two rode away still hungry.

The next day as the column moved toward Cincinnati, the city of Indianapolis, seventy miles away, went berserk. Church and fire bells rang all day, keeping the Home Guards in a perpetual state of useless but frenzied activity. The situation throughout the forty counties south of the National Road was not appreciably different. So widespread was the panic that a local poet was moved to place the prevailing attitude in verse:

> Morgan, Morgan, the raider, and
> Morgan's terrible men
> With Bowie knives and pistols
> Are galloping up the glen.

On the twelfth, Morgan thundered into Versailles, captured three hundred militiamen and took five thousand dollars from the tax collector. He then split his column to speed up travel and moved toward Milan. Detachments were dispatched to rush through Pierceville and Aurora, further spreading confusion and panic. At dark, the totally exhausted troopers, who were averaging twenty-one of every twenty-four hours in the saddle, stopped near Milan and slept where they fell. Within twenty miles around them, fifteen thousand Union troops waited for daylight. Not one approached the camp or, for that matter, even knew it existed!

With three hours' rest the command moved again. Hobson was now only five miles behind and was slowly closing the gap between them. The raiders destroyed the bridge over the Whitewater River and pushed on to Harrison for another three hours of rest. Morgan, having decided it would be insane to attack Cincinnati, swung aside, crossed the Big Miami River and passed through New Baltimore, Bevis, New Burlington, Glendale, Sharonville, and Montgomery.

As they rode, such intense darkness settled over them that the trailing units had to strike a light and watch the dust settle to see which direction the leaders had gone. Choking dust, stifling heat, and excruciating fatigue combined to pour misery on the semiconscious troopers as they plodded numbly through the long summer night. Rocking along in an almost somnolent state, Johnson remarked, "I'd give a thousand dollars for an hour of sleep."

Shortly after daybreak, they overran Camp Dennison, a convalescent center, wrecked a train, and burned seventy-five wagons. Then, on to Batavia, through Williamsburg, and into camp, sleep grasping every rider the moment motion stopped. They had just completed the longest, continuous cavalry ride in history—ninety-five miles in thirty-five hours without stopping and with frequent skirmishes along the way.

Pursuit had been disrupted by everyone converging on the panicky city of Cincinnati. But, a wary Hobson again took up the trail while Judah steamed furiously up the Ohio past gunboats hovering at every crossing. Ahead, the Ohio Militia blocked roads and set up ambushes in the path of the raiders.

Morgan now split his force, sending a small group toward Ripley, hoping to give the impression he was anxious to cross the river. The main body swept through Sardinia and Winchester to Locust Grove where the feinting column rejoined, then on to Jasper and across the Scioto River to Piketown where they burned the bridge. En route, they constantly found roads blocked and frequently were forced to engage in sharp clashes with groups of militia. These constant delays were again shrinking their lead over Hobson, which had been stretched to more than twelve hours because he had been briefly diverted toward Cincinnati. That morning Morgan had told his men, "All our troubles are now over. The river is only twenty-five miles away and tomorrow we will be on Southern soil." Somehow, the words had a hollow ring.

Desperate to relieve the pressure, Morgan had Elsworth send a dispatch advising that he was heading directly to Chillicothe to cut the railroad. Again, the ruse worked as the Federals frantically rushed to protect that city. The raiders swept away to the south through Jackson, Wilkesville, and Rutland. Pressing toward Middleport, they ran into a strong force of entrenched militia that forced them to veer eastward. Under constant fire, the Rebels slowly made their way through a stretch of country broken by steep hills and deep ravines. Unable to come to grips with their tormentors, the gray riders could only endure until they broke into the open at noon on the eighteenth. Given room to maneuver, they rode the pesky militia down, scattering it into the nearby hills, and jogged into Chester.

Burnside, frantic that he was about to suffer a repeat of the catastrophes that had engulfed him at Antietam and Fredericksburg, now had 125,000 men committed to Morgan's capture. Aware the raiders were within hours of escaping, the anxious Union general was pouring his entire force into the Chester area. Unknown to him, Kautz had learned that Morgan intended to cross the rising Ohio at Buffington Island. Kautz quickly passed this word to Hobson and rushed the still-smarting Judah to this crucial point.

In Chester, the Rebel chief halted to hold a council of war with his commanders. Quickly, the decision to cross at Buffington Island was reconfirmed but Morgan decided to wait until a guide could be found. This took ninety minutes—just enough time for the Union to block the crossing.

Behind, the stubborn Hobson closed in, his troops urged on by anxious citizens still fearful for their lives and property. He later reported that they were met everywhere by large bodies of people enthusiastically singing "Rally 'Round the Flag Boys." For the blue troopers, it was six hundred miles of fried chicken and the incessant singing of this song. Hobson later grumpily observed that, "Even the katydids learned the damned tune!"

Underway after the lengthy delay at Chester, the raiders hurried forward until they pushed out of the woods bordering the river. Ahead, dimly visible through the fast fading twilight, they saw a network of trenches and barricades blocking their way to freedom. Scouts scuttled forward and returned to report the fortifications were manned by a large body of troops. Morgan knew his time was rapidly running out. Still, faced with the strong blocking force, he decided to gamble that darkness would slow the pursuit and he could afford to wait until daylight to attack.

With darkness, a heavy fog started to seep into the valley. Above it, a brisk wind sent fragments of cloud scooting across a sliver of moon that soon gave up its futile effort to provide light and dropped from sight. The Fifth and Sixth Kentucky slithered up through the impenetrable blackness that ensued to lay close to the breastworks, waiting for dawn and sufficient light to attack. Behind them, the Parrotts were dug in on a low hill that provided enough elevation to permit them to fire directly over the attacking force into the fortifications.

Unable to see, the two hundred defenders huddled in the darkness. As time throbbed by in slow motion, their straining ears could hear the muffled noise of over two thousand men and horses shuffling about in the night. Soon the strain, induced by the night sounds and magnified by fear, exceeded their capacity for courage. Silently, they crawled out of their positions and drifted away in the concealing blackness. Unknown to the raiders, only the swollen river hissing through the fog barred them from escape.

As day began to rip the fog apart, the Fifth and Sixth charged the breastworks. To their amazement, not a sound greeted them as they poured over the ramparts into deserted firing positions. Realizing the way was open, they sent word back and swung toward Pomeroy to watch for any approaching enemy. After a short distance, they ran into heavy fog. They continued to move gingerly forward through this swirling cloud when a hole suddenly appeared to reveal advancing troops—Judah's point. The Rebels instantly opened fire. The Yankees, caught off guard, retreated in confusion while the Rebels quickly started digging in for the counterblow they knew was coming.

Their wait was short. Three regiments of blue cavalry stormed out of the fog, pinned the Fifth and Sixth down and captured the Parrotts. Behind them, as Morgan frantically tried to organize the remainder of the command, the vedettes from the Chester Road tumbled in ahead of Hobson's troops. Retreat to the north now became Morgan's only hope of salvation. But, just as he started, the troops of Wolford and Kautz poured out of the fog in a headlong charge, pennons whipping in the breeze above the thundering rumble of galloping hoofbeats. Desperately, the Confederates stood their ground, grimly refusing to budge despite the horde of blue troopers pressing in on them. Then, the fog evaporated and horrified Rebel eyes saw the ugly snouts of gunboats burst into view in the glaring sunlight. In seconds, twenty-four-pound Dahlgrens were dropping rounds into their ranks. Then, Hobson's guns added their bass voices to the artillery choir singing a funeral anthem over the embattled raiders.

Slowly the graybacks were pushed into a U-shaped formation that placed them in a cross fire and enabled only a portion of their force to be effectively employed. Although the Rebels showed no sign of breaking, Morgan knew his only alternatives were retreat or extermination. Ordering Johnson and Duke to hold, he began to withdraw the remainder of the division. As they pulled out, those left behind fought with redoubled fury, giving up ground an inch at a time.

By midmorning, the pressure became unbearable and, knowing the rest of the division was gone, the two colonels agreed to fall back simultaneously. At a signal, the graybacks swung to horse and moved off at a trot in columns of fours from right of companies. Behind them, the battered Sixth Kentucky three times swung into line and charged pell-mell into the Union cavalry, finally throwing it into panic. For a mile, the retreating rear guard moved as if on parade. Then disaster struck. Recklessly pushing their way into a narrow chute, the gunboats brought the horsemen under almost point-blank fire. Shot and shell poured in on the hapless riders from three sides in a deluge. Screams, dust, and explosions filled the air as destruction swaggered at will through the Confederate ranks. "The scream of shells drowned the hum of bullets," Duke remembered. "The air seemed filled with metal, and the ground was torn and ploughed into furrows."

Under this assault the iron courage of the Rebels snapped and their retreat dissolved into a scrambling rout. This was the moment for which the Michigan cavalry had been waiting. They swept over the suffering rear guard like a hailstorm pounds a field of wheat. Soon a white flag waved and the battle's ocean of sound receded, leaving the screams and groans of the wounded hanging in the hot summer air. Seven hundred despondent graybacks turned themselves over to the Federals—but, Morgan and one thousand more were gone.

The victors had no time to celebrate, for the central question remained—how to catch Morgan? First, though, the question of command, which had already embroiled Hobson and Judah in a quarrel, had to be resolved. Burnside attempted to squelch the argument by promising, ". . . either one that retards this [pursuit of Morgan] will assume a heavy responsibility, which will bring its retribution."

In truth, the question was answered by the condition of the men and horses. This forced the chase to be turned over to Shackleford and Wolford. They were given one thousand men and told not to rest until the raider was captured.

While the Union argued, Morgan dashed to Reedsville where he found the crossing open except for the surging river. One look at the shore of West Virginia and the escaping riders plunged into the flood. Despite the danger and, indeed, losses to the vicious current, the crossing was going well when the late-afternoon quiet was splintered by a grumbling roar and a geyser erupted in the midst of the swimming horse soldiers. The gunboat *Moose* had ignored the fight downriver and pushed on upstream to catch the cavalry in this watery element. As shells rained down on them, the escaping column split and thrashed toward land as fast as possible, seeking cover. Morgan and about seven hundred men were forced to turn back into Ohio while Johnson and three hundred others huddled in the willows of the eastern shore.

As the sun used its last rays to paint the western sky scarlet, Morgan led his weary men into a dark ravine. There he halted. He told his men he intended to press on, but offered them the opportunity to fall out and individually try to cross the river under cover of night. Not a man accepted. Greatly pleased by this show of loyalty, Morgan again reached into his bag of tricks. He had his men gather wood and stack it for campfires. Then, the main body rode off to the west while a rear guard waited for full darkness. Once it fell, they lit the stacks of wood and galloped after their comrades.

Shackleford's men were not long in spotting the distant fires. Messengers raced across the countryside carrying the word and summoning scattered regiments to the capture. As soon as his force had gathered, Shackleford had them stealthily surround the camp and scouts slipped in to get the lay of the land. Shortly, they returned to report only empty ground and the dying embers of untended fires.

Meanwhile, Morgan pushed on to the vicinity of Tupper Plain and went into camp at midnight. Within two hours, Shackleford's wide-ranging scouts found him and the Union pursuit rushed to the scene. Even in the darkness, it was obvious to Shackleford that Morgan occupied an extraordinarily strong defensive position. Unwilling to commit his troops to the fierce gunfire that awaited them as surely as death, the Union commander held back. This was all Morgan needed. Swinging to saddle, the raiders dashed away toward the ford at Eight Mile Island.

This ford was protected by militia cut from different cloth than those who had abandoned Buffington Island. Their commander, aware that his troops were no match for the battle-hardened raiders, searched for gunboat support but could find none. Finally, in desperation, he acquired a side-wheeler and positioned it as if were a gunboat. For once, the wily Morgan took the bait. Spotting the ersatz war vessel from a distance, he swung off and took up a position near Cheshire. Here, he waited for the pursuit.

At 3:00 P.M., Shackleford's force arrived and deployed. A flag of truce was sent forward and its bearer demanded Morgan's surrender. The Rebel chief asked for an hour to think it over. Shackleford gave him forty minutes. The Union force, poised expectantly for the attack, fidgeted as the minutes ticked slowly away. In the Confederate position, there appeared to be little activity until, on the fortieth minute, a white flag waved and a group of gray troops moved forward. It was the work of only a few minutes for the chagrined Federals to discover they had captured about one hundred sick and wounded men. Morgan and the other six hundred had vanished.

Before the furious Shackleford could recover, Morgan sped through Vinton, by McArthur, and disappeared into the tumbling hills of Vinton County headed toward the Muskingum River. This area was now a vacuum of communications as a result of the raiders' earlier activity. Nevertheless, word that the Union had lost the raiders spread rapidly and panic again swept the countryside.

The early stage through Nelsonville brought welcome news on the twenty-second—the Rebels had been captured at Hamden. This news flashed through the village and soon the entire population was engaged in a wild celebration. An hour later, the merriment was abruptly snuffed out as the terrified townspeople stared at the gray mass of bitter, weary, hard-eyed Southern cavalry filling their streets. These riders swept through the normally quiet village burning bridges and canal boats and taking what they wanted in supplies. Then, they rode on toward Eagleport on the Muskingum River; but the Federal bloodhound was again loping along their backtrail.

By midafternoon the twenty-third, Wolford was beyond the Muskingum and in front of Morgan. This forced the raiders to double back, then head down the Muskingum toward Blennerhassett Island on the Ohio. As they hurried along, sharp-eyed Union scouts spotted their dust cloud and the pursuers swung inexorably into position to pin the fleeing riders. At ten o'clock, the job was done. Strong forces were ahead and behind. Hobson lay across the Muskingum on their right and a sheer cliff blocked them on the left. With nowhere to go, Morgan reined in at the base of the cliff and the exhausted riders dropped to the ground. On three sides of them, campfires sprang to life as their opponents rested, content to wait for daylight to finish the job.

Unwilling to accept defeat, Morgan sent scouts to search for a way up the bluffs. By the time the Federal campfires had died down, the scouts returned. They told Morgan they had found a way out if the riders could substitute desire for footholds. The Rebel leader never hesitated. In single file, leading their horses, the weary raiders began scrambling up the cliffside like goats. Panting, sweating, slashed by invisible vines and branches, slipping to within centimeters of disaster, every man made the climb. The last man reached the top at mid-

night, leaped into his saddle, and scooted away northward. Below
and behind them, the Federals slept peacefully until dawn.

No record exists of the pursuers' reaction when they discovered
the Rebels missing, but it is safe to say they were apoplectic. As for
the overall commander, Burnside, 24 July may not have been the
most miserable day of his life but it ranked near the top. He was literally swamped with messages from Halleck and Rosecrans that were
couched in unfriendly terms demanding the answers to unanswerable
questions. What hurt the embarrassed and frustrated general most,
however, was a caustic one-liner from a certain A. Lincoln. It asked,
"What, if anything, further do you hear from John Morgan?"

The shaken Burnside, trying frantically to recover, demanded more
troops and began furiously reshuffling his forces. Fortunately for the
Union, Shackleford and Hobson ignored their leader. White-hot with
rage, they again rushed after the ghost they had been chasing for
twenty-four days.

Following their escape the raiders took Cumberland without firing
a shot, rested a few hours, then moved on through Senecaville to Old
Washington. Here, despite the precariousness of their situation, they
had a leisurely meal at the American Hotel. Then, the Ohio drawing
them like a magnet, they swung east on the National Road heading
for Coxe's Riffle. Londonderry, Smyrna, Moorefield, Hopedale,
Bloomingdale, and Wintersville all fell behind before constant pressure from militia again forced them to turn away from their goal. The
raiders now knew beyond the shadow of a doubt that the game was
up. Still, they pressed on to Bergholz where they spent the night.

The next morning in the brilliant light of a new day, they moved
toward Salineville, pursuit only minutes behind. Just beyond this
town, they hit a force of 350 men of the First Michigan Cavalry. A
running fight ensued until finally Company C of the Second
Kentucky turned. Forming into line, these plucky riders charged
while Morgan escaped. But, he left 275 men of his dwindling band
behind as the price of a few more short hours of freedom.

The Confederates again turned toward the Ohio aiming for
Smith's Ford. At one o'clock they ran into a company of militia.
Persuading them to let him pass, Morgan took their commander,
Capt. James Burbick, with him. In another hour, the baying hounds
of the pursuit were on his heels, their dust cloud showing they were
gaining rapidly. The last grain of sand had run through the hour-
glass and Morgan knew it. Turning to Burbick, Morgan asked if he
would accept his surrender. Burbick assured him he would be
delighted to do so.

Still, Morgan hesitated. Then he said, "But, perhaps you would not give me such terms as I wish."

"General Morgan," Burbick assured him, "You may write your own terms, and I will grant them."

"Very well then, it is a bargain. I will surrender to you," Morgan told him. He then proposed parole for all the raiders with everyone to keep his horse and the officers their side arms. Burbick nodded agreement and the motions of a formal surrender were rapidly completed.

Minutes later the pursuing force descended on the now docile Confederates. Burbick was shoved unceremoniously aside as Federal commanders vied to claim credit for the capture. Wolford demanded the surrender terms be honored but Shackleford would not hear of it. He carried the argument, and Morgan and a large number of his men were eventually confined in the Ohio State Penitentiary as criminals. Later some, including Morgan, would escape and return to the South. But, for now, the weary riders simply dropped in their tracks and rested.

The merits, or lack thereof, of Morgan's raid can be argued interminably without consensus. There were, however, several positive results from the Confederate viewpoint. He pulled fourteen thousand soldiers from other duty, caused 120,000 militia to be mustered, captured and paroled six thousand of the enemy, destroyed thirty-four major bridges, demolished the railroad in over sixty locations, burned warehouses, trains, plants, mills, boats, wagons, and depots and delayed the fall of East Tennessee significantly. Further, to some degree he reinspired the flagging South while bringing terror to an untold number of Northerners who had previously felt immune to the war. The cost to the Confederacy was about twenty-four hundred men and horses.

At four o'clock in the afternoon, a column of blue and gray troopers trotted away from the surrender site with Morgan and Shackleford in the lead. As they rumbled across a small wooden bridge, Morgan turned to a Federal officer following him. With a broad smile and a twinkle in his eye, the Rebel leader said, "Adjutant, see that that bridge is burned."

Prison lay ahead but the captured horsemen riding into the late afternoon had made history. Never before or again would there be a cavalry exploit to match the one just completed by Morgan and Morgan's Terrible Men.

CHAPTER XII

Ride Down the Valley

Eyeing each other as warily as strange dogs, two cavalry forces moved northward through the flat bottomland of the Tennessee River Valley. Between them, the shining river rushed past, its surging current and broad expanse effectively separating mortal enemies as they rode parallel on its banks. On the western bank, the flatland quickly ascended to the left of the blue troops of Maj. Gen. George Crook to a hulking mountain called Walden's Ridge. Its forbidding slopes provided a bulwark between the river and the spectacularly beautiful Sequatchie Valley that lay behind it. The softly undulating bottom of this valley, tinted lightly with the first colors of autumn, stretched away until it reached the mountains of the Eastern Highland Rim, barely visible through the bluish haze of early fall. Along the valley floor a rutted, narrow wagon road wound for sixty tortuous miles. This tenuous string of ruts, laughable in ordinary times, had through circumstance assumed an importance of major proportions. It was now the principal target of Maj. Gen. Joseph Wheeler's gray troopers jogging along the eastern shore, seeking an opportunity to cross the river with minimal contact with the enemy.

Their presence in this area was the result of the situation that had developed following Chickamauga. As that struggle wound to an end,

Maj. Gen. William S. Rosecrans's battered Union army had fled to Chattanooga, Tennessee in search of a safe haven. They had hardly huddled there, critically short of supplies and ammunition, however, when the realization dawned that they had leaped headlong from the frying pan into a very hot fire. For as they moved into the city, Lt. Gen. James Longstreet's troops swept onto Lookout Mountain perching like hungry predators over their normal supply route. At the same time, Gen. Braxton Bragg took control of the eastern bank of the Tennessee River, moving northward until he confronted the army of Maj. Gen. Ambrose Burnside.

Rosecrans's survival depended on either resupply by the questionable Sequatchie Valley Road or relief from Burnside. The latter offered little promise, however, since that army faced the merciless cavalry of Maj. Gen. Nathan Bedford Forrest and, in addition, was charged with the heavy duty of guarding the Cumberland Gap. Reluctance to challenge Forrest and fear that Bragg might suddenly sweep through the Gap caused Burnside to select the easy decision— do nothing. Thus, the fate of an army was left to hang on a miserable set of ruts hardly more dignified than a pig trail.

Bragg, sitting comfortably in the catbird's seat, watching the trapped Rosecrans, mulled over the situation carefully. He concluded he had two alternatives: He could wait patiently and starve the Federals out or move quickly and force a retreat, which was certain to be disastrous. Uncharacteristically, the controversial North Carolinian chose the latter.

On 27 September 1863, to the astonishment of experienced cavalry officers, who predicted loss of at least half the command, Bragg ordered Wheeler, the Confederacy's little dynamo, across the river to cut the Sequatchie Valley road. The attacking force was to be composed of Brig. Gens. John A. Wharton's and W. T. Martin's divisions from Wheeler's cavalry and three brigades of Forrest's cavalry led by Brigadier General H. B. Davidson and Cols. John S. Scott and George B. Hodge. Both Wheeler and Forrest were appalled at the order and pleaded that both horses and men were completely worn out and were incapable of meeting the demand being placed upon them. Bragg, brushing aside the pleas of his subordinates, was not to be dissuaded.

Forrest, not a man to shirk a challenge, argued the matter until Bragg summarily ordered him to move his men. Reluctantly starting them south, the enraged Forrest, galled by what he considered a usurpation of his prerogatives, told Bragg, "You have threatened to arrest me for not obeying orders promptly. I dare you to do it, and I say to you that if you ever again try to interfere with me or cross my path, it will be at the peril of your life!" He then concluded this tirade by telling his commander, "You are unfit to command an army!"

Oddly, this blatant display of insubordination went unpunished by the strict disciplinarian Bragg and was left to the Confederate president. Rather than calling the obstreperous Forrest to account, Jefferson Davis not only ignored what should have been intolerable but rewarded him with an independent command.

While the insubordinate Forrest was raving against his leader, the ever dutiful Wheeler went quietly about the business of carrying out his orders. Gathering the part of his new command that was with him, he set out on what could only be called a desperate mission. Short of ammunition, separated from supplies, and traveling through a depleted countryside with Burnside's army on his flank and to his rear, he led his tired, worn-out troopers up the river under the watchful eyes of the Fourth Ohio Cavalry. Finally, irritated by the persistence of his Yankee shadow across the river, the peppery little general swung his artillery into position and ordered his troops across. Led by Col. James Hagan, the Third Alabama plunged into the river and a storm of Federal gunfire. Sheltered in timber and covered by two six-pound Parrotts, the blue troopers turned the rushing river into a churning mass of miniature geysers. Struggling with the tugging current, water three feet deep, and tiny spouts of death, the Rebels pushed doggedly forward ignoring suddenly empty saddles and the cries of wounded men. Pulling from the grasping current at last, they charged into the woods, routing the opposition.

The remnants of this river guard rushed to the rear, losing no time in informing Crook of Wheeler's crossing. Startled by this development he played a safe hand and did nothing to turn the Rebels back. He was seriously concerned about the impact this might have on him personally, however, and hurriedly wired Chattanooga of the Rebel success. Then, in an effort to absolve himself of responsibility and to avoid the criticism he felt was coming, the man, who would later gain fame as an Indian fighter in the West, lamely added, "It was impossible for me to resist the crossing, as there was no ford at the river where they crossed, until they made it last night."

Galvanized into action by this news, Federal commanders hurriedly took steps to reinforce the cavalry patrolling the Tennessee with three regiments of infantry and a section of artillery. This force was then ordered to ". . . move with all dispatch . . . to Anderson's Cross Roads, in the Sequatchie Valley, to protect our wagon trains."

Once on the western shore, Wheeler regrouped his command and moved to Cottonport. Here he was joined by the brigades Forrest had so grudgingly supplied. He found them in terrible condition and critically short of supplies. Undaunted by this discouraging state of affairs, he weeded out the completely unfit and reorganized his force into three divisions under Wharton, Martin, and Davidson. Satisfied he had done the best he could in preparation for the task ahead of him, Wheeler was ready to move out. At dusk on 1 October "Boots and Saddles" sounded and the command moved toward the scowling heights of Walden's Ridge.

During the preceding day heavy clouds had slowly formed, spreading across the river valley until they obliterated the sky. Late in the afternoon, a quiet rain began to fall, turning into a downpour as darkness fell. Probing through the driving rain in inky blackness, scouts found a narrow, winding trail leading up the steep flank of the mountain. Grunting from exertion, slipping and sliding in treacherous mud, the column felt its way slowly up the slopes of the ridge while occasional bursts of lightning fitfully illuminated the almost absolute darkness and thunder muttered sullenly through the deluge. As they groped their way slowly up the mountainside without an inkling of trouble, they blindly crashed head-on into a regiment of enemy riders.

Almost instinctively, Wheeler shouted, "Charge!" The Rebels surged forward and the Yankees, as startled as their opponents, scattered like frightened quail. The Confederates then resumed their plodding climb. The Union regiment's collapse without any attempt to resist the Confederate incursion allowed another opportunity to disrupt the Rebel foray to slip away virtually uncontested.

Late in the day on 2 October, the Rebels made camp on the crest of Walden's Ridge and gazed into the shadow-filled Sequatchie Valley. As night closed in, Wheeler settled comfortably before a crackling log fire and summoned Martin and Wharton to join him. While his lieutenants listened, Wheeler outlined his plans. He would, he told them, take a detachment of about fifteen hundred men, descend into the valley, and attempt to destroy a huge wagon train on its way to resupply Rosecrans. The remainder of the command, under Wharton, would proceed in the direction of McMinnville. Martin and Wharton were instantly on their feet in protest. Wharton pointed out that dividing a small force surrounded by larger forces and behind enemy lines was contrary to all the maxims of war. Wheeler listened patiently to the impassioned arguments of the former lawyers now serving as his lieutenants, then terminated the discussion by saying, "I have my orders, gentlemen, and I will attempt the work. General Martin will accompany me. General Wharton will go on with the remainder of the command to the vicinity of McMinnville, where I shall join him tomorrow night, if I am alive."

Crook, with Rosecrans's ultimatum, "They must not be allowed to enter Sequatchie!" echoing in his brain, arrived at Walden's Ridge about the time Wheeler was having his meeting. He immediately wired Chattanooga that Wheeler had passed his location about noon and that he expected to catch him the next day. Then, at least tacitly recognizing he could not meet the terms of Rosecrans's command, added that he would catch them, ". . . if I have to go to Nashville." The reality was that no blue-suited soldier was in position to avert the catastrophe poised above them on the crest of the ridge.

The countryside was still swaddled in darkness when Wheeler's tired troopers hit the saddle and headed for the valley floor. They had traveled about ten miles before the feeble light of the coming day revealed thirty-two six-mule wagons under heavy guard groaning toward Chattanooga. Without ceremony, the Rebels charged out of the fading darkness to crush the wagon train escort, taking them by surprise. The captured wagons were quickly rounded up and turned over to the Fourth Alabama to control while the remainder of the force moved forward.

As Wheeler trotted by the captured train, he spotted a Rebel rifling a captured vehicle. "Come out, there, and go to meet the enemy," the little general sternly ordered.

"Yes, General," answered the forager who was only a youngster. "I am very hungry and am filling my haversack," he told Wheeler as he swung to horse. With that, the boy rode off to combat side-by-side with the general he had served under for months but to whom he had never spoken.

As they rode, the rising sun crawled over the hump of Walden's Ridge, scattering the remaining darkness. As the last fragments of night scuttled into hiding, the bright rays of a new day revealed a sight that caused Rebel wonder and anticipation. As far as the eye could see stretched a line of snow-white canvas covering the largest wagon train any of them had ever seen. As the enormous line of wagons bounced heavily along the deeply rutted roadway, a force of

Union cavalry and infantry fanned out along its flanks determined to protect this fat worm from any early bird seeking it.

Wheeler rapidly formed up his force with Col. John T. Morgan in the lead. Then, as a bugle screamed "Charge" the raiding horsemen swept down on the hapless wagons. Morgan's men hit the front ranks of the escort with a crash, riding over them only to be thrown back in disorder by the reserves. Now, leaving the wagons behind, Colonel A. A. Russell's Fourth Alabama charged at a gallop, ripping the heavy morning air with their screeching Rebel yell. At point-blank range, these reckless riding troopers took a volley without faltering and rode their opponents down. Although split into two groups, the escort continued to fight stubbornly. For two hours, the air was filled with the rattle of gunshots, yells, screams, and curses as the fighting swirled aimlessly along the line of wagons. Finally, the last bluecoat gave up the fight and the bonanza of wagons lay helpless before the victorious Confederates.

For the next eight hours the Rebels devoted themselves to an orgy of destruction. The Union teamsters had abandoned their charges in panic, leaving the terrified teams to run free. For miles, the road was a mass of overturned wagons and entangled teams. The Confederates now raged down this line firing wagons and sabering or shooting mules. As they worked, a towering column of smoke visible for miles around billowed high into the clear morning sky above the stricken wagon train. Periodically, drowning out the clamor that accompanied the train's destruction, an ordnance wagon would explode with a reverberating roar that could be heard clearly in Chattanooga twenty miles away.

In that city, Rosecrans pondered a message from Crook that said, "The Rebels must have 10,000 men, from the most reliable information I can get." Actually, Wheeler had less than four thousand, but numbers, which he did not believe anyway, were not of any great interest to the Union commander at the moment. He was both worried about the future of his army and chagrined at the ease with which the Rebels had gotten into the valley. He knew something had to be done immediately to prevent Wheeler from succeeding and he also wanted to make sure he didn't inherit the blame if the "War Child" prevailed. With the sound of explosions still hanging hauntingly in the air, he shot off a message to Burnside urging him to act and complaining because Wheeler had been permitted to cross the river. He ended the bitter message by telling his counterpart,

"Heaven only knows where the mischief will end. If you don't unite with us soon you will be responsible for another catastrophe, I fear."

Rosecrans's attempt to place blame and at the same time get help apparently fell on deaf ears. Even the reminder of past disasters that haunted Burnside, and which he was not anxious to repeat, had no effect. Burnside stolidly held his position. Lesser commanders were more responsive, however, as they hastened to stave off complete disaster. Troops under Brig. Gen. Robert B. Mitchell and Col. Edward W. McCook rushed up the valley while Crook, at last motivated and supported by Col. John T. Wilder's mounted infantry, plunged down Walden's Ridge riding pell-mell for the valley floor.

Late in the day, a weary Confederate force regrouped and moved out, leaving a small rear guard. This latter group sparred with the leading elements of the Federal pursuit when it made belated contact with them. Falling slowly back, they kept up the appearance of wanting to fight, without actually coming firmly to grips with the pursuing force until darkness fell. Then, they slipped away leaving the crestfallen bluecoats to survey the smoldering remains of perhaps one thousand wagons. In Chattanooga, Federal forces immediately went on one-quarter rations.

At ten o'clock the following morning, the leading elements of Wharton's force under Hodge reached McMinnville. Hodge quickly drove in the pickets and took possession of a series of outlying rifle pits. When Wharton arrived, he found Hodge's troopers deployed in line of battle preparatory to assaulting the town. Anxious to avoid a street fight, Wharton sent in a flag of truce demanding the unconditional surrender of the city. Maj. Michael L. Patterson, the garrison commander and the son-in-law of Andrew Johnson, soon to be vice president, read the demand, noting that it claimed he was surrounded by four divisions of cavalry and artillery. Doubting the accuracy of this statement, he naively asked permission to count the raiders. The request was promptly and emphatically denied. Patterson, lacking the nerve to test his doubts of the Confederate's strength, meekly gave up. Rushing through the town like water looking for a low place, the raiders captured 587 prisoners, 250 horses and mules, a wagon train, a railroad train, and a huge store of supplies.

Wheeler's men, fresh from their destruction of the wagon train, rejoined just as the town was secured and pitched in to spend the remainder of the day destroying the captured booty as well as the bridges over Hickory Creek and Collins River. Their work complete, the Rebel column whipped onto the Nashville Road and headed for Murfreesboro. Behind them a soaring pillar of boiling black smoke hung heavily in the melancholy sky to mark their passage.

Behind the marauders, twenty-five thousand Federals were scrambling frantically to catch them. Crook had been in almost constant contact with the persistent Rebel rear guard but had been totally unable to come to grips with it in force. At McMinnville, Crook was joined by Mitchell, who was then sent to Shelbyville in an attempt to cut Wheeler off. Concurrently, McCook was ordered to Unionville while Crook and Wilder continued in the general direction of the Farmington Road trying to maintain pressure on the raiders' rear.

Wheeler's troopers galloped down on Murfreesboro finding it both strong and ready for them. Unwilling to commit his command to a drawn out fight, Wheeler destroyed a stockade on the edge of town and rode out. On their way the raiders destroyed a bridge over Stone's River, tore up several miles of railroad track, and moved toward Wartrace, capturing supply trains at Christiana and Fosterville. At Wartrace, they tore up more track and destroyed the trestle there as well as the one over Duck River. From Wartrace, the raiders swung south. They found Shelbyville deserted and promptly sacked the town, which contained large stores of Federal supplies. Fifty miles away the Union garrison in Columbia gave in to panic, set fire to their supplies, and abandoned their post.

The blue cavalry had now closed the gap and was inflicting heavy punishment on the Confederate rear. Deeply concerned with the deteriorating situation, Wheeler decided to get out of the state as quickly as possible and swung toward the Tennessee River and safety. At nightfall on 6 September, he went into camp at Crowell's Mill on the Duck River. Davidson stopped near Warner's Bridge with Martin two miles below him and Wharton still farther downriver. Discovering Crook and Mitchell were near Davidson, Wheeler ordered him to watch all roads, to fall back on Wheeler if attacked, and to make absolutely sure the Union force did not get between them. Worrying about the situation through the evening, Wheeler became more and more concerned about Davidson's position. Finally, he modified his last order by telling Davidson to fall back on him immediately. Unfortunately, and for no good reason, Davidson, a disciplined soldier whose valiant service as a private in the Mexican War and as a sergeant in the First Tennessee had earned him an appointment to West Point, ignored both orders.

Morning burst over the quiet, rolling Tennessee countryside on the seventh, its spectacle masking the danger streaking along in its wake. Davidson's tired riders got the first taste of it when they rolled grudgingly out of their blankets into a heavy shower of Yankee bullets. Crook's riders hit the disconcerted Rebels like a hand grenade, turning their ranks into a disorganized mob of scrambling bodies frantically seeking safety. Fighting sporadically and ineffectively, the confused Rebels began to fall back toward Farmington instead of Wheeler, leaving the crumpled bodies of their downed comrades spotting the autumn-browned earth like heaps of discarded litter. Davidson, who had lost control almost from the first shot, made no attempt to tell Wheeler where he was going—he just went, his troops battered, gray leaves flying before the blue gale which threatened to blow them away.

At ten o'clock in the morning, Scott's brigade, as yet relatively unscathed, caught the full force of the Union attack and shattered like an overstressed pane of glass. In seconds, what had been a well-disciplined unit dissolved into a panic-stricken mob charging wildly to the rear. Their commander, who would be prevented from promotion to brigadier general by Forrest, could not regain control of his troops as they reeled away from their attackers. Soon, they ran into Hodge's men who were advancing to support them. Now, little better than a mob, the thoroughly routed brigade simply rode its intended reinforcements down.

Frantically, Hodge and his officers rushed in, shouting orders in an effort to keep their men from joining the rout. Discipline told finally and gradually Hodge's troops extricated themselves and formed into line behind a fence running at right angles to the road. From this position, they opened fire on the greatly superior Union force bearing down on them. But, without support, their position was hopeless and they knew it.

Davidson, finally regaining his composure, attempted to halt and reform his men. The fight was gone from them, however, and he soon gave up, contenting himself with drifting along with them, leaving the sound of desperate fighting behind him. Hodge, an Annapolis graduate who had left the naval service as a passed midshipman, was alone, facing a force that had the taste of victory in its mouth. He described the result, "For five hours and a half, over seven miles of country, the unequal contest continued. My gallant brigade was cut to pieces and slaughtered. I had informed the officers and men that the sacrifice of their lives was necessary and they manfully made the sacrifice."

As soon as Wheeler heard Davidson was moving toward Farmington, he sent Wharton with the captured wagons toward the Tennessee River and took Martin's division at a gallop for the Lewisburg Pike. By three o'clock in the afternoon, he was behind the retreating force and going into position in a thick cedar forest. At four o'clock, his lines opened to let Davidson through followed by the bloody remnants of Hodge's brigade.

Crook's victory-flushed force, unaware of Wheeler's location, rushed ahead with abandon. As the pursuing Yankees swept into view disdaining cover and caution, Wheeler cut them down with a deluge of grape, canister, and small-arms fire. What had been a noisy mass of elated men was suddenly a silent carpet of blue, etched with an irregular pattern of red and splotches of white.

Crook's remaining soldiers were not easily dissuaded, however. They reformed and again pressed forward into a gray-green curtain of cedar. For twenty minutes, unbridled fighting raged, the cedars swaying to the cacophonous music of war. Men screamed in agony as the Grim Reaper's scythe found them, cursed at the sharp pain of bullet-driven cedar splinters, or prayed silently as they squinted through the rolling smoke of battle searching for a target. Through this maelstrom of destruction, a horde of leaden pellets whispered a mocking promise of death as they sought the yielding flesh of men, while above the frightening roar, the banshee wail of ricochets howled a song of frustrated death. At last, the blue line wavered and Martin's mounted troopers pounced on them to hack and slash their fleeing ranks to pieces. Darkness finally brought a halt and both sides dropped for a few hours' rest. Tomorrow they would race for the river.

The Confederates moved at daylight with the Federals right behind them. The previous day's battle had cooled the Union troop's ardor, however, and the expected race was run very carefully. The pursuers followed closely enough to keep their respect, but not so close as to precipitate an all-out fight. Wheeler's troops hit the river at Mussel Shoals and immediately started streaming across. The river, low at this time of year, was a series of large boulders and deep pools. Crossing consisted largely of scrambling up slick rocks and plunging with a prodigious splash into green depths that covered both man and horse. One trooper said. "Everyone got about six duckings as we crossed."

At midnight, under rapidly increasing Union small-arms fire, the last of the rear guard forded the stream. As the last dripping figure alighted on Alabama soil, the troops got a good look at the tiny figure with the heart of a giant who led them. Joe Wheeler had remained on enemy soil until the last of his battle-worn troopers reached safety.

The raid had been a resounding success for the little general. He had destroyed well over one thousand loaded wagons; destroyed or captured hundreds of mules and horses; destroyed several locomotives and trains; destroyed five major bridges and many smaller ones; wrecked miles of railroad track; captured, wounded, or killed two thousand Federals; recruited over three thousand men; destroyed hundreds of thousands of dollars worth of supplies; and circled Rosecrans's army, traveling about three hundred miles in nine days. The raid cost him 212 killed and captured. The impact on Rosecrans's army was tremendous. After he had the opportunity to inspect it, Grant described its condition, "The artillery horses and mules had become so reduced by starvation that they could not have been relied on for moving anything. Any attempt at retreat must have been with men alone and with only such supplies as they could carry. A retreat would have been almost certain annihilation."

Within two weeks, Rosecrans was relieved by Maj. Gen. George Thomas who was, in turn, relieved by Major General U. S. Grant. Of these actions, Maj. Gen. David Hunter, who had been sent by Secretary of War Edwin Stanton to review the condition of the army, said, "I am convinced the change of commanders was not made an hour too soon and that if it had not been made just when it was we should have been driven from the valley of the Tennessee, if not from the whole state." It was most fortunate for the Union that Bragg did not act as decisively in moving against Chattanooga as he did in sending his lieutenant to destroy that city's supply line.

Once in Alabama, Wheeler discovered he was on the property of Col. Richard Jones, one of the largest landowners in the state. He promptly dispatched a staff officer to request permission to camp on the colonel's property. Approaching the colonel, Wheeler's emissary saluted and said, "General Wheeler presents his compliments and asks your permission for his men to camp here for the night."

As the colonel nodded his consent, he was joined by his pretty, young, and recently widowed daughter. "General Wheeler, did you say?" she asked. "I'd like to see him."

The staff officer bowed and with a laugh answered, "Well, Madam, you won't see much when you do."

However adept Wheeler's emissary may have been in other areas, he obviously lacked proficiency in matters of the heart. For, when Joe Wheeler rode out, the romance was on. He eventually married the lady he met fresh from his foray through the Sequatchie Valley, and he later came into ownership of her father's extensive holdings. As the years passed, he became active in politics, serving the state of Alabama as one of its representatives in the U.S. Congress. Then, in another time and another war, he again wore the stars of a major general, only this time on a blue uniform, as he served in Cuba and the Philippines, a member of the army he had once fought to the edge of death. Finally, he retired, full of honors, as a brigadier general of the Regular Army of the United States, the only officer to command a corps in both the Union and Confederate armies—a soldier to the last.

CHAPTER XIII

Until Forrest Is Dead

Atlanta, the mainspring of the Confederacy, was the prize that lured Maj. Gen. William T. Sherman out of Tennessee in the spring of 1864 on a mission of destruction that would earn him the enduring hatred of the South. As his army marched into the piney woods of Georgia's hill country, it became enmeshed in a running battle with the Rebels of Gen. Joseph E. Johnston, one of the South's most capable senior commanders. Masterfully employed by their commander, these stubborn fighters viciously disputed every square inch of soil coveted by the invaders. As a result, Union progress was slow and their losses heavy. Still, Sherman was confident he could achieve his objective if he could keep his supply line open. That he could do so was by no means certain. Lurking behind him in northern Mississippi was his gray-clad nemesis, Maj. Gen. Nathan Bedford Forrest.

Sherman's regard for Forrest's ability was so great that he had offered to make any brigadier general who killed the Rebel cavalryman a major general. None had been able to cash in on the offer, however, leaving Sherman with a constant, nagging worry for the safety of his rear. An expedition in late April and early May designed to alleviate this worry had driven Forrest out of Tennessee for the moment, but had failed to eliminate him. Brig. Gen. Samuel

185

D. Sturgis, who had won a brevet at Wilson's Creek and had been commended on his "handsome success" for his operations in East Tennessee, had been a leader in that effort. On 13 May, he wrote to Sherman, "My little campaign is over, and I regret to say Forrest is still at large. . . . I regret very much that I could not have the pleasure of bringing you his hair, but he is too great a plunderer to fight anything like an equal force, and we have to be satisfied with driving him from the State. He may turn on your communications—I rather think he will, but I see no way to prevent it from this point with this force."

Sturgis was absolutely correct in his speculation about Forrest's intentions. Sherman, however, was unwilling to accept the "no way to prevent it" point of view of his subordinate. By the end of May, uncertainty about Forrest and his intentions had become unbearable to the fiery Union commander. He ordered Maj. Gen. Cadwallader C. Washburn, commanding District of West Tennessee, to send Sturgis into Mississippi to ravage the countryside and, if not kill him, at least tie Forrest in position. Washburn, not a man to take chances, put together a stronger force than Sherman had recommended and, on the first of June, sent Sturgis south. That same day, Forrest left Tupelo, Mississippi headed for Tennessee and Sherman's lifeline.

The force under Sturgis was by far the largest and best equipped ever sent out for the specific purpose of finding Forrest. It consisted of a division of cavalry under Brig. Gen. Benjamin H. Grierson, one of the North's best cavalry commanders. He divided this force into two brigades, commanded by Cols. George E. Waring, Sr. and E. F. Winslow, totaling thirty-three hundred men and ten guns. They were supported by Col. William L. McMillen's infantry division made up of three brigades under Cols. A. Wilkins, George B. Hoge, and Edward Bouton—forty-eight hundred men and twelve guns. For logistical support, the force had a supply train of 250 wagons and ambulances. Every requirement had been anticipated and Washburn later asserted, "The number of troops deemed necessary by General Sherman was six thousand, but I sent eight thousand. Everything was in complete order, and the force consisted of some of our best troops. I saw to it personally that they lacked nothing to insure a successful campaign."

Torrential rains, flooded streams, incredibly bad roads, and a countryside pitifully barren of forage made Sturgis's progress painfully slow. As his troops slogged through the morass that passed for roads, their commander complained of moving in the blind with "information exceedingly meager and unsatisfactory." By the eighth, when they had reached Ripley, Sturgis was ready to return to Memphis. He called Grierson and McMillen into conference, telling them he feared the enemy would overwhelm them further south and that they would certainly lose the wagon train if this happened. He suggested these two possibilities were strong arguments in favor of an immediate return north. Grierson agreed but McMillen objected, pointing out that they had used this excuse before and suggested that if they used it again it would most likely not be well-received by Sherman. Sturgis reluctantly agreed, later reporting, "All agreed with me in the probable consequences of defeat. Some thought our only safety lay in retracing our steps and abandoning the expedition. It was urged, however, (and with some propriety, too) that inasmuch as I had abandoned a similar expedition only a few weeks before . . . it would be ruinous on all sides to return without first meeting the enemy. . . . Under these circumstances, and with a sad foreboding of the consequences, I determined to move forward. . . ." The march resumed.

Forrest reached Russellville, Alabama on the third of June. There he received news of the Union movement and orders from Maj. Gen. Stephen D. Lee, commanding Department of Alabama, Mississippi, and East Louisiana, to return immediately. Forrest promptly pivoted his command and began a forced march to head off the invaders. Arriving in Tupelo on the fifth, he threw his force along the Mobile and Ohio Railroad toward Corinth until he could be sure of the Federal line of march. The answer came on the ninth when Sturgis moved toward Guntown, concentrated his force, and went into camp at Stubb's Farm. His target was Tupelo.

Forrest's supporting force was badly scattered—Col. Tyree H. Bell's brigade of twenty-eight hundred men, a part of Brig. Gen. Abraham Buford's division, was at Rienzi; Cols. Hylan B. Lyon and Bushrod Johnson were at Baldwyn with thirteen hundred men; and Col. Edward W. Rucker with seven hundred men and Capt. John W. Morton's artillery were at Booneville with Forrest and his escort of two hundred thirty-five men.

While awaiting further orders, the troops encamped at Booneville received a chilling lesson in military justice. Two men and a boy had been convicted of desertion in the face of the enemy and sentenced to death. On the night of the eighth they were confined in a boxcar to await their execution the next morning. Sgt. Frank T. Reid, a member of Morton's Battery, described the event years later when he wrote, "A preacher was with them and I can still hear their loud voices in prayer and singing hymns." At daybreak they were brought out before open graves dug in the sedge field. The firing squad took its position, the boy received a last-minute pardon, and the final act took place. Reid continued, "A sharp command, a crack of musketry, and two lives were snuffed out like worthless candles."

Shortly after this event, despite the scattered disposition of Forrest's force, Lee directed Forrest to intercept Sturgis and to lure him toward Okolona where the two of them would combine and destroy him. Forrest accepted the order but warned Lee he might have to fight Sturgis before he could join up with him. Lee left the matter to Forrest's discretion and departed south. Orders went out immediately to Forrest's commanders to move at first light to Brice's Cross Roads. Sturgis was only eight miles from that point while the Rebels were from six to twenty-five miles away and only thirteen hundred of the Rebel troops were closer to the crossroads than the Yankees.

In the first weak light of dawn on the tenth, Forrest moved forward down a narrow road surrounded by thick woods. At this time, the Rebel leader announced his decision to fight a force that outnumbered him almost two to one and outgunned him three to one. Riding along with Rucker, he laid out his strategy, "I know they greatly outnumber the troops I have at hand, but the road along which they will march is narrow and muddy; they will make slow progress. The country is densely wooded and the undergrowth so heavy that when we strike them they will not know how few men we have. Their cavalry will move out ahead of the infantry, and should reach the crossroads three hours in advance. We can whip their cavalry in that time. As soon as the fight opens they will send back to have the infantry hurried up. It is going to be hot as hell, and coming on a run for five or six miles over such roads, their infantry will be so tired out we will ride right over them. I want everything to move up as fast as possible. I will go ahead with Lyon and the escort and open the fight." It was typical of the daring Rebel that he did not concern himself that most of his men would have to travel further under the same conditions. And, it was typical of them not to let it make any difference.

Grierson's Federal cavalry left their encampment at five-thirty in the morning. Their route through the heavily timbered countryside followed a narrow, soggy road that wound along a branch of the Tallahatchie River. Waring, out in front, was ordered to send a heavy patrol up the Baldwyn Road when he reached it. Intelligence received the previous evening indicated both Lee and Forrest had gone in that direction.

Day broke in the fury typical of that season in the Deep South. It had rained for several days before, ending in a cloudburst that had fallen until the previous midnight. Now, the sun, a brass incandescent ball, poured its scorching rays on the saturated ground. The temperature and humidity soared, creating a steamy, smothering atmosphere that quickly drained the energy from every living thing that moved.

Waring's patrol had gone only about a mile toward Baldwyn when it collided with Lyon's advance. The bluecoats immediately yelled for help and their commander threw his full brigade and six guns into the fight. The Rebel opposition was only a bit more than two companies. Their commander, Captain H. A. Tyler, positioned them so well and used them so effectively as they fell back through the thick underbrush, however, that the Federals believed their strength was much greater. Waring, convinced he had a strong force on his hands, dismounted his troopers and placed them in the heavy undergrowth at one end and on both sides of a narrow field. From this position, he prepared to launch a general assault.

Realizing he faced an overwhelming force, Tyler sent a courier on the run to advise Forrest. He responded by speeding up Lyon and telling the advance, "Fight on, men, and keep fighting 'till I come."

In a short while, Forrest and Lyon were on the scene. Their newly arrived troops were quickly dismounted and thrown into position behind a heavy rail fence reinforced with the thick brush that surrounded the field. The daring Rebel leader, who would "give more for fifteen minutes of bulge on the enemy than for a week of tactics," was greatly concerned that his small force would be overrun before the remainder could come up. In typical Forrest fashion, he decided to try to prevent this by a fake attack. He ordered Lyon forward, making a feint that Waring called "exceedingly fierce," before falling back behind the rail fence. In this manner, he held the superior force at bay for over an hour.

Now, Rucker arrived with seven hundred more troops. He found Forrest sitting on his horse in the middle of the road calmly surveying the battlefield. "What is it, General?" he asked.

"Yankees and lots of them," Forrest replied.

"Is it a battle?" Rucker wanted to know.

"Yes," Forrest assured him, "it is a battle. Never took a dare from them yet, and won't do it today."

Rucker's men were thrown into the line on Lyon's left and immediately a second fake charge was made. By the time the Confederates had returned to cover from this feint, Johnson had joined them. His group was positioned on Lyon's right while Colonel W. L. Duff's regiment of Rucker's command remained mounted and moved far to the left. Now, Forrest sent a courier at a long gallop to, "Tell Bell to move up fast and fetch all he's got." But, Bell, along with Morton's artillery, had a long way to come and horseflesh could only do so much.

Meanwhile, on the Federal side, Winslow's eighteen hundred men and four guns had arrived and gone into position on Waring's right. Grierson now had a front that stretched from just across the Baldwyn Road to slightly past the Guntown Road. Behind them, the ground sloped gently away to the bank of slow-moving Tishomingo Creek. Its simple wooden bridge, bounded on both sides by cornfields, offered the Federals their only access to the battlefield.

Forrest now decided he could wait no longer but would have to fight the blue cavalry with the force he had at hand. He calmly moved down the line bracing his troopers for the fight, telling them to charge at the sound of the bugle. Momentary silence fell across the woodlands. Then, as clear and compelling as the last trumpet, the notes of "Charge" rang from the timber's edge. As one, the gray riders rose and, with a hair-raising Rebel yell, rushed from cover.

A sheet of lead met the attackers and staggered their line. Here and there, troopers dropped, hugging the ground for protection from the whispering death that engulfed them. Their commanders ran down the line shouting for them to continue. And, continue they did, hunched up like livestock in a sleet storm, until they hit the fence on the opposite side of the field. Here, the fence and a blackjack thicket behind it halted them momentarily while Union rifles continued to exact a murderous toll. "Pull out a tree, boys!" someone yelled. In a heartbeat, a few of the blackjack saplings were jerked out by the roots and the Rebels poured into the thicket.

Amid the remaining scrubby blackjacks, six-guns came out and rifles were converted to clubs as the fight degenerated into a wild, hand-to-hand *melee*. Crashing and floundering in the thick underbrush, the two groups swayed to and fro for several minutes before Rucker's men suddenly surged forward. Waring quickly concentrated a brutal fire on that unit and saw it falter. Instantly, he threw the Second New Jersey and the Seventh Indiana against it. But, the determined graybacks would not give.

Lyon and Johnson redoubled their efforts on the Union left while Duff concentrated a blistering fire on the right. This relieved the pressure on Rucker and his hard-bitten Southerners again surged forward. The pressure was too much for the Union center which started to collapse. Recognizing impending disaster, Grierson fell back trying to reform in a new line. But, the die had already been cast. The Union horse soldiers were whipped at every point. It was now twelve-thirty in the afternoon and no infantry had arrived. Forrest had successfully carried out the first half of his strategy.

The Union infantry had left camp at seven o'clock in the morning. As they slogged forward through the steaming heat, word came back that a battle was underway in front of them. In a short while, urgent messages to "make all haste" and "lose no time in coming up" caused their commanders to order them to quick time. As they strained through the clinging mud, the merciless sun bore down on them with strength-sapping heat that soon began to exact a toll on the bluecoated foot soldiers. But, even more speed was demanded in the form of a "peremptory order," under the premise that only they could save the day. Finally, near complete exhaustion, they arrived at the double-quick to find, in the words of McMillen, ". . . everything at the Cross Roads was going to the devil as fast as it possibly could."

Hoge's brigade, first on the field, started moving rapidly into the line. Before they had completed their maneuver, Wilkins arrived and went into position on their left. Supporting artillery was placed on high ground behind them near Brice's house, the house that marked the crossroads and for which they were named. The remaining force, Bouton's brigade of black troops supported by artillery, was held in reserve on the Ripley Road. The beaten blue cavalry, "exhausted and well-nigh out of ammunition," was taken out of the line, some of it departing the field without orders.

Help was arriving on the Confederate side at the same time. Morton's artillery had thundered up and gone into position at Lyon's rear. Bell's brigade arrived and was placed on Rucker's left. Duff moved farther left to the Pontotoc Road and most of Forrest's escort and Tyler's battalion went into position on the extreme left. Colonel C. R. Barteau's tough Second Tennessee Cavalry, detached at Old Carrollsville, was sweeping wide to the right. Their purpose was to hit the Federal left rear. Now, command of the Confederate right was given to Brigadier General Buford, a 320-pound former dragoon who had remained neutral a year longer than his native state of Kentucky. Forrest personally commanded the left.

Forrest had no intention of allowing the Yankees to regain their composure after their grueling march. Quickly, Morton's guns opened the ball with deadly accurate fire, every round dropping on the opposing artillery's position. Under this barrage, Bell's men, struggling through the entangling underbrush, charged into a storm of Yankee bullets. For a time they held on grimly in the teeth of this withering fire, but they were then forced back. Hoge, moving quickly to take advantage of the breaking Rebel line, ordered his infantry forward. The blue troops charged with such force they quickly threatened to overrun Bell's men. Forrest countered the threat by throwing his remaining escort and Capt. Henry Gartell's Georgians into the fight. By dent of hard fighting and, with the help of this additional force, the Rebels were able to stabilize the line.

Part of Hoge's assault had splashed over onto the Rebel left. Rucker, watching the heavy thickets in front of him, saw them part. Out of this tangle of growth a grim line of blue troops, bayonets fixed, bore down on his thin line. Rucker, startled, shouted to his troopers, "Kneel on the ground, men, draw your six-shooters, and don't run!"

The gray defenders dropped to the earth to discover that the heavy fire had stripped the foliage from the lower branches of the underbrush. Before them was a forest of Yankee legs that immediately became the target for a hail of pistol bullets. The legs were literally cut from under the attackers as they received a never-to-be-forgotten demonstration that bayonets could not match six-guns in hand-to-hand combat. The Federal charge rapidly rebounded into better cover.

Lyon and Johnson on the right and Duff on the left had also struck McMillen hard. As a result, individual lower-echelon commanders reported to McMillen that they were the object of the main attack and the other actions were merely demonstrations. In fact, everything was a "main" attack, for Forrest's aim was to roll Sturgis's entire command back on the Cross Roads.

For almost two hours, the fighting raged, men groping through the thickets to engage in bitter, face-to-face combat. The ground shook with the shattering sound of desperate battle as the outcome swayed in the balance. Time was rapidly running out for the Rebels, however. At this critical juncture, Barteau arrived. From the Federal rear came the notes of a bugle wildly sounding "Charge!" Barteau's bugler, Jimmy Bradford, was galloping through the edge of the woodland behind the Yankees, his instrument commanding phantom regiments to attack. As Barteau's 250 Tennesseans ploughed into the Union rear, the Federal troops swung to meet the new threat. Believing a large force was coming onto the field, Waring and Winslow took their entire cavalry forces to counter it. Pressure was immediately increased on the Federal front by Forrest and, without cavalry support, it wavered backward.

Now, as if by common agreement, both sides paused. Except for the occasional nasty snap of a sharpshooter's rifle, silence fell across the field of battle. Not a leaf quivered as the air lay dormant in the stultifying heat that blanketed the arena. Exhausted men on both sides dropped to the ground to rest. One Rebel recalled that there was ". . . a bountiful supply of water from the rills fed by the recent rains. I never tasted better and the cessation of battle was as grateful as the water, but there was intense anxiety to know the final result. An order to retire from the field would have brought no surprise."

Forrest had no thought of retiring. He recognized the crux of the issue had been reached, however, and knew the next assault would tell the tale. He rode along the line among his men telling them the Yankees were beaten and preparing them for the next attack. "Get up, men," he told the troops. "I have ordered Bell to charge on the left. When you hear his guns, and the bugle sounds, every man must charge; and we will give them hell."

When he reached Morton's guns, the young artilleryman, who was in an exposed position, cautioned him, "General, you'd better get down the hill. They'll hit you here."

Stunned at his audacity in speaking to his commander in this manner, Morton was surprised when the tired Forrest agreed, saying, "Well, John, I will rest a little."

He rode a few yards to a large tree, dismounted, and propped himself against it. Then, he signalled Morton to join him. As he leaned against the tree, Forrest told the artilleryman that he believed Sturgis was whipped. He went on to say that in ten minutes he was going to order a charge all along the line. When the heavy firing started on the right, Morton was to take four guns, double-shotted with canister, charge as near as possible to the enemy, and blast them at close range.

Finished with Morton, Forrest remounted and rode over to Buford to give him his orders. When told the artillery's instructions, the surprised Buford asked, "General, don't you think it's dangerous to have the artillery charge without support?"

"Buford," Forrest assured him, "all the Yankees in front of us can't get to Morton's guns."

An incident occurring after the battle suggests Forrest may not have been as confident as he sounded. Riding up to Morton as he returned to his battery, Forrest put his hand on the young officer's shoulder and said, "Well, John, I think your guns won the battle for us."

Slightly embarrassed but beaming with pride, Morton said, "General, I'm glad you think so much of our work, but you scared me pretty badly when you pushed me up so close to their infantry and left me without protection. I was afraid they might take my guns."

As he rode away, Forrest replied, "Well, artillery is made to be captured, and I wanted to see them take yours."

After Forrest's exchange with Buford he went to Lyon. His instructions were simple and to the point. "Charge and give them hell; and when they fall back, keep on charging and giving them hell; and I'll soon be there with you and bring up Morton's Bull Pups."

A ringing Rebel yell split the oppressive silence to signal the new attack. A rising crash of rifle fire followed in its wake as the gray line moved forward. Morton's guns rumbled down the narrow road at a gallop, swung into position, and unlimbered. When the blue defenders rose from cover, the guns spewed a storm of canister in salutation. Their line was blasted to shreds as the artillery was moved forward by hand between salvos of the murderous canister.

Forrest was in the thick of things urging his troops forward. One Rebel later reported, "I noticed some writers on Forrest say he seldom cursed. Well, the fellow who writes that way was not where the Seventh Tennessee was that day. . . . Our movement was too slow to suit Forrest, he would curse, then praise and then threaten to shoot us himself, if we were so afraid the Yanks might hit us. . . . He would praise in one breath, then in the next would curse us and finally said, 'I will lead you.' . . . We hustled, and across that narrow field was a race—double quick nowhere in it."

Lyon, Bell, and Rucker now began slowly but inexorably to fold up the Union line. Johnson rolled wide to his right and fell on the wagon train guard. In a desperate attempt to escape the doom building before them, the wagoners put the train in motion trying to get it back across Tishomingo Creek's single bridge. The far left of the Confederate line now got the order to, "Hit 'em on the e-e-end!" This force immediately launched a vicious charge that carried them out into the open bottomland along the creek bank. In a short while, they were across the creek and charging toward the wagon train that was still struggling vainly to escape. Now, the Federal line began to suffer a general collapse.

Sturgis, attempting to join Bouton, reported, "The main line began to give way at various points. Order soon gave way to confusion, and confusion to panic. . . . The army drifted toward the rear and was beyond control. The road became crowded and jammed with troops; wagons and artillery sank into the deep mud and became inextricable. No power could check the panic-stricken mass as it swept toward the rear."

Bouton's brigade still remained uncommitted. Just north of the Cross Roads, the Fourth Iowa Cavalry dug their heels in for a last stand. Bouton's troops quickly joined them in a frantic effort to stem the gray tide about to sweep over the Union army. These fresh troops fought hard but to no avail. Johnson's men swept up the bank of Tishomingo Creek to crash into their left flank. Simultaneously, the escort under Lt. George Cowan and Captain Tyler's horsemen galloped into the right flank behind a cloud of revolver fire. As the Union force shuddered under this double blow, Morton's guns came within range. Their charges of double-shotted canister settled the issue in minutes. The blue soldiers melted away.

Indescribable confusion followed as the Federals tried to escape the victory-flushed Rebels. A wagon overturned on the bridge, blocking it and causing the loss of a large part of the wagon train. The fleeing Yankees poured into Tishomingo Creek and many of them were shot or drowned as they struggled to cross. On all sides, blue soldiers threw arms, ammunition, and equipment away as they raced frantically for the rear. Wild-eyed gray troopers were everywhere shouting, shooting, and slashing in the midst of the fleeing, demoralized Federals.

At this point, several wagons that had escaped were plunging wildly toward the rear. Sturgis ordered an officer to halt the racing wagons beyond a point where he hoped to make a stand. Once the wagons were stopped, the officer was told to "issue rations and ammunition to the troops" and then "burn the goddamned train with the remaining supplies." Before these orders could be carried out the pursuing Rebels were on them. The terrified teamsters cut their teams from the wagons, using them for mounts as they again fled for safety. Some wagons were set on fire but most of these were saved with little damage when Forrest shouted to his troopers, "Don't you see the damned Yanks are burning *my* wagons? Get off your horses and throw the burning beds off!"

Darkness had now fallen, but it brought no respite to Sturgis as Forrest grimly pushed the pursuit. But, Bouton still felt that something could be saved. With this in mind, he appealed to Sturgis, "General, for God's sake don't let us give up so!"

"What can we do?" demanded the flustered commander.

"I told him [Sturgis]," Bouton reported, "to give me the ammunition that the white troops were throwing away in the mud and I would hold the enemy in check until we could get those ambulances, wagons, and artillery all over that bottom and save them. I told him that if he would give me one of those white regiments to help me lift the wagons and artillery over, that I would stake my life, that I would save the whole of them."

Sturgis stared in disbelief when he heard these words. Without further consideration, he told Bouton, "For God's sake, if Mr. Forrest will let me alone, I will let him alone. You have done all you could and more than was expected of you, and now all you can do is save yourselves."

Leaving Sturgis alone had never entered Mr. Forrest's mind. His philosophy of fighting was to ". . . get 'em skeered, and then keep the skeer on 'em!" This philosophy was now applied with a vengeance and the Union force was blown away like chaff before the wind. Every effort of the Federals to reform was crushed without a slackening of the pace of the pursuers. Away from the main conflict, small bands of Rebel horsemen ranged the countryside like ravening wolves, snapping up any Yankees unfortunate enough to be in their path. Under this extreme pressure, the Union force ceased to exist as an organized unit.

William Witherspoon gave an excellent description of the state of the Union force when he wrote, "Somewhere between midnight and day we came to a wide slough or creek bottom; it was miry and truly the slough of despair and despond to the Yanks. Their artillery and wagons which had heretofore escaped capture were now bogged down and had to be abandoned. This slough was near knee-deep in mud and water, with logs lying here and there. On top of every log were Yanks perched as close as they could be, for there were more Yanks than logs—reminded me of chickens at roost. . . .We who were in front were ordered to pay no attention to prisoners, those in the rear would look after that."

The pursuit was so rapid that the pursuers often caught up to and joined with members of the fleeing army. During the night, one Yankee, who had been joined by a silent companion, commented, "Old Forrest gave us hell today."

The only response this brought was a brief grunt.

Determined to make conversation, the retreating Union man said, "Yes, and we were fooled about Old Forrest's strength. He certainly had fifty thousand men in that fight. The woods were full of them, they were everywhere."

Tired of the chatter of his loquacious companion, the silent one terminated the talk by informing his companion that he was now a prisoner of one of "Old Forrest's" men.

Throughout the night, the next day, and the following night, the persistent Rebels hounded the shattered army. Pursuers and pursued alike were near a state of total collapse from the unbelievable pace to which they had been subjected. The commanders were also showing signs of complete exhaustion as nerves frayed to the breaking point.

Late on the eleventh, a courier charged up to General Buford to tell him Forrest wanted him to "gallop up."

"Tell General Forrest, by God, that my men can't gallop up!" Buford exploded.

"Very well, sir," the messenger replied. "I'll tell the General what you say."

The rider was hardly on his way back to Forrest when he heard the sound of bugles. Hard behind him, Buford's men were "galloping up." Not even exhausted generals commanding divisions dared trigger the black temper of Bedford Forrest.

Finally, on the twelfth, Forrest gave up the pursuit and the remnants of Sturgis's shattered command trickled into Colliersville. Here a fresh Union force dispatched by Washburn offered them protection. It had taken Sturgis ten days to reach Brice's Cross Roads from that point. The return had required only sixty-four hours!

No defeat inflicted on either side during the war ever matched the one Sturgis suffered. Years later, Major E. H. Hanson, Adjutant, Fourth Missouri Cavalry, wrote, "The bitter humiliation of this disaster rankles after a quarter of a century. . . . If there was, during the war, another engagement like this, it is not known to the writer; and in its immediate results there was no success among the many won by Forrest comparable to that of Guntown."

Although Forrest did not lose a single man as a prisoner or a piece of gear to the Union and achieved an incredible victory, he had paid a high price. Casualties were twenty percent in Lyon's outfit and twenty-three percent in Rucker's. A total of 493 of Forrest's scrappy horse soldiers were killed or wounded—evidence that though the Union force was blown off the field, it fought stubbornly for the time it did fight.

Sherman had achieved his purpose of keeping Forrest off his life-line. He had not in his wildest dreams, however, anticipated the price. In killed, wounded, captured, and missing, the Union lost 2,612 men of which 1,618 were taken prisoner. Forrest also captured 250 wagons and ambulances, five thousand stands of small arms, 500,000 rounds of small-arms ammunition, almost one thousand rounds of artillery ammunition, sixteen pieces of artillery, and huge amounts of medical, quartermaster, and other supplies and equipment. In addition, the South realized a considerable strategic gain from Forrest's victory. The forces under Major General A. J. Smith, Brigadier General J. E. Smith, and Colonel J. H. Howe had to be diverted to keep watch on Forrest and whip him if possible. Sherman urgently needed these troops elsewhere and could ill-afford their loss. But, Forrest was so great a danger to him that he had to pay the price.

Perhaps of equal significance was the anxiety and doubt created in Grant's headquarters and in Washington by Sturgis's stunning defeat. Secretary of War Edwin Stanton wanted to know, why. To the Secretary's query, Sherman answered in exasperation, ". . . the chief object (of Sturgis's expedition) was to hold Forrest there and keep him off our road. . . . Forrest has only his cavalry; I cannot understand how he could defeat Sturgis with eight thousand men." In a cold fury, he promised Washington, "I will have the matter of Sturgis critically examined, and if he should be at fault he shall have no mercy at my hands. I cannot but believe he had troops enough. I know I would have been willing to attempt the same task with that force; but Forrest is the devil, and I think he has got some of our troops under cower."

An investigation was duly conducted as Sherman promised. When all the evidence was in, the unfortunate Union commander was weighed in the balance and found wanting. He was promptly consigned to oblivion and remained there until late 1865. He then came partially out of the shadows of obscurity and was posted to frontier duty at Austin, Texas. He ended his career as a colonel with another ill-fated organization, the Seventh U.S. Cavalry, which also would suffer disaster in the rolling hills of eastern Montana on the banks of another stream, the Little Bighorn River.

What Sherman wanted most, however, he did not get. Forrest was still on the loose. And, as long as he was, he remained an unacceptable threat to the Union. Sherman was determined to eradicate him. In tones that were apoplectic, he vowed to Washington that he would order his generals ". . . to make up a force and go out to follow Forrest to the death, if it costs ten thousand lives and breaks the Treasury. There will never be peace in Tennessee until Forrest is dead!" It was a vow that would never be kept.

Perhaps the crushing totality of Forrest's supreme victory is best summed up in this story: After the war, Brig. Gen. Basil Duke was telling the saga of Tishomingo Creek to a pair of visiting French cavalrymen, a colonel and a captain. As Duke unraveled the tale, the young captain translated for the colonel who did not speak English. Duke, warming to his task, brought the colonel closer and closer to the edge of his chair as the story progressed. When it ended, the colonel leaped up, his eyes shining, threw his arms high in the air, and exhausted his English vocabulary, "*Sapristi!* Goddamn!"

CHAPTER XIV

Take No Prisoners

Northern Virginia lay stifling hot and dusty dry in July 1864. Miles south of Washington, D.C. the U.S. Army was stolidly applying pressure to the Confederates along the Richmond Front. In many areas, however, the countryside had subsided into a relatively quiescent state that was broken from time to time by slashing raids by partisan rangers against the Union camps and picket lines dotting the area. These impetuous mounted guerillas ranged about hitting unexpectedly with an effectiveness belying their numerical strength. This shifting pool of turmoil caused constant uneasiness in the capital and forced its defending forces to swing back and forth in front of it in pendulumlike movements that accomplished nothing.

Superficially, near Washington the scene was peaceful enough, despite rumors that Confederate Lt. Gen. Jubal Early was moving on the city, for a group of young people to plan a picnic just outside the outer perimeter near Falls Church, Virginia. This group set out in carriages early on the morning of the ninth, driving by the Lee Mansion to a secluded, shady area they had selected. Preparations were quickly made for the lunch. Then the instruments came out and the air was filled with music as the couples began whirling in a gay dance. Abruptly the music stopped and soft cries of surprise routed laughter as the heavy undergrowth hiding the glen parted and about twenty-five riders trotted into the open area. The gray uniforms and upturned hats marked the new arrivals as Brig. Gen. John Mosby's men.

Admonishing the picnickers not to be afraid, the newcomers swung from their horses and mingled casually with the crowd. Shortly, the music makers were signaled to play and in moments the Rebels were dancing with the ladies as if war and Union lines did not exist. Their entertainment needs satisfied, the riders turned to the picnic baskets and, with lavish thanks and praise of the food, had a full meal. At a signal from the leader, all gave the ladies a sweeping bow, swung to horse, and disappeared as quickly and silently as they had arrived.

The visiting Rebels had more on their minds than a few hours of lollygagging with some Yankee belles. A few days earlier one of the group, Henry Wheaton, a former staff officer of Early's, had visited his old boss. The general, already preparing to move on Washington, sent Wheaton back with a request that Mosby strike into Maryland. Early wanted him to enter the state in the vicinity of Point-of-Rocks, do as much damage as possible to the railroad and telegraph, then wait at Frederick. On the eleventh, Mosby was ready.

Leaving camp, the Rangers galloped into Maryland, destroying some isolated blockhouses in the Poolesville area. From there they raced to Seneca, hoping to surprise the Eighth Illinois Cavalry. When they arrived on the morning of the twelfth, they found their quarry gone and had to content themselves with burning several buildings and all the supplies they could find. That night they were back in Virginia.

While the raid was in progress, Early and his III Corps had brushed Maj. Gen. Lew Wallace's VIII Corps aside, crossed the Potomac, and stood in front of Washington. They were immediately assaulted by the VI Corps and a division of the IXX Corps. The pressure from these units was too much. On the fourteenth, they had to recross the river at White's Ford and seek safety in Virginia. As they fell back toward Winchester on the sixteenth, Mosby met them and, after short conference, the guerilla agreed to continue his efforts to provide support. A few days later, the situation completely changed when Early's pursuers were called off and sent to help at Petersburg. The Confederate general promptly reversed course, hit Brig. Gen. George Crook's First Infantry Division at Kernstown, forcing him back toward Martinsburg and Harper's Ferry, and hustled away north into Pennsylvania.

While all this was going on, small groups of Mosby's men harassed the Union at widely scattered points throughout the Shenandoah Valley. On the twenty-eighth, Mosby called them together in preparation for another foray into Maryland. Early the thirtieth, he positioned artillery at Cheek's Ford and Nolan's Ford. Leaving the guns with a small force to protect them, Mosby took the rest and dashed into lower Maryland, cutting telegraph lines and attacking pickets. As soon as his activity had caused confusion to reach a crescendo, the raiders dropped from sight, taking seventy-five horses and about thirty prisoners with them. Smarting at the effrontery of this raid, Brig. Gen. Robert Tyler, commanding the forces along the Monocacy River, grumbled petulantly, "It is evidently the intention of Mosby to continue his raids upon the railroad when stealing will not pay him better."

In Washington, a thoroughly irritated Major General C.C. Augur, commanding XXII Corps and the District of Washington, shot off a smoking message to the commander at Muddy Branch telling him, "I wish you as fast as possible to get those thieves and marauders out of Maryland."

More importantly, the Rebel activity had gotten the attention of President Abraham Lincoln and Lieutenant General U. S. Grant. The latter, despite some misgivings on the part of the president and Secretary of War Edwin Stanton, called on hard-nosed Maj. Gen. Phillip Sheridan, commanding the Army of the Shenandoah, to take command. Then he headed for Monocacy Junction, spurred on by a message from Lincoln clearly expressing both his impatience with the situation and his opinion that Grant's presence in the area was required immediately.

Sheridan met his commander at Monocacy Junction on 4 August to get his marching orders. The first order of business, Grant told him, was to stop the army from swinging back and forth like a slightly addled snake. Then, he was to concentrate his force near Harper's Ferry and drive Early, who was back in the vicinity, out of the country. At the same time, he wanted an adequate force sent after Mosby to at least control, if not destroy, him. "Bear in mind," Grant concluded, "the object is to drive the enemy south, and to do this you want to keep him always in sight. Be guided in your course by the course he takes." Good advice when applied to an army, but exceedingly difficult to employ when dealing with guerrillas.

Sheridan immediately set to work trying to put fight into a badly demoralized, tired army. As he struggled with this problem and organized to move against Early, constant reports of partisan activity poured into his headquarters. On the eighth, Sheridan passed the word that Mosby was at Point-of-Rocks but, when nothing developed, he finally wired Augur, "Have heard nothing from Mosby today."

That evening, as sixty men of the Sixteenth New York Cavalry neared Fairfax Station, Mosby and about twenty men suddenly appeared. Before the astonished Yankees could overcome their surprise, Mosby yelled, "Go through 'em boys!" And the "boys" did.

The chagrined Federal commander, upon learning his troops had been soundly whipped by about one-third their number, glumly wired Sheridan, "I have nothing to report except disgraceful mismanagement and consequent complete rout of our men." Then, he added lamely, "A board of investigation has been called." Sheridan had just received his first practical lesson in the art of guerrilla warfare.

At the main army encampment near Halltown, Sheridan grimly read the message, shrugged the attack off for the moment, and gave his full attention to the impending movement of his army. It was scheduled to move out the next morning and his day was already largely gone, the harried general still plagued by a seemingly infinite number of details to resolve.

Finally, the day wore away and the sun, a fiery ball of sullen red, dropped from view. As darkness closed in, stars popped out by the millions to dimly light a beautiful but hot and sticky night. Later, mountainous clouds slowly crept over the army, thunder muttering hoarsely as erratic streaks of lightning etched the night sky, but no rain fell. Finally, the exhausted commander sought his quarters in an old hotel and stillness settled over the sprawling camp.

Once the area was quiet, except for the slight noise of sentries moving about, a small group of guerillas entered the camp and proceeded through the sleeping soldiers in a confident, businesslike manner. Occasionally, a sentry would challenge and received a crisp, "106th New York," in reply.

At one point, the group stopped while a member dressed a guard down. Then, they moved on again, the speaker saying disgustedly, "What a hell of a way to stand on duty!"

About three hundred yards from where Sheridan slept, the group disappeared into a ravine that cut a dark slash through the camp. There they huddled in the concealing blackness while one, John Hearn, climbed the far bank and moved onward. Keeping well clear of the flickering light of dying fires, he sauntered up to a rail fence surrounding the general's quarters. He looked about him quickly, then sprang over the fence, landing in the midst of a group of sleeping men and almost on a sentry.

"Who are you?" the startled sentry gasped.

"Hundred and sixth New York!" Hearn snapped and grabbed the guard's rifle.

Briefly the two struggled silently in the darkness until the sentry, suddenly realizing his peril, screamed, "Help! Murder!"

With a savage jerk, Hearn pulled the rifle free, leaped the fence, and ran to the ravine carrying it as a trophy. Sliding down into concealment, he alerted the others. Without hesitation, the group ran up the ravine, hunched over in the covering night, and disappeared into the darkness. Sheridan had barely missed his second, and what would have been his last, lesson in guerrilla warfare.

Morning broke hot, dry, and dusty on the tenth. As its light flooded the countryside, the army, traveling in three parallel lines, moved out toward Charles Town and Winchester. By the next day, contact had been made with the Confederates and skirmishing started as the blue troops drew up along Cedar Creek in preparation for battle with Jubal Early.

As the army moved, Sheridan was plagued by both rumors and guerrillas. Rumor told him that a large Rebel force was moving through Chester Gap toward Front Royal. If this were true, it could strike his exposed rear and crush him against Early's army. The guerrillas, unlike the rumored force were real. John M. McNiell and his men were constantly pecking away at the Baltimore and Ohio Railroad and at Brigadier General B. F. Kelley's forces, Department of West Virginia troops, which, situated west of Sleepy Creek, were trying to protect it. At the same time, Mosby's Rangers were hovering on the flanks and rear of the army, snapping up stragglers and providing a constant source of harassment.

In an effort to corral the guerrillas, Sheridan detached the Eighth Illinois Cavalry on the twelfth, sending them to Loundon County to hunt the partisans. Their efforts were wasted, for they were now running a cold trail. As they searched futilely for the elusive Mosby, he was leading his men through Snicker's Gap into the Shenandoah Valley. His target was Sheridan's supply line.

The blue army depended on supply from Harper's Ferry by wagon train. As the Illinois cavalry rushed through Loundon County and Mosby streaked for the valley, the first units of a train of 525 wagons rolled forward under an already blazing midmorning sun. As the five-sectioned train got underway, a guard of about three thousand

Ohioans and Marylanders strung out from the front and the rear toward the center to shield it. In the lead rode Brig. Gen. John R. Kenly, the wagon train commander. As he rode, Sheridan's orders ran through his mind, "It is of importance that the train should reach Winchester as speedily as possible. Commanding officers will be held responsible that no unnecessary delays occur."

It quickly became obvious to even the most optimistic that there was simply no way to move a train of that size rapidly. First, there was trouble getting everyone moving, then there was a constant hassle trying to keep the units closed up, and finally, adding insult to injury, a herd of cattle accompanying the train absolutely refused to hurry through the heat. Any chance of partial concealment of the movement was also hopeless. The noise of squeaking axles, swearing teamsters, braying mules, thumping hooves, lowing cattle, and rumbling wheels combined in an earsplitting din that echoed off the hills and could be heard for miles. Over, around, and behind the train a great pillar of dust rose into the burnished sky to hang for over two hours at any given spot, an orangish beacon of dirt signalling to the world the train's location. And, when the dust did settle, it left a carpet of dirty powder marking a broad swath across grass, bushes, and trees to trumpet the train's passing.

Kenly gradually pulled ahead of his command, the weight of his responsibility, the slowness of movement, and the heat and stifling dust combining to fray his temper and jangle his nerves. He kept a constant stream of couriers dashing to the rear demanding to know why the train could not be kept closed up. No suitable answer was forthcoming. Behind him, shrouded in dust, perspiration streaking their caked faces, teamsters and guards strained on doing the best they could and praying for night.

At last the sun dropped from sight and night closed in giving only small respite from the rigors and discomforts of the day. To the astonishment of all, no order came to halt. Neither was any indication of their commander's intentions given. Up ahead, Kenly rode stoically onward, slumped in the saddle under the weight of his responsibility. Now, his worries had increased. Before leaving Harpers Ferry, he had received word that Mosby was in the vicinity. Despite himself, he had the feeling that the Rebel chief was even now pacing him through the darkness patiently awaiting an opportunity to strike.

Finally, at eleven o'clock at night, with Berryville in reach, Kenly halted near a small stream. He gave orders that each section could stop here long enough to water their weary animals and make coffee for the men. The night quickly became a bedlam as fires sprang to life and shouting, cursing men tried to water stamping, braying, bellowing, thirsty animals in an orderly fashion. Time after time, groups of wild-eyed, dust-caked animals, saliva stringing stickily from their mouths and foam streaking their flanks, were allowed to rush to the muddy stream, and then were kicked and beaten back into line after they drank. Near one o'clock, the first section got underway again, moving slowly off into the darkness. As it left, Kenly, preparing to go with it, rode up to Captain J. C. Mann, First Division, IXX Corps, and told him, "I consider this the most dangerous point in the route. I desire you to remain here, therefore, until every wagon has passed."

The last section of the train arrived at two o'clock in the morning. The leader of this section explained his lateness by blaming inexperienced drivers and mules unused to harness. Now, Mann waited impatiently as group after group slowly moved out, disappearing into a heavy mist that had formed over the valley. At four o'clock, fingers of fear tickled up his spine and an almost paralyzing premonition of disaster seized him. He swung to horse, trotted quickly to the head of the last section of the train, located the officers in charge and told them to hurry the harnessing of their teams and to get underway. "Start immediately," he insisted. "We're in danger of attack!"

As Mann watched them stumble off to carry out his orders, the first soft light of day began to seep through the thick mist. In this feeble light, he could see teamsters and guards sprawled everywhere, sound asleep. The first threads of panic coursed through him as he realized pickets had not been posted. As his panic grew, he began to rush about the train yelling at the men to get up and get moving. At the reserve brigade, he discovered that nothing was being done and he could not find the people in charge. Swearing in disgust and panic, he dismounted and started waking drivers himself, trying to put some spirit in their lethargic movements.

Time seemed to stand still for Mann as he raced around threatening and cajoling in a frantic effort to get underway. At last, the first wagon moved and relief washed over the harried captain. He remounted and trotted up and down the line, pausing to shout at the reserve to hurry. Suddenly, he was transfixed in his saddle. Off in the distance a cannon coughed. A split second later its ball screamed out of the mist and decapitated a mule.

Under cover of the confusion at the watering stop, Mosby had moved up. With the first streaks of dawn, he led his troops forward, bringing their howitzer up at a gallop and unlimbering it on top of a

low knoll overlooking the road. Instantly, the gunners found themselves in deadly combat with an unexpected enemy—they had unlimbered the gun on top of a yellow jacket nest. These ill-tempered
insects launched a full-scale attack and, in seconds, the dreaded partisans scattered like a covey of quail, horses rearing, while riders
slapped fruitlessly about them trying unsuccessfully to ward off the
stings of their assailants. Mosby later remarked that he felt ". . . a
good deal like Hercules did when he put on the shirt of the Centaur
and couldn't pull it off."

The yellow jackets, their domain again secure and one howitzer
captured, broke off the attack leaving the partisans in a quandary.
Mosby had split his force into four groups; three of which were to
attack while the fourth waited in reserve and guarded the artillery.
Two of the attacking groups were out of earshot waiting for the signal to attack. That signal was to be three shots from the cannon now
solidly in the possession of a horde of greatly offended, testy insects.
Fortunately, a hero arose in the form of A. G. Babcock, First Sergeant
of Artillery. Whipping the air wildly with his hat, Babcock dashed
back into no man's land. Engulfed in a cloud of buzzing, stinging yellow jackets, he managed to grab a chain on the gun and pull it free of
their territory. Now, the other war could begin.

The shot that had wreaked havoc on the unfortunate mule was
quickly followed by a second and a third. Before the sound of the
detonations had died, pandemonium struck the wagon train. Most of
the startled guards ran frantically for safety leaving their weapons
behind. Teamsters leaped aboard the nearest horse or mule and galloped wildly away into the cloaking mist, going whatever direction
their steed happened to be aimed when they mounted. Behind them
mules brayed and cattle bellowed as the fear-crazed animals surged
aimlessly through the train, upsetting wagons and generally reducing
the area to chaos.

Mann, regaining his wits after the first artillery round, galloped to
the position of the guard commander. That officer was frantically
attempting, with small success, to rally what was left of his demoralized command. Since the guard commander was senior, Mann asked
for instructions and received a "thousand meter stare" in reply.
Then, through the lifting mist, he saw a charging line of gray riders
bearing down on the train, revolvers blazing. This sight drove all
indecision from the captain's mind. Sinking spurs to his horse, Mann
left the field of honor at a long gallop, convinced that all was irretrievably lost.

Under cover of steady fire from the howitzer, Mosby led his men at a gallop across the intervening space between it and the stricken wagon train. Firing handguns as they rode, the partisans swept among the wagons. It was the work of seconds to kill, capture, or rout the troops that had remained at their posts with the train. So unexpected and overwhelming had been the Confederate attack, that little real resistance was offered. The main body of raiders now started gathering up animals and looting and burning wagons while two groups broke off to silence the remaining opposition.

Some distance away, a small group of guards had taken shelter behind a stone fence. They now opened a brisk fire on the raiders. Capt. William Chapman, a former member of the Dixie Artillery, gathered his squadron and led them in a reckless charge across the open area between them and the fence. The defenders folded under this onslaught and Chapman captured the lot.

Captain A. E. Richards took the First Squadron and went after the last remaining pocket of resistance, a group of guards who had taken refuge in a brick church building in the direction of Berryville. From the security of this position, they directed a hail of fire at the attackers. Richards moved up quickly, taking advantage of the sparse cover, until his men were in position to bring fire to bear on all the building's windows. Once settled into position, they put such a murderous cross fire into the structure that its defenders surrendered.

Back at the wagon train, smoke was beginning to rise from burning wagons and prisoners and animals were herded into groups. As rapidly as they could, the raiders loaded badly needed supplies on any animal available. Some distance away a single wagon lay smashed against a tree with most of its load, including a chest, scattered about it. As some raiders moved to burn it, a group of Federals dashed into view, drove them back, grabbed the chest, and galloped away. With them, in the chest, went a payroll of $112,000.

Mosby now signaled his men to move out. As they rode away the smoke of seventy-five burning wagons boiled up in a towering black cloud. With them went two hundred prisoners, about six hundred horses and mules, almost two hundred beef cattle, and a large amount of supplies.

The news of the debacle hit Sheridan like a sledgehammer. Frantically, the officers under him tried to keep the news from Washington. Their efforts were to no avail for a Union scout who talked to Mosby immediately after the raid made a full report to Maj. Gen. Henry Halleck, the Army's chief of staff. The Union's senior

general immediately wired Sheridan for full information. Halleck
included in his message details of the scout's report saying, "Mosby
told him that he captured one of your wagon trains of seventy to
eighty wagons, with five hundred mules and horses. Is that true?"

An embarrassed Sheridan told him it was. Then added, "It was said
everything was recovered except six wagons, but this was not true."

Newspapers quickly reported the event in something less than a
favorable light. One even went so far as to say the entire matter was
due to carelessness. Here, at last, Sheridan found an enemy he could
temporarily handle. He summarily ordered all correspondents to
report to him. Once they gathered, he delivered a scathing talk to
them that called all the maledictions he could think of down on their
heads. His speech finished, he ordered every one them out of his
department.

Lincoln was running for reelection and facing a strong group in
opposition who were insisting the war was a failure. This consideration was brought forcefully to Sheridan's attention along with the
point that news of a major defeat would not be well-received by the
president. On the heels of this came word that Early might have forty
thousand troops at his disposal and advice to Sheridan that he ". . .
be cautious and act now on the defensive." The final ingredient making Sheridan's life miserable was difficulty in maintaining contact
with Washington and with Grant's headquarters because of partisan
activities. In fact, it had taken a regiment of cavalry to deliver word
of Early's reinforcement and current strength. When he added these
factors to the guerilla activity swirling around him and the obvious
fact that a long supply line would not work, he decided to fall back
to Halltown where he had started on the tenth.

As Sheridan prepared to retreat, he recalled Grant's recommenda-
tion, ". . . it is desirable that nothing should be left to invite the
enemy to return. Take all provisions, forage, and stock wanted for
use of your command. Such as cannot be consumed, destroy." These
words were now followed up with an even stronger admonition,
"The families of most of Mosby's men are known, and can be collect-
ed. I think they should be taken and kept at Fort McHenry, or some
secure place, as hostages for the good conduct of Mosby and his men.
Where any of Mosby's men are caught, hang them without trial."

Without hesitation, the Union commander began enforcing his
leader's orders. Moving slowly toward Halltown, his harassed army
began to leave a swath of destruction in its wake. Burned buildings,
crops, and slaughtered livestock gave mute testimony to the thor-

oughness of the Union efforts to make the valley, as Sheridan said, ". . . as untenable as possible for a Rebel force to subsist."

The ruthlessness of the retreating army brought a scream for vengeance from the valley's inhabitants. Their cries fell on receptive ears and the partisans set about exacting it in full measure. In one incident, a ranger rode up to a lone Union soldier skinning a sheep. Without a word, the guerrilla drew his pistol, took deliberate aim and killed the hapless forager. Dropping to the ground, the ranger quickly turned the dead man over and propped him up against the partly skinned animal. A few strokes of the partisan's knife severed one of the sheep's feet which the guerrilla stuck into the dead man's mouth. To it, he attached a note that read, "I reckon you got enough sheep now." Then, he silently rode away.

Later at a farmhouse near where a group of the Fifth Michigan Cavalry was camped, a man rode up in the darkness to deliver a death message. Members of the family struck a light to read the note. Shortly afterward, a band of partisans struck savagely at the Union pickets, leaving several them sprawled lifeless in the hot Virginia night.

The commander of these cavalrymen, Brig. Gen. George Armstrong Custer, who was beginning to compile a creditable record against the gray cavalry that was now a shadow of the force it had been, listened intently to the report of this attack on his men. When told they believed the light might have been a signal to the partisans, he quickly exercised the snap judgment that in later years would leave him and his command lying face up under the Big Sky of Montana. With no thought for where his actions might lead, he instantly decided to retaliate. Quickly selecting some homes that happened to be handy, he ordered two companies to burn them to the ground. They were also told to show no mercy to the owners. Hurriedly, the men split into groups and rushed off to carry out Custer's wishes.

Some distance away, a group of partisans led by William Chapman spotted the flames and smoke rising high into the air. Without hesitation, the Rebels drove spurs to their horses and raced toward the burning buildings. As they approached the offending blue soldiers, Chapman, who later said he led with murder in his heart, shouted, "Wipe them from the face of the earth! No quarter! Take no prisoners!"

The charging horsemen quickly took up the cry, "No quarter!" Storming past crying women and children, the gray riders crashed into the enemy. For a short span of time, the world dissolved into whirling horses, shouting, cursing men, and brief staccato bursts of gunfire. Then, all was silent except for the muffled sobbing of homeless residents. One rider gruffly described the action, "It was a sharp, quick, and clean little fight, no prisoners."

The Yankees were preoccupied when attacked. As a result they were completely surprised and ill-prepared to fight. In addition, the bloodcurdling promise of no quarter greatly magnified their fear and helped to drive them into panic. A woman witness, who saw the entire episode, said of them, "They hid behind burning ruins, they crouched in the corners of fences, they begged for life, but their day of grace was past. . . . Two came to us, the most pitiable objects you ever beheld, and we did what we could for them; for, after all, the men are not to blame half so much as the officers. . . ."

But, this was "Mosby's Confederacy" and no one in their right mind could have expected Mosby to give less than he got. That was not the character of John Singleton Mosby! So, unfortunately for the two men, the lady's protection was insufficient. "These two wounded men," she continued, "were removed that night."

As the Rebels took them away, one of the partisans bluntly remarked to her, "If we leave any of them with you all, Mosby will come and kill them over again."

"We have since heard that those men died that night," she concluded.

As the gray horsemen rode back up the mountain away from the scene of devastation below them, they discovered a prisoner in their midst. As soon as Chapman heard the news, he halted the column. The prisoner was hauled to the ground and told to quickly make peace with his Creator. In a trembling voice, the doomed man said his prayers beneath the spreading arms of the mountain forest. When the man's fervent prayer ended, a crash of gunfire shattered the early evening air. Moments later only the trees stood mute watch over his lifeless form and the sound of muffled hoofbeats faded away as the group resumed their way up the mountain.

Scenes such as these were repeated again and again as the Union Army struggled toward safety. Finally, they stumbled into Halltown on the twenty-second, having fought every foot of the way with a merciless enemy that shifted around them as formless as a shadow. Yet, everywhere the shadow touched, broken Yankee bodies lay in the dust to mark its passing.

Once the gray horsemen, who had so recently left the scene of battle and execution, reached the crest of the Blue Ridge Mountains, they turned to look down from the heights. Their view was a thick haze of smoke hovering over the valley floor, wafting slowly in the light breeze. Before them, as far as the eye could see, stretched the blackened and broken debris that marks war's passing. What had been a beautiful, softly undulating landscape lay disfigured; scarred by the footprint of Mars.

Total war had come to the Shenandoah.

CHAPTER XV

A Perfect Piece
of Rascality

When a Yankee bullet cut Jeb Stuart down at Yellow Tavern, his mantle of leadership fell on the shoulders of a hulking South Carolinian named Wade Hampton. This aristocratic, amiable giant lacked Stuart's glamour but was an exceptional leader and Bedford Forrest's equal as a fighter. Son and grandson of veterans of the Revolution and the War of 1812, he grew up steeped in military tradition but had no formal training as a soldier prior to joining the Confederate Army. Nevertheless, when war came, he raised Hampton's Legion and served brilliantly as a part of Stuart's command. Absolutely fearless in action, he was always in the thick of any fighting, riding, according to Lt. John Wise of Gen. Robert E. Lee's staff, like a centaur. Despite his ferocity in combat and his patrician background, Hampton, now a major general, was democratic with his troops and extremely popular with them. Strangely enough, this was also the case with his enemies.

His popularity with his opponents stemmed from many sources but can be illustrated by this incident: Riding along a slow-moving Virginia stream one day, Hampton spotted a Yankee blissfully skinny-

213

dipping to relieve the heat. The Confederate general trotted over to where the Federal had left his clothing, dismounted, and scooped it up. Pointing a pistol at the startled bather, he identified himself and announced to the swimmer that he was a prisoner. Terrified at the thought of prison, the soldier begged eloquently to be set free. Hampton listened to the frantic begging for a while then said the man could go. Inspired by his success, the newly freed prisoner asked for his clothes. To this request, Hampton shook his head and said, "Ah! No! I can't let you have them. My men are too much in need of clothes. I can't spare them."

Slowly, the naked swimmer crawled out of the water continuing to beg earnestly. Hampton, back on his horse, simply sat there, a broad smile creasing his thick beard and a twinkle sparkling in his brilliant, blue eyes, while he slowly shook his head. Despairing of regaining his cover, the embarrassed Yank thanked his captor for his release and started to walk away with what little dignity he could muster. After a few steps, he turned around, looked back, and to express his grateful-ness said with some fervor, "I'll name my first son Wade Hampton!"

Years later, then Sen. Wade Hampton stepped on an elevator in a Washington, D.C. hotel. As he did so, a young elevator occupant asked, "Are you General Wade Hampton?"

"I am," Hampton acknowledged.

"Do you remember capturing a naked Union soldier in Virginia during the war and releasing him?" the young fellow inquired.

"Yes," Hampton answered, "I recollect it perfectly."

"Well, he is my father. My name is Wade Hampton. Good morning, sir," his namesake said and stepped off the elevator.

Such was the man who led the Army of Northern Virginia's cavalry as it locked in mortal combat with Grant's at Petersburg in 1864.

Problems always exist for any army at anytime and they are com-pounded when the army enters combat. Lee's army was no exception as it fitfully struggled to hold back the Union river threatening to wash it away. Not the least of the problems Lee faced was a desperate need to obtain adequate rations for his soldiers. In fact, so over-whelming was this need that a major portion of the Union strategy was to starve the Confederacy into submission.

Despite the life-and-death battle being waged, both Union and Confederate cavalry activity was at an ebb. This lull in action prompted Hampton to decide to engage in a little aggression of his own. He selected Sgt. George B. Shadburne to assist him in imple-menting his decision. He kept the sergeant and his Iron Scouts busy scurrying to and fro through the blue lines, doing both their regular intelligence work and keeping an eye peeled for a lucrative target for a raid.

On 5 September, Shadburne rode out of his camp deep in the Blackwater Swamp to scout the Federal headquarters at City Point, Virginia. After a brief reconnaissance, he returned to Rebel lines and sought Hampton out. He briefed his leader on troop dispositions, then added a tidbit that caught the cavalryman's fancy. The sergeant told him that about five miles east of City Point, at a place on the James River called Coggin's Point, there was a herd of about three thousand fat beef cattle being held for the Union Army. Hampton had found his target.

The Rebel cavalry chief hastily sketched out the plan for a raid in his mind, then sought an audience with Gen. Robert E. Lee. He outlined the proposed raid to the commander, pointing out that it would embarrass the Union and, above all, provide much needed rations to the Army of Northern Virginia. Lee agreed, promising to provide a diversion to assist Hampton. Then, perhaps remembering Stuart's proclivity for sometimes stretching authorizations beyond the breaking point, added, "Your chief object is to get the beef. Avoid a fight if you can, but be prepared for one."

"If I can get to the cattle without being discovered, I can bring them out," Hampton assured him.

"When will you move?" Lee asked.

"As soon as I find Grant gone, General," Hampton replied.

The last thing Lieutenant General U. S. Grant, commander in chief of the United States Army, wanted was to be gone from the area. He lacked confidence in his subordinates, especially Maj. Gen. George G. Meade, commanding the Army of the Potomac, and was uncertain what the Rebels might attempt to do in his absence. Still, he urgently needed to visit Maj. Gen. Philip H. Sheridan, commanding the Army of the Shenandoah, and had reluctantly decided to do so on the fourteenth. Worried about Confederate reaction to his absence, he attempted to keep his trip a secret until the last moment, waiting until the day of his departure to tell both Meade and Sheridan his plans.

Meade, fully aware of his commanding officer's lack of confidence in him, immediately wired an earnest assurance that he would maintain the highest degree of vigilance. This pledge worried the Rebels, who knew of Grant's plans five days earlier, as little as it comforted Grant.

Hampton had already sent out the call and the last of the cavaliers had assembled. These cavalry captains represented some of the brightest stars remaining in the Confederate firmament. They were: Big, reckless Maj. Gen. Thomas Lafayette Rosser, who had resigned from West Point two weeks before graduation to join the Confederate Army and was the survivor of two serious battle wounds. Leader of the Laurel Brigade, he came from Texas and was an accomplished cattle thief. Handsome, blond Maj. Gen. "Matt" Galbraith Butler who had lost a leg in South Carolina. His battle cry was, "Charge 'em! Show 'em the steel!" Of him, Sheridan said, "That damned man has caused me more trouble than all the rest of the Rebel cavalry put together. Big, burly Maj. Gen. William Henry Fitzhugh "Rooney" Lee. A Harvard man and son of the Confederate commander, he had been twice around McClellan with Stuart. The boy brigadier, James Dearing, a tall, good-looking ex-artilleryman. He lacked the flair of the others but was a fearless, steady commander who got the job done. Sleepy-eyed, mean as a devil, Col. Elijah "Lige" White, leader of the Thirty-fifth Battalion, Virginia Cavalry, the Comanches, who had fought long and well as a regular and as a partisan. A man who would charge hell with a pint of ice water, Hampton said of him, "I never ordered White to clear the road of the enemy that he didn't ride over everything in sight."

Once assembled, Hampton brought his commanders together and thoroughly briefed them on the plan. He ended his comments by saying, "We're riding directly behind Grant's army. Our chief and only object is capture of his main cattle herd at Coggin's Point on the James. And, bring it back! Beefsteaks, gentlemen! Two million pounds of them!"

Soft whistles and low exclamations of surprise greeted the announcement. Then, Butler spoke, "Sounds like riding around McClellan at Richmond only we weren't so goddamned hungry then."

Hampton warned his subordinates not to talk about their objective. He pointed out they had over sixty miles, one-way, to travel, much of it through Union-held territory. Word must not get out, so it would be necessary to travel fast, light, and quiet if they hoped to be successful.

The moon clung reluctantly to the horizon in the early morning hours of the fourteenth as the riders began to fall in. Above them, millions of stars sparkled in the chilly autumn sky. Their light, added to that of the moon, revealed fingers of white fog stretched along ravines, blanketing the small streams that trickled lazily along their bottoms. No flare of fire or note of bugle broke into this peaceful setting as the raiders quietly mounted and moved out to the soft sound of spoken commands.

Leaving their camp on Boydton Road near Gravelly Run, they headed south, three thousand of the finest cavalrymen left in the embattled Confederacy. They held their course for an hour until they hit a fork of Flat Foot Road. Here, they turned southeast along Rowanty Creek, far wide of any blue pickets that might be out.

Morning softly blossomed, its pink hues swiftly fading as the sun rose in autumn splendor. In the ravines etching the landscape, the mist slowly dissolved to the accompaniment of birds singing in the woodland. From time to time, roosters strutting about scattered farmsteads issued their challenges to the new day. Heavy woodlands, lightly touched by fall's first color, crowded in on the road to conceal the band of armed riders jogging along. The only indication of their presence was a light dust cloud rising upward in the rapidly warming air. Through the day, the column moved at a steady pace over hills, through streams, and past isolated farm houses, the pastoral beauty of their surroundings only occasionally marred by blackened ruins marking the results of Union raids. At dusk, they stopped at Wilkinson's Bridge over the Rowanty and went into camp. As tired troopers dropped to the ground to sleep on their reins, quiet settled in, the silence of the darkness broken only by the sounds of snoring men, the gruff hoot of hunting owls, and the melancholy crying of whippoorwills.

Up before daybreak, the troopers crossed the Rowanty to the Jerusalem Plank Road, passed over the destroyed Norfolk and Petersburg Railroad tracks, and rode by Ebenezer Church, arriving at Cook's Bridge over the Blackwater at noon. The bridge had been destroyed but Hampton had known about it in advance and had brought Lt. John F. Lanneau and his engineers along to replace it.

After surveying the situation, accompanied by the engineer, Hampton asked, "How long will it take to get us over?"

"By night, sir," Lanneau told him.

"Good enough," Hampton said and ordered out a rear guard, posting two guns with them. The Union left had now been completely outflanked.

Through the lazy afternoon some of the troopers idled away the time speculating about where they were going. Others dozed in the shade of the spreading trees, the reins of their mounts caught in the crook of their elbows. As dusk fell, Lanneau reported to Hampton that the bridge was ready—unsteady but sound. The troops were quickly assembled and told the objective of their mission. The news galvanized the already eager raiders, excitement giving vent to whoops of elation and bursts of song, causing officers, fearing discovery, some anxious moments.

Almost immediately the troops started crossing the Blackwater by the sooty light of burning pine knots. Near midnight, the last man, Hampton, rode over the bridge behind guns rolling on wheels muffled by grain sacks. Moving some distance away from the troops, he ordered a small fire built, then called his commanders to a war council. Huddled in the flickering light of the tiny fire, they listened as their leader gave them their marching orders.

Rooney Lee was ordered to move up Layton's Road to the Powhatan Stage Road and establish cover on the east and west approaches. This done he was to continue up Stage Road to Coggin's Point. Here he was to go into position directly behind the Union Army.

Dearing was told to go northeast along Hines Road to Cocke's Mill on Stage Road. He was instructed to hold at this point until he heard firing and then to drive toward Sycamore Church and cut off the Fort Powhatan garrison.

Using Shadburne and his scouts to guide him, Rosser was to take the lead. He would go north to Walls Road and then to Sycamore Church. Here he could expect to find a portion of the First District Cavalry entrenched behind pine log barricades. He was told to pace his march to assure arrival just before daybreak to allow him to hit and destroy the enemy cavalry in the dark. At the first sound of firing, he was assured Lee and Dearing would push hard to join him.

Haunted by an active sense of intuition, Union Colonel A. V. Kautz, a veteran of heavy Indian fighting in the Northwest in which he was twice wounded, smelled something in the air but could not figure out exactly what it was. As a precaution, he alerted his superiors to the possibility of an attack but was ignored. On the fifteenth, Hampton had been spotted and a report had been flashed up the line; but this too was ignored. Kautz did alert Maj. J. Stannard Baker of the First District Cavalry, but he took no action of any significance. So unconcerned were Union commanders that at dusk on the fifteenth all Federal signal stations were shut down. Meade's promise of vigilance was being honored in the breach.

At three o'clock in the morning, with the moon down, Lee's men began to peel off, vanishing into the chill blackness of night. As they departed, their commander jogged over to where Hampton waited, saluted, and said, "Good-bye. But, not forever, sir. I'll see you at breakfast."

The big South Carolinian returned the salute with a smile, saying, "Maybe a beefsteak breakfast."

Two miles more and Dearing disappeared into the night, headed up Hines Road. Rosser continued north on Walls Road, moving gingerly forward through the pitch black night. Three times he halted, nervously waiting for the scouts to report. Finally, Scout Jo McCalla materialized out of the darkness to tell Rosser the Yanks were only a mile in front and obviously knew something was up.

The Twelfth Virginia was ordered forward. Moving stealthily through the blackness that was just beginning to faintly give way to the beginning of light in the east, they halted momentarily when scouts whispered the Yankees were only one hundred yards ahead. After a last minute check of their arms, they again moved slowly forward. Suddenly, the night blossomed with flickering lights as a shower of Federal repeater bullets staggered the attackers. Above the ripping sound of rifle fire, Rosser shouted, "Go in hard!"

With a wild yell, the Virginians charged full tilt into the yammering repeater fire. Although hampered by darkness, the First District kept up a steady fire that emptied saddles as the Twelfth milled in front of the barricade. Flesh could take only so much though, and the attackers broke under the storm of leaden pellets, falling back in confusion.

As Rosser shouted commands in an attempt to restore order, some Rebels yelled for the First District to surrender. To the Confederate urging, a Union voice responded, "Come and get us if you want us!"

When order was finally restored, Rosser called the commander of the Twelfth over. "Colonel Massie, try it again," he ordered. "We've got to clear the road and clear it fast."

Massie hurriedly reformed his men and ordered them to charge. As they rushed forward, Rosser yelled, "Use your pistols, men!" But, his advice was of no avail as the charge broke in the face of the Union repeaters and the survivors wheeled back to safety.

Rosser now dismounted the Seventh Virginia and sent them forward in a skirmish line. Hunched over in the darkness to escape the probing Federal bullets, they slowly encircled the barricade to bring the defenders under a blistering cross fire. In the center, a group finally made it to the pine logs and began tearing them out. At last a trooper shouted, "It's wide open enough for an elephant!"

The Eleventh and Twelfth Virginia and Lige White's Comanches hurriedly lined up and prepared to charge. "Use your sabers, men," Rosser told them. "Ride through and cut 'em down!"

As a bugle began singing "Charge," the gray horsemen plunged forward. The First District fought valiantly but futilely as they were overwhelmed. Behind them, four sutlers ran wildly to save their wagons but were cut down in full stride as the raiders pounced on them, determined not to lose this unexpected find. As the graybacks tore into the contents of the wagons, the sound of distant firing floated in on the night air. Lee and Dearing had engaged the enemy.

Day was rapidly breaking as the Rebels moved out again. They whipped through the picket line on Stage Road and thundered down on the 150 men of the Thirteenth Pennsylvania under the command of Capt. Henry H. Gregg who were guarding the cattle herd.

Earlier, Gregg had made his rounds, stopping to talk to Sgt. Albert Kenyon who had charge of the night herders. Kenyon reported that he had heard heavy firing to the south earlier, but Gregg shrugged it off as guerrilla activity. Returning to camp, he had just dismounted when a crash of gunfire announced Rosser's arrival.

Halting short of the camp, Rosser sent Pvt. Cary Selden of the Twelfth Virginia forward with a flag of truce waving from his saber. Selden trotted up to Kenyon and announced, "General Rosser demands your surrender."

"Go to hell," Kenyon snapped. Then he added, "Tell General Rosser if you come to us again with that damned rag, I'll shoot you."

Selden carried the word back to Rosser who simply nodded his head that he understood. Turning to White, he said, "Come down on them, White."

The leader of the Comanches needed no urging. With a wave forward, he sank spurs to his horse, plunging ahead of his charging troops. Behind them, Rosser shouted, "Go get 'em boys! Chop them down!"

The cattle guard melted in front of the yelling Comanches like cold grease on a hot stove. Without slowing pace, the charge quickly turned into a race as the Rebels spotted their bovine quarry running headlong away from them. In an effort to save the cattle, the herders had stampeded them. The raiders' tired horses had difficulty catching the running cattle but they finally made it, surrounding both the herd and its keepers. Not interested in any long negotiations, the Rebels quickly lined the herders up and gave them their options in little, bitty words—herd or be shot. It took but a heartbeat for the captives to decide. They herded.

It was the work of only a few minutes to turn the cattle and start them moving down Walls Road toward Sycamore Church. By six o'clock in the morning, the herd was fully underway. As they moved out, two Federal gunboats on the James River opened an ineffective fire, but it was too little, too late.

News of the raid hit Meade's headquarters with the terror of Judgment Day. With estimates of the enemy strength running as high as twenty-five thousand, panic took charge. The Union leadership belatedly concerned, fussed about the cattle herd and started to fret about the safety of their giant supply depot located in the area. Warnings were flashed in all directions, gunboats were ordered up, and several batteries were pulled out of the line at Petersburg. Finally, by ten o'clock, the commotion subsided sufficiently for the demoralized Federal leadership to figure out what had actually happened and to start delayed actions to deal with it.

Meade, mindful of Grant's distrust and his promise to him, instantly started looking for a way out. He sent Grant a long, complicated, wheedling message announcing what had happened. In it, he tried to excuse himself by saying, "This raid was one which I have feared for sometime, as with the limited force of cavalry under my command and the great extent of country to be watched, I have always considered Coggin's Point an unsuitable position for the cattle herd."

Grant read the message stoically, while Sheridan silently observed him. When he finished, he handed it to him with the comment, "See what happens when I leave." He then fired off a message to Meade telling him to get with it and recover the stolen cattle. This brought two more mewling messages from Meade as he tried to shed the cloak of responsibility.

His efforts not only didn't move Grant, they brought on condemnation in northern newspapers, one writer saying, "Meade had nothing to do with it except that, in Grant's absence, he commanded every man in the Armies operating against Richmond, one hundred thousand of them, from general to drummer boy—and the responsibility lay at his door."

Hampton had different problems. He had sixty miles to travel, twenty-five of them just to cross the Rowanty. Heavy Union forces were all around him and his booty was strung out in a long line of prisoners, wagons, and cattle. He had what he'd gone after, but could he keep it?

Rooney Lee had fought hard with the Third New York and Eleventh Pennsylvania Cavalry, defeating them both. Momentarily, he had toyed with the idea of attempting to capture Meade but had given the idea up as foolhardy. Instead, he broke off and fell back along Wall's Road to protect Rosser's rear.

Rosser and Lee reported to Hampton at Sycamore Church while Dearing, who had defeated the remainder of the First District Cavalry, was hurrying to get in front of them. Hampton was in a rush and made his sense of urgency clear. "Don't let them stop or slow up this side of the Blackwater," he told his commanders, adding, "Dearing will meet us at the Hine's Road fork and take over the advance."

Steadily the raiders pushed south leaving behind a towering cloud of dust to mark their passage. As they traveled, the peace of the countryside was destroyed by the cracks of the herders' whips, bawling cattle, and the pleading curses of both raiders and herdsmen as they tried to hurry the booty along. All efforts were wasted on the plodding cattle. They refused to be rushed despite the frantic efforts of their keepers.

Kautz started moving his force as soon as he heard of the attack. But, he did not really know the reason for the raid until about eight-thirty in the morning. Then, Meade ordered him to follow the retreating Rebels and told Brig. Gen. Henry Davies, a former New York City attorney, to head down the Jerusalem Plank Road to intercept them. Davies moved out smartly but Kautz dawdled along. He was extremely concerned because he had received reports that the enemy numbered fourteen thousand and he wanted no part of a group of that size. At 12:30 P.M., Kautz finally arrived at Sycamore Church to find devastation. He now knew exactly what had happened and had a good feel for the size of his opposition. If he had moved out briskly and in concert with Davies, Hampton could have been crushed. But, he waffled.

The raiders crossed Cook's Bridge at ten o'clock in the morning. Here, Hampton gave the lead to Dearing and sent Rosser with his brigade and Chew's guns to block the Jerusalem Plank Road at Belsche's Mill. Lee was told to destroy the bridge as soon as all the raiders were over.

Lee ordered the bridge blown up only to be told there were no charges available. He then ordered it to be burned. Unfortunately, fire proved to be an unsatisfactory substitute for explosives. The frustrated Rebels discovered that the bridge would not burn. Frantically, they fell to work tearing it down. This proved to be the answer, although they finished the job not a second too soon. Just as the last pieces fell into the water, the Yankees galloped up and opened fire. To the disgust of the Federals, the jeering Rebels trotted off filling the air with taunting yells, obscenely suggesting what the Yanks could do. Kautz, watching the graybacks disappear, gave in to despair.

Five miles below the river, Hampton swung south through Hawkinsville and on toward Neblitt's Millstream. He now heard gunfire indicating that Rosser had engaged Davies. Dearing was dispatched to bolster Rosser, Hampton fully aware that if Lee failed to hold Kautz and Davies broke through, he could lose it all.

Now, to add to Hampton's troubles, the cattle stampeded to water. By the time the recalcitrant beasts were regrouped, Hampton was certain from the sound of the battle that Rosser was falling back. This was confirmed shortly when a sweating messenger arrived to report on the situation. Lee had rejoined by this time, which gave the beleaguered Hampton the additional force he needed. Taking Lee and all but one regiment of his command, Hampton set out at a gallop toward the sound of battle.

Davies had two thousand troops and the guts and sense to use them. They were about to overwhelm Rosser's men when Dearing arrived. He hurried his troops into combat and was able to somewhat stabilize the situation. At best, the battle was a seesaw affair with the Union possessing a slight advantage, when Hampton and Lee arrived at twilight. The South Carolinian had his entire force form up as rapidly as possible. Then, in the last minutes of the fading day, his bugler sounded "Charge." The two forces met with a resounding crash, quickly splintering into a swirling mass of desperately struggling men and horses. After a few minutes, new Rebel strength finally told and Davies withdrew into the covering darkness.

A small force led by Maj. Reid Venable remained in the area while Hampton moved out. After a short wait, the last of the raiding force followed, hurrying south. After full night had fallen, they crossed the Nottoway at Freeman's Ford where the exhausted men and animals stopped to rest. Meanwhile, Hampton, leaving a few men at Ebenezer Church, moved down the road to the turnoff to Wilkinson's Bridge and bivouacked, expecting the Federals to arrive at any minute. He need not have worried, however, for Davies had had enough.

The now supercautious Kautz finally crossed the Blackwater and moved slowly forward. At 9:00 P.M., he hit the small outpost

Hampton had left at Hawkinsville. After a brief brush, he pulled back, put out pickets, and barricaded the road. He was now out of the fight.

All of Hampton's command rejoined the next morning at a fork of Flat Foot Road. At noon, they were met by Brig. Gen. John Dunovant's South Carolinians sent to act as their escort. The raid was over.

Hampton had covered over a hundred miles, captured 304 of the enemy and eleven wagons, burned three camps, taken a large load of supplies, captured three flags, and rustled 2,468 fat steers weighing, according to the *Richmond Dispatch* 1,988,800 pounds. He had lost ten killed, forty-seven wounded, and four missing.

The *Washington Star* said of the raid, "As a piece of raiding rascality it was perfect."

Lincoln agreed, saying, "It was the slickest piece of cattle stealing I ever heard of."

Grant would drive the point home even more forcefully several days later when he invited Kautz and several generals to dinner. A fine meal was served but beef was noticeably lacking. After the rather strained dinner, cigars were passed around and all the attendees sat quietly, puffing, waiting for Grant to speak. When he didn't, one diner summoned up enough courage to ask, "General, how long will it take you to starve out Lee and capture Richmond?"

Grant removed his cigar from his mouth, studied the ash intently for a minute, then quietly answered, "Forever, General, if you keep feeding Lee's army with beef."

On the nineteenth, with the cattle rested, the Rebels paraded into Petersburg. It was a glad day for the city's residents as the raiders put on a "Stuart Show." Swinging onto Washington Street with Hampton in the lead, the Rebel riders pranced their horses to the music as the band struck up "Jine the Cavalry." Then, the notes of the music bringing back haunting memories of the days when the laughing Cavalier had led such parades, the strains of "Lorena" filled the air and voices rose in song. But, the sounds of gaiety were strained, for deep in their hearts, they knew the days of glory were gone forever.

CHAPTER XVI

Devil on the River

Fatigue-etched lines lacing the gaunt face of the gray-clad general spoke mutely but eloquently of the ravages war commits on the bodies of men. Nearly three years of perpetual combat had drawn the planes of his sharply defined features ever tauter until they had become a study of deepening weariness. His heavy shock of prematurely gray hair contrasted sharply with a crow's wing black, short beard and mustache framing a mouth little given to laughter. A prominent, high-bridged nose ran straight up his face to bisect a heavy brow. Beneath the shaggy brows, dark, penetrating eyes revealed the determination, still undiminished, of their owner. Here, barely visible at rest, smoldered the volcanic force of will that had driven the largely uneducated, but shrewd and naturally able, backwoodsman from private to the stars of a major general. Nathan Bedford Forrest had become the Confederacy's premier cavalry leader, indispensable to those who still harbored vain hope of prolonging a fading dream.

The exhaustion so plainly visible in the general was endemic in the troopers under his command. They had just returned from a raid deep into west Tennessee in a state of near collapse. Their condition and his own bone-aching weariness had led Forrest to request a short furlough from the constant campaigning that had been their lot. It was not to be. The dispatch from the department commander, Lt. Gen. Richard Taylor, that he now held in his hand was lavish in its praise of his efforts, but denied the respite he had sought. Instead, it informed him that he must again raid in the Union rear in an effort to relieve the unremitting pressure being applied to the Confederate Army. October of 1864 was a time of unparalleled danger to the Confederacy and no man who wore the gray would ever again rest as long as the Stars and Bars waved above a square centimeter of the continent.

Forrest wasted no time in fruitless argument. Acknowledging the order, he informed his commander that his first action would be to move into west Tennessee where he could obtain the supplies necessary to sustain his force. Once he had accomplished this, he would move against the Federal forces that were moving to the east. He told Taylor, "It is my present design to take possession of Fort Heiman on the Tennessee River below Johnsonville, and thus prevent all communication with Johnsonville by transports. It is highly important that this line be interrupted, if not entirely destroyed, as I learned during my recent operations in Middle Tennessee that it was by this route that the enemy received most of his supplies at Atlanta. I shall exercise diligence in gathering up the large number of deserters and absentees in Tennessee. As fast as these are gathered up I would suggest that they be sent to you and placed at once in the infantry service. The facilities of these men for running away is much greater in the cavalry service, and they should be placed in positions remote from their country. The great, predominating, absorbing desire is to cut Sherman's line of communication."

Forrest wasted no time in preparing his ragged troops to depart Corinth, Mississippi. Concerned about the sagging strength of his command, he fired off a message to Brig. Gen. James Chalmers, commanding a division, Forrest's Cavalry Corps, Department of Alabama, Mississippi, and East Louisiana, to join him en route and to, "Fetch your wagons and the two batteries with you." Adding, "I will supply you with the artillery ammunition at Jackson."

In the mellow light of daybreak on 16 October, Col. Tyree Bell led the first contingent out of Corinth with instructions to proceed to Lavinia, Tennessee. On the eighteenth, Brig. Gen. Abe Buford with Capt. John Morton's and Captain E. S. Walton's batteries got underway, headed for Lexington. Forrest, with Rucker's brigade under Colonel D. C. Kelley, brought up the rear. He left Corinth on the nineteenth and arrived at Jackson on the twenty-first where he set up his headquarters. There, he was joined by Chalmers with 550 men of Mabry's and McCullough's brigades giving him a force of about 3,000 men.

The condition of the command continued to be a matter of major concern, however. Forrest reported to his superior that much of the command bordered on the edge of being unserviceable. He noted that they had lost a large number of horses from exposure and fatigue during their recent hard campaigns and that many of the men were sick and worn out. He added that he had been forced to permit a large number of his troops to go to their homes in west Tennessee and Kentucky to procure horses and clothing so they could continue their service. This sorry state of affairs weighed heavily on the commander's mind but in no way deterred him from pressing forward to attack Sherman's lifeline.

The bright flashes of autumn color speckling the woodlands, the fresh tinge of crispness in the October air, and the building excitement of anticipated battle pumped new vigor into the worn bodies of the troopers. Men sat a little straighter in the saddle or walked a bit taller as the miles between them and the enemy fell steadily behind. This human revitalization was not reflected in the tired horses the men rode, however. Immune to such mundane things as color, crisp air, and human anticipation, they persisted in dropping from exhaustion or limping along on sore, poorly-shod or bare hooves. Their refusal to rise to the demands of the moment led to a dragging pace that was unbearable to Forrest. Finally, he called a halt and asked for ten volunteers from each regiment. Goaded by the sting of past experiences when response had not been sufficiently prompt, the needed volunteers were assembled before him in minutes.

Forrest surveyed the ragtag group with a jaundiced eye. "Well, you think you're mighty fine roosters, don't you? You think you'll git out and drink a gallon of buttermilk don't you?" He paused briefly, then in a different tone of voice continued, "Well, I hope you do. But, I'll tell you what you have to do now. You there," he said pointing, "down that road you'll find a bunch of wagons in a barn lot. Strip off all the tires and bring 'em back, and before sundown." Turning to the remainder, he told them, "Now you go up that road to the west until you come to a crossroads. You'll find a blacksmith there. It's full of iron. Bring it all back, and before sundown."

A brusque wave of the general's hand sent them scurrying off in search of the desired metal. The main force lounged about, grateful for the chance to rest, while the daylight hours slowly wasted away.

At last, with the late evening sun still clinging tenaciously to the rim of the world, the foragers reappeared. Each, loaded with wagon tires, hub hoops, or other pieces of iron, deposited his booty before Forrest and received a nod of approval for his efforts. Blacksmiths searched out of the ranks quickly produced glowing fires. In the gathering darkness, the red tongues of flame and pungent clouds of smoke created a scene approximating that of a miniature hell with the ringing sound of hammers on white-hot iron replacing the anguished screams of tortured souls. On the edge of the circle where the flickering firelight struggled to hold the shadows of night at bay, other men grasping still warm horseshoes and nails cursed the poor light and uncooperative horses in a massive shoeing effort. As the last wisps of smoke faded into hazy morning light, two brigades, mounted on well-shod animals, resumed the march.

Wary of the enemy, Forrest moved his force northeast in a shallow curving swing that led through Huntington to Paris. Convinced by this time that no force was after them, the raiders abruptly turned east, crossed the Big Sandy River and arrived at Paris Landing below Fort Heiman on the Tennessee River on the twenty-eighth. Buford, in the lead, placed Walton with two twenty-pound Parrotts in the old Confederate works of the fort and a section of Morton's Battery about six hundred yards downstream. Bell, with the remainder of Morton's Battery, went into position five miles upstream at Paris Landing. By late afternoon the Tennessee was effectively blockaded.

As darkness fell, four small boats, riding high in the water, were sighted moving downstream. The Confederate gunners anxious to go into action made ready to fire. Buford would not have it. "Keep quiet, men, don't fire a gun," he ordered. "Those are empty boats going down after more supplies for Sherman's army. I want a loaded boat, a richer prize. Just wait until one comes up the river, and then you may take her if you can."

Forrest was on the scene early the next morning. He made a hurried inspection while Buford watched tensely, knowing the mercurial temper of his leader would explode if he were dissatisfied. Finally, the grim visaged general nodded his approval. But, before Buford could relax, a steamer swung into view around a bend just below Fort Heiman.

The *Mazeppa,* riding deep in the water, towing a barge, her boilers straining to overcome the current, chugged furiously past the first concealed battery into the Rebel trap. Both lower batteries opened, the seasoned gunners putting every round into the hapless vessel. The third salvo hit with such punishing force that the *Mazeppa*'s pilot ran her aground on the opposite shore. As soon as she touched the bank all the crew, except the captain and two men, took to the bushes at a long run, showing a sudden affinity for dry ground.

The Confederate jubilation quickly subsided as the realization that they had no way to secure their prize slowly spread through the ranks. After some milling around, Private W. C. West of Barteau's Second Tennessee solved the problem. He stripped, hung his pistol around his neck, and, using a plank for flotation, swam to the beached steamer. The three remaining crew members offered no resistance, the captain promptly surrendering and offering his hand to help West on board. With the help of the remaining crew, the conqueror of the steamboat launched the boat's yawl and used it to get a hawser to the other shore. Once this had been accomplished, the crippled steamboat was warped into the arms of her eager captors.

The almost destitute Rebels now found themselves the possessors of a large amount of clothing, blankets, food, and equipment. They were ordered to quickly unload the vessels and move the supplies to a safe place. As the raiders started unloading the seven hundred tons of cargo on board the *Mazeppa* and her barge, a private found a jug of brandy. Buford quickly appropriated the demijohn. Once the rotund leader had it in hand, he scampered to the hurricane deck and waved it before the troopers. Immediately shouts went up for him not to drink it all. Buford shook his head sadly and shouted back, "Plenty of meat, boys, plenty of hardtack, shoes, and clothes—all for the boys, but just enough whiskey for the General."

Late in the afternoon, three gunboats poked their noses around the bend and opened up on the troops unloading the *Mazeppa*. The Rebel shore batteries returned the fire vigorously and soon convinced the gunboat commanders that discretion was the better part of valor. As the intruders slipped out of sight downriver, the *Mazeppa* was fired and the exuberant raiders retired for the night.

Business started briskly the next morning when the *Anna* appeared, headed downriver. As soon as she entered the trap, Buford, anxious to capture an undamaged vessel, hailed her, promising not to fire if she would pull in to the bank. The *Anna*'s pilot answered he would "round to" at the lower landing. As he neared that point, he ordered, "Full ahead," racing to pass the last battery. Enraged at this display of "Yankee perfidy," that battery opened with all guns. They were too late. Although badly damaged, the *Anna* scooted from sight, her wake mocking the gullible Rebels.

The *Anna* had been escorted by the gunboat *Undine* to within a few miles of the blockade. The captain of the *Undine,* who had headed back to his base at Johnsonville, heard the Confederate guns. He immediately cleared for action and headed full speed toward the sound of combat. Her eight, twenty-four-pounders bellowing, the *Undine* engaged Bell's guns. For fifty-five minutes the river valley echoed the drumming roar of cannon fire. By this time, the *Undine* with her escape pipe shot off, four gun casements suffering from direct hits, four of her crew dead and three wounded, was becoming unmanageable. Desperate to save her, the captain moved her into shore midway between, and out of range of, both Confederate positions.

Now, Colonel C. R. Barteau arrived with a regiment. Spotting the stricken gunboat, he deployed his troopers along the shore, commanding them, "Halt! Dismount and prepare, on foot, to fight gunboats."

The gray riders immediately peppered the crippled vessel with musket balls. Their efforts were successful in slowing repair work on the *Undine* but got them an occasional broadside of shrapnel from the wounded gunboat as the Yankee rivermen worked and fought at the same time.

Meanwhile, the *Venus* came downriver towing two barges. Ignoring frantic signals from the *Undine,* her captain opened the throttle and churned by the first Rebel battery. His poor judgment cost him his life in a hail of artillery fire. The salvo caused little damage otherwise, but a much chastened *Venus* quickly changed tactics and anchored under the protective guns of the *Undine.*

Within twenty minutes, the *J. W. Cheeseman,* also ignoring signals from the *Undine,* tried to run the blockade. She was less fortunate, for Rebel fire quickly disabled her, driving her to the shore where her crew surrendered. The raiders rapidly unloaded the badly damaged steamer and burned her to the waterline.

Chalmers, who had been joined by Colonel E. W. Rucker, now arrived with the last of Forrest's cavalry and two batteries. Rucker personally scouted through the maze of scrub timber, underbrush, and drifts along the riverside protecting the *Undine* and *Venus.* After much searching, he found a passable way to a spot near the river's edge. With much sweating, tugging, and swearing, two pieces of artillery were finally moved into position. In a few deafening moments these guns destroyed the safe haven the two boats occupied. The *Venus* surrendered in place but the severely damaged *Undine* ran across the river and beached before her crew abandoned ship. Kelley immediately boarded the *Venus* with two companies, crossed the river, and took control of the *Undine*. Another gunboat, the *Tawah,* taking advantage of the distraction of the Rebels, approached and began shelling the upper battery. Chalmers quickly moved into position and drove her off upstream.

A hallmark of Forrest was his inclination to take immediate advantage of any opportunity that passed his way. In keeping with his proclivity for doing the unusual and unexpected, he decided on the spot to create himself a navy. Since it was natural for him to view the boats as simply a new way to use artillery, he called for Morton. When his chief of artillery reported, Forrest complimented him profusely on the captured prizes, then asked, "John, how would you like to transfer your guns to these boats and command a gunboat fleet?"

Morton, acutely conscious that he was as ignorant as his commander of maritime warfare, declined. "Not at all, General," he told him. "My whole knowledge is of land batteries. I know nothing of water and I prefer to stay on terra firma."

Although reluctantly willing to let Morton off the hook, the determined Forrest was not about to accept his as the final answer. He promptly ordered Capt. Frank Gracey, an ex-steamboat captain and artilleryman, to assume command of the *Undine*. Colonel W. A. Dawson was appointed "Commodore" and told to put the Parrotts on the *Venus* and assume command of her and the fleet.

Dawson, who had seen the black temper of Bedford Forrest in action and wanted no part of it, braced himself and laid out some terms. "Now, look-a-here, General," he said. "I'll go with these gunboats wherever you order but I want to tell you now that I know nothing about them. I want you to promise me now that, if I lose the fleet and come in afoot, you'll not cuss me out for it."

A momentary darkening of Forrest's stern features gave way to the flash of white teeth as the terrible temper sparked briefly then collapsed in humor. "All right," Bedford agreed. "If you can't hold your water dogs, run their noses in the mud, fire them, and head for safer ground."

The new sailors spent Halloween practicing their newly acquired trade, free of interference since all traffic on the river had stopped. On 1 November, "Forrest's cavalry afloat" got underway toward Johnsonville under strict orders to stay within reach of the artillery following on shore.

Rain started falling early in the day, making life hell for the troops on shore as they struggled to move artillery along a narrow road that had become a morass. With a soldier's characteristic lack of sympathy for the discomfort of his messmates, the waterborne cavalrymen shouted commiserations to those on shore in terms calculated to raise bile in a saint. Their tired, mud-caked comrades had to content themselves with calling maledictions down on them and predicting all sorts of dire consequences for their tormentors once the Yankee gunboats appeared. The command finally stopped and pitched camp in a driving rain. They spent the night huddled near the river with the boats anchored near the abutments of an old railway bridge.

Late the next afternoon, the *Venus*, overconfidently and contrary to orders, steamed ahead well out of range of both the *Undine* and the shore batteries. Rounding a bend near the Green Bottom Bar she met the gunboats *Key West* and *Tawah* head on. Completely overmatched and ineptly fought, the *Venus* was rapidly driven ashore where her crew escaped. The *Undine* made a move to come to her rescue but was forced downstream, leaving the victorious Federals to exult over the recapture of their property and the two Rebel Parrotts.

Desultory action in the form of random shelling went on until after dark. As night fell, a massive thunderstorm blanketing the area fitfully lit the forbidding night with crashing bolts of lightning. The darkness, cannon fire, and storm were too much for one new Rebel regiment. Its members decided to fight with their feet by finding a safe locality. As they ran from the area, one passed near a beef that had been slaughtered but not distributed. His passing coincided with an ear-numbing crash of thunder as a huge lightning bolt momentarily dissolved the night with a flash of blue-white brilliance. The sight overwhelmed him. As he added speed to his already flying feet, he shouted, "There, by God, a shell has split a horse wide open!"

Told the story the next day, Barteau shook his head absently and mused, "He must have thought that was a wonderful shell—to split a horse open and skin him at the same time!"

On the third, Forrest started his final move on Johnsonville, the original target of the raid. To mask his intention, he emplaced two small batteries on Reynoldsburg Island and sent the *Undine* to entice the blue gunboats into battle. Three times she steamed impudently out into the open, daring the enemy. Federal commanders, rightly suspecting that land batteries were lying in wait on the island, declined the invitation. While this game of bluff occupied Union attention, Forrest, with the remainder of his force, was rapidly pushing on to a point opposite Johnsonville.

The position chosen by Forrest to attack Johnsonville was separated from the river by a wide, low-lying bottom that was virtually a swamp. Fighting almost bottomless mud, tangles of fallen timber, and huge rotting drifts, the struggling troopers slaved through the night to position the artillery. By morning it was done. Captain J. C. Thrall's battery was placed slightly above the town while Morton's and Hudson's batteries were situated directly opposite it. Most of the field pieces were dug in for protection, but a few were left capable of rapid movement. The raiders cut hickory saplings and wove them into the ones standing along the river as camouflage to conceal the raiders. An observer glancing across the river from the city in the bright morning light would have seen nothing to tell him that destruction crouched in the muddy river bottomland.

Surveying his position in daylight, Morton decided he was not satisfied with it. Searching out Forrest, he explained his misgivings and requested permission to do a careful survey in an effort to improve the location of his guns. After some discussion, the general reluctantly agreed and Morton scurried off. In a short while, he found a spot that would give him unobstructed command of the far shore and hurried back to tell his leader. Forrest quizzed him thoroughly on his proposal, then said, "No, that's gittin' too close. They'll knock you all to pieces from the fort and gunboats too."

"No, General," Morton argued, "I have examined the location well. The fort is so elevated that they can't depress their guns sufficiently to effect me and the gunboats are so much below in the river that they will fire over me. I'll be at an angle of comparative safety." At last Forrest agreed and Morton's men set to building a roadway through the fetid marshland.

Meanwhile, the Union gunboats were making a determined effort to rid the Tennessee River of the "Confederate Navy." Six gunboats came upriver and three down to converge on the *Undine* and the Reynoldsburg Island batteries. Trapped between these forces, Gracey had no alternative but to beach and destroy the *Undine*. Mattresses filled with shavings were ripped open, soaked with oil, and set on fire. As the pirate crew of the *Undine* raced to safety through the woods, the last "dreadnaught" of Forrest's fleet disappeared in a spectacular explosion.

The waterborne threat disposed of, the gunboats now engaged the land batteries. The upriver vessels took nineteen hits in twenty minutes. This was enough to convince its commander that this was not an engagement likely to end in his favor. He disengaged and steamed back to Johnsonville. The lower flotilla remained in the area but could not pass the island since a narrow chute at this point would permit only one boat to approach at a time. To have made such an approach would have been to invite certain disaster. Thus, these boats had to sit impotently within sound of the cannon fire while the attack on Johnsonville developed.

Across from that city, Forrest scanned the area through binoculars while anxious gunners stood by their pieces awaiting the signal to fire. Gunboats, transports, loaded barges, and acres of supplies piled on the bank filled Forrest's field of vision. People moved casually about their normal activities oblivious to the fact they were under the hawk-eyed stare of a man bent on their destruction. At 2:00 P.M., Forrest signaled, "Fire." Instantly, the massed cannon belched a cloud of metal destruction.

Smoke, fire, steam, and flying debris racked the river fleet as the salvo smashed home. Panicky crews jumped into the river or ran wildly up the shore while the barrage methodically hammered their vessels to bits. Fire spread rapidly as burning boats broke from the moorings, drifting aimlessly in the current until they collided with other vessels. In forty minutes every boat and barge was burning furiously. The Federals watched helplessly as one by one the flame-swept fleet slipped, hissing, and steaming, beneath the boiling waters of the Tennessee. Union efforts to counter the Rebel fire proved futile as the few rounds that landed near their targets penetrated so deeply in the mud that their explosions did no damage.

Now, the Rebel gunners shifted their attention to the great mounds of supplies lining the riverbank, some already burning, having caught fire from the now sunken boats. As the incoming artillery fire marched across the storage area, spotty fires turned into a conflagration. Forrest ordered the rifled guns of Brigg's Section to concentrate on a stack of barrels he had spotted hidden under a canvas cover. The first rounds caused a blue haze to form in the smoke-filled sky. Then, in a heartbeat, the haze turned into a towering ball of orange fire as exploding barrels of whiskey sent geysers of flame spurting upward and rivers of fire streaming down the shoreline.

Carried away with the excitement, the normally taciturn Forrest decided to become a cannoneer. Drafting Bell and Buford to assist him, he placed an officer up on the bank behind a tree as observer. When the observer reported the first round a miss, Forrest, a satanic gleam in his eye, gleefully shouted, "Rickety-shay! A rickety-shay! I'll hit her next time. Buford, elevate the breach of that gun lower!"

Darkness had fallen before Forrest was satisfied his work was done. As the attackers withdrew, their way was lighted by the glare from the wild, wind-whipped inferno behind them. Their foray had netted four gunboats, fourteen steamboats, seventeen barges, thirty-three guns, 150 prisoners, and over seventy-five thousand tons of supplies. Forrest estimated the damage at $6,700,000.

Despite all the activity, most Union commanders seemed at a loss as to Forrest's location. Consequently, a series of fantastic stories regarding his activities and intentions were in circulation. Sherman, a man not given to belief in the incredible, settled the question by bluntly telling Grant, "That devil Forrest was down about Johnsonville making havoc among the gunboats and transports."

As the weary Rebels streamed south, Forrest rode up to Thrall's Battery which had done exceptional work. This group, made up of men from the White River Country of Arkansas, had been dubbed the "Arkansas Rats." Now, their proud leader told them, "Well, boys, after this fight, we'll have to find a better name for you than 'Arkansas Rats.' I'm agoin' to baptize you, right now, the 'Arkansas Braves.'"

A sergeant emboldened by their success hollered back, "Gen'l, talkin' may be all right but somethin' to eat would sound a heap better. We've been livin' on wind fer two days."

A smiling Forrest accepted the mild rebuke. Turning to a staff officer, he told him, "Go back to my headquarters wagon where you'll find four boxes of hardtack and three hams. Have them brought right up here and issued to Captain Thrall's men."

Forrest now took Morton and went back for one last look at his handiwork. As they sat on their horses atop the riverbank overlooking a scene of complete devastation, Forrest spoke in a voice choked with emotion. "John," he said, "if they'd give you enough guns and me enough men, we could whip old Sherman off the face of the earth."

And, they probably could have too!

EPILOGUE

Glory at a Gallop

As magnificent at it was, the gray cavalry, like the Rebel cause, faded, then succumbed to the inexorable blue force squeezing the life out of it. Its decline became readily perceptible in early 1864 as remounts, supplies, and men became more difficult to find. While the months passed, these problems mounted until at last they were insuperable. In midspring of 1865, the proud gray cavalry, like the nation it had served so well, could no longer rise to meet the challenge. Reluctantly, defeat like gall in their mouths, the exhausted troopers raised the white banner and rode no more. Hotheads among them talked of going south to Mexico to continue the struggle in another place at another time. But, cooler, wiser heads prevailed. The survivors broke up and headed homeward to help rebuild and expand a shattered nation.

Unrecognized by all the participants was the fact that horse cavalry had passed its zenith with the end of this great conflict. For, before the last bugle note had faded into a haunting memory, an event had transpired that spelled finis to the horse soldier. In the gray, windy city of Chicago a man named George Gatling had put the final touches on a new weapon. His Gatling gun and its successors gave the foot soldier such awesome firepower that cavalry could not surmount it. Still, the horsemen survived the better part of a century, doing yeoman service in the American West. And, even after the shattering experience of World War I, the cavalry hung on, a beloved relic of the past, until World War II when the panzers of Germany demonstrated once and for all that horses were totally incompatible with automatic weapons and the internal combustion engine.

Cavalry died only as a military force, however, its usefulness in that arena relegated to ceremonial duties. For, as the cavalryman changed his horse for a rumbling tank or screaming fighter plane, the horse soldier passed from life directly into legend. He survived in countless books regaling his exploits and lived in glory in thundering charges across the silver screen. And, his spirit lived on too. It rode with his descendants across the gritty sands of Africa, the soggy, snow-covered fields of Europe, the icy skies of Korea, the SAM-filled air over Thud Ridge, and across and above the burning desert of the Arabian Peninsula. The horses were gone; but the men who had ridden them left a legacy of grit, guts, and glory that will never die.

And, maybe the horse soldiers are not really gone either. Long after the war, an old veteran speculated hopefully that another life awaited those who had worn the blue and the gray. He suggested that in some ethereal land they would all meet again. Then, on Elysian fields under cobalt skies, the great battles would be fought again. And at day's end, the dead would spring to life, the wounded become whole, and all would gather around the campfires. Here amid good-natured laughter, old animosities would be buried in soldier-talk as the day's adventures were recounted. Thus, throughout eternity, they would relive, without pain and suffering, the cataclysmic event that had once engulfed their lives.

If this Valhalla exists and you should visit there, the gray troopers will be easy to find. Just go to the fire where you hear Sweeny's banjo tinkling out "Jine the Cavalry" and they'll be there. In the front row you will see their leaders—the laughing cavalier, Jeb Stuart, debonair John Morgan, diminutive Joe Wheeler, hard-eyed Nathan Bedford Forrest, hulking Wade Hampton, dashing Earl Van Dorn, and fiery John Mosby. And, circled about them, their white smiles flashing in the gathering dusk, will be the superb riders who followed them to glory at a gallop.

Bibliography

A Confederate. *The Grayjackets*. Philadelphia, 1867.

Abbott, John S. C. *The History of the Civil War in America*. Springfield: Gordon Bill, 1866.

Agnew, Rev. Samuel. *Southern Sentinel*. Ripley, 1895.

Albaugh, William R., III; Simmons, Edward N. *Confederate Arms*. New York: Bonanza Books, 1957.

American Heritage Picture History of the Civil War. American Heritage Publishing Co., 1960.

Angle, Paul M. *A Pictorial History of the Civil War Years*. Garden City: Doubleday & Co., 1967.

_____ ; Miers, Earl Schenck. *Tragic Years: 1860–1865*. New York: Simon & Schuster, 1960.

Baker, Gen. Lafayette C. *Spies, Traitors, and Conspirators of the Late Civil War*. Philadelphia: John E. Potter & Co., 1894.

Barron, Samuel B. *The Lone Star Defenders: A Chronicle of the Third Texas Cavalry, Ross Brigade*. New York: The Neale Publishing Co., 1908.

Boatner, Mark M., III. *The Civil War Dictionary*. New York: Vintage Books, 1988.

Boykin, Edward. *Beefsteak Raid*. New York: Funk & Wagnalls Co., 1960.

Blackford, Lt. Col. W. W., CSA.*War Years with Jeb Stuart*. New York: Charles Scribner's Sons, 1946.

Brocke, Heros von. *Memories of the Confederate War for Independence*. 2 vols. London, 1866.

Brooks, U. R., ed. *Butler and His Cavalry in the War of Secession*. Columbia: The State Co., 1909.

Brown, A. F. "Van Dorn's Operations in Northern Mississippi." In *Southern Historical Society Papers*. October 1878.

Brownlee, Richard S. *Gray Ghosts of the Confederacy: Guerrilla Warfare in the West, 1861–1865.* Baton Rouge: Louisiana State Univ. Press, 1958.

Bryan, J., III. *The Sword Over the Mantle.* New York: McGraw-Hill Book Co., 1960.

Cadwallader, Sylvanus. *Three Years With Grant.* New York: Charles Scribner's Sons, 1881.

Catton, Bruce. *The Centennial History of the Civil War.* 3 vols. Garden City: Doubleday & Co., 1961–1965.

———. *Grant Moves South.* Boston: Little, Brown & Co., 1960.

———. *This Hallowed Ground.* Garden City: Doubleday & Co., 1956.

———. *Mr. Lincoln's Army.* Garden City: Doubleday & Co., 1962.

———. *Glory Road.* Garden City: Doubleday & Co., 1952.

———. *A Stillness at Appomattox.* Garden City: Doubleday & Co., 1953.

Coffin, Charles Carleton. *Marching to Victory.* 2 vols. New York: Harper & Bros., 1889.

Commager, Henry Steele. *The Blue and the Gray.* 2 vols. New York: Bobbs-Merrill Co., 1950.

Confederate Veteran. 40 vols. Nashville, January 1893–December 1932.

Cooke, John Esten. *Wearing of the Gray.* Bloomington: Indiana Univ. Press, 1959.

Davis, Burke. *Jeb Stuart: The Last Cavalier.* New York: Rinehart & Co., 1957.

Davis, Maj. George B.; Perry, Leslie J.; Kirkley, Joseph W.; Cowles, Capt. Calvin D. *The Official Military Atlas of the Civil War.* New York: Arno Press and Crown Publishers, 1978.

DeForest, John William. *A Volunteer's Adventures.* New Haven: Yale Univ. Press, 1946.

Dinkins, Capt. James. *Personal Recollections and Experiences in the Confederate Army.* Cincinnati, 1897.

Dodson, William Carey, ed. *Campaigns of Wheeler and His Cavalry 1862–1865.* Atlanta: Hudgins Publishing Co., 1899.

Dubose, John Witherspoon. *General Joseph Wheeler and the Army of Tennessee.* New York: The Neale Publishing Co., 1912.

Duke, Basil W. *A History of Morgan's Cavalry.* Bloomington: Indiana Univ. Press, 1961.

———. *Reminiscences of General Basil W. Duke, CSA.* Garden City: Doubleday & Co., 1960.

Dupree, J. G. "The Capture of Holly Springs, Mississippi, December 20, 1862." In *Publication of the Mississippi Historical Society.* Vol.4. 1901.

Dyer, John P. *"Fightin' Joe" Wheeler.* Baton Rouge: Louisana State Univ. Press, 1941.

Eisenschiml, Otto; Newman, Ralph. *The American Iliad.* New York: The Bobbs-Merrill Co., 1947.

———. *The Civil War.* 2 vols. New York: Grossett & Dunlap, 1956.

Everhart, William C. *Vicksburg.* National Park Service Handbook, Series no. 21. Washington: Government Printing Office, 1954.

Faust, Patricia L., ed., *Historical Times Illustrated Encyclopedia of the Civil War.* New York: Harper & Row, 1986.

Foote, Shelby. *The Civil War.* 3 vols. New York: Random House, 1958–1974.

Ford, C. Y. *Letter to The Confederate Veteran.* 22 March 1897.

Freeman, Douglas Southall. *Lee's Lieutenants.* 3 vols. New York: Charles Scribner's Sons, 1942–1944.

———. *R. E. Lee.* 4 vols. New York: Charles Scribner's Sons, 1935.

Grant, U. S. *Personal Memoirs of U. S. Grant.* 2 vols. New York: Charles L. Webster & Co., 1885.

Greeve, Francis Vinton. *The Mississippi.* New York: Alfred A. Knopf, 1955.

Hancock, Sgt. R. R. *Hancock's Diary or A History of the Second Tennessee Cavalry, CSA.* Nashville, 1887.

Hanson, Lt. G. A. *Minor Incidents of the Late War.* Bartow, 1887.

Hartje, Robert G. *Van Dorn—The Life and Times of the Confederate General* Nashville: Vanderbilt Univ. Press, 1967.

Harwell, Richard B. *The Confederate Reader* New York: Dorset Press, 1992.

Henry, Robert Selph. *"First with the Most" Forrest.* New York: The Bobbs-Merrill Co., 1944.

———, ed. *As They Saw Forrest: Some Recollections and Comments of Contemporaries.* Jackson: McCowart-Mercer Press, 1956.

History of the United States Secret Service. Privately Printed, 1867.

Holland, Cecil Fletcher. *Morgan and His Raiders.* New York: The Macmillan Co., 1943.

Howe, M. A. Dewolfe, ed. *Home Letters of General Sherman.* New York, 1909.

Johnson, Robert U.; Buel, Clarence C., eds. *Battles and Leaders of the Civil War.* 4 vols. New York: Century Co., 1887.

Johnson, Rossiter. *Campfires and Battlefields.* New York: Civil War Press, 1967.

Jones, Virgil Carrington. *Gray Ghosts and Rebel Raiders.* New York: Henry Holt & Co., 1956.

———. *Ranger Mosby.* Chapel Hill: Univ. of North Carolina Press, 1944.

Jordan, Brig. Gen. Thomas; Pryor, J. B. *The Campaigns of Lieutenant General N. B. Forrest and of Forrest's Cavalry.* New York, 1868.

Jordan, Robert Paul. *The Civil War.* Washington: The National Geographic Society, 1969.

Keller, Allan. *Morgan's Raid.* New York: Bobbs-Merrill Co., 1961.

Knapp, David, Jr. *The Confederate Horsemen.* New York: Vantage Press, 1966.

Leckie, Robert. *The Wars of America*. 2 vols. New York: Harper & Row, 1968.

Lindsley, John Berrien, ed. *The Military Annals of Tennessee, Confederate*. Nashville, 1886.

Lord, Francis A. *Civil War Collector's Encyclopedia*. New York: Castle Books, 1963.

———; Wise, Arthur. *Uniforms of the Civil War*. New York: South Brunswick, 1970.

Lytle, Andrew. *Bedford Forrest and His Critter Company*. New York: McDonnell, Obolensky, 1960.

Lee, Robert Edward, Jr. *Recollections and Letters of General Robert E. Lee*. New York, 1904.

Longstreet, James. *From Manassas to Appomattox: Memoirs of the Civil War in America*. Philadelphia, 1896.

Mason, Mrs. "Raid on Holly Springs." In the Van Dorn Collection. Montgomery.

Massey, Mary Elizabeth. *Bonnet Brigades*. New York: Alfred A. Knopf, 1966.

Mathes, Capt. J. Harvey. *Bedford Forrest*. New York, 1902.

McClellan, H. B. *I Rode with Jeb Stuart*. Bloomington: Indiana Univ. Press, 1958.

McClure, A. K. *Lincoln and Men of War Times*. Philadelphia, 1892.

McGuire, Judith White. *Diary of a Southern Refugee*. New York: E.J. Hale & Son, 1868.

Miers, Earl Schenck. *Robert E. Lee*. New York: Alfred A. Knopf, 1958.

Miller, Francis Trevelyan, ed. *The Photographic History of the Civil War*. New York: The Review of Reviews Co., 1912.

Mobile Register and Advertiser. Mobile, 27 December 1862.

Moehring, Eugene P; Keylin, Arleen, eds. *The Civil War Extra*. New York: Arno Press, 1975.

Moore, Frank, ed. *The Rebellion Record*. 11 vols. New York: D. Van Nostrand, 1861–1868.

Morton, Chief of Artillery John W. *The Artillery of Nathan Bedford Forrest's Cavalry*. Nashville, 1909.

Mosby, John S. *Mosby's War Reminiscences*. New York, 1958.

Myers, F. M. *The Comanches: A History of White's Battalion, Virginia Cavalry, Laurel Brigade, Hampton's Division, Army of Northern Virginia, CSA*. Baltimore, 1871.

Newman, Joseph, ed. *A Bicentennial Illustrated History of the United States*. 2 vols. New York, 1973.

Nye, W. S. *Here Come the Rebels!* Baton Rouge: Louisiana State Univ. Press, 1965.

Paris, Louis Phillipe Albert D'Orleans, Comte de, *History of the Civil War in America* 4 vols. Philadelphia, 1875.

Plum, William B. *The Military Telegraph During the Civil War.* Chicago: Jansen, McClure, & Co., 1882.

Pollard, Edward A. *The Lost Cause.* Baltimore: E. B. Treat & Co., 1867.

————. *The Early Life, Campaigns and Public Service of Robert E. Lee, with a Record of the Campaigns and Heroic Deeds of His Companions in Arms.* New York, 1870.

Pratt, Fletcher. *Ordeal by Fire.* New York: Harrison Smith & Robert Maas, 1935.

Price, Lt. R. Channing, CSA. Letter to Mother, 5 October 1862. Southern Historical Collection. Chapel Hill: Univ. of North Carolina.

Richmond Dispatch. 15 January 1863.

Rose, Victor M. *Ross' Texas Brigade.* Louisville: Courier-Journal, 1881.

Russell, Charles Wells. *The Memoirs of Colonel John S. Mosby.* Bloomington: Indiana Univ. Press, 1959.

Sandburg, Carl. *Abraham Lincoln.* New York: Harcourt, Brace & Co., 1954.

Scott, John W. *Partisan Life with Mosby.* New York: Harper & Brothers, 1867.

Sheads, J. Melchoir. "Border Raids into Pennsylvania During the Civil War," M.A. thesis. Gettysburg: Gettysburg College, 1933.

Schriver, Miss S. C. Letter to Mrs. Thomas J. Meyer, 29 June 1863. Klein Papers. Lancaster, PA: Franklin and Marshall College.

Sifakis, Stewart. *Who Was Who in the Civil War.* 2 vols. New York: Facts on File, 1988.

Sorrel, Gen. G. Moxley, CSA. *Recollections of a Confederate Staff Officer.* New York: The Neale Publishing Co., 1905.

Simmons, Henry E. *A Concise Encyclopedia of the Civil War.* New York: Bonanza Books, 1965.

Southern Historical Society Papers. 49 vols. Richmond: The Southern Historical Society, 1876–1944.

Stern, Philip Van Doren. *Secret Missions of the Civil War.* New York: Rand McNally & Co., 1959.

Swiggett, Howard. *The Rebel Raider.* Garden City: The Garden City Publishing Co., 1937.

Tanner, Robert G. *Stonewall in the Valley.* Garden City: Doubleday & Co., 1976.

Thomason, Capt. John W., USMC. *Jeb Stuart.* New York: Charles Scribner's Sons, 1930.

Tilberg, Frederick. *Gettysburg National Military Park Pennsylvania.* Washington: Government Printing Office, 1954.

W. L. F. Letter. *Missouri Democrat.* 22 December 1862.

Waring, Col. George E., Jr. *Whip and Spur.* Boston, 1875.

Warner, Ezra J. *Generals in Gray.* Baton Rouge: Louisana State University Press, 1959.

War of the Rebellion: Official Records of the Union and Confederate Armies. 130 vols. Washington: Government Printing Office, 1880–1901.

Wellman, Manly Wade. *Giant in Gray.* New York: Charles Scribner's Sons, 1949.

———. *Ride Rebels.* New York, 1959.

Wells, Edward L. *Hampton and His Cavalry in '64.* Richmond: B.P. Johnson Publishing Co., 1899.

Williams, Alfred B. *Hampton and His Red Shirts.* Charleston: Walker, Evans, & Cogswell Co., 1935.

Williamson, James J. *Mosby's Rangers: A Record of the Operations of the Forty-Third Battalion, Virginia Cavalry.* New York: Ralph B. Kenyon, 1896.

Witherspoon, William. *Tishomingo Creek or the Battle of Brice's Cross Roads as I Saw It.* Jackson, 1906.

Wyeth, John Allan, M.D. *Life of General Nathan Bedford Forrest.* Dayton: Morningside Bookshop, 1975.

———. *That Devil Forrest.* New York: Harper & Brothers, 1959.

INDEX

Ranks shown are in most cases, the highest rank the individual held during the war. No distinction is made between Regular United States Army, United States Volunteer, and Brevet ranks.

Alabama, State of, 183–84
Aldie, VA, 129–30
Alexandria, VA, 70
Alexandria, TN, 102
Allen, Thomas, Capt., CSA, 26
Altamount, TN, 36
American Hotel, 171
Ames, James F., Sgt., USA, 130–32
Anders, Jack, Cpl., USA, 62
Anderson's Cross Roads, TN, 176
Antietam, MD: Battle of, 46, 49, 70, 116, 166
Antietam Creek, 46
Appalachian Mountains, 155
"Arkansas Braves," 235
"Arkansas Rats," 235
Armfield, Mrs., 36
Army of Northern Virginia, 2, 16, 46–47, 49, 140–41, 143, 146, 149, 153–54, 214–15
Army of the Potomac, 1–2, 6, 8, 16–18, 46, 68–69, 140–41, 145–47, 215
Army of the Shenandoah, 202, 215
Army of Tennessee, 131
Ashland Station, VA, 5
Atlanta, GA, 185, 226
Augur, Christopher C., Maj. Gen., USA, 202–3
Aurora, IN, 164

Austin, TX, 198
Averell, William W., Brig. Gen., USA, 55

Babcock, A. G., 1st. Sgt., CSA, 209
Bacon Creek, 106, 109
Baker, J. Stannard, Maj., USA, 218
Baldwyn, MS, 187, 189
Baldwyn Road, 188, 190
Bardstown, KY, 110, 159
Barker, Augustus, Capt., USA, 132, 136
Barnesville, MD, 64–65
Barteau, C. R., Col., CSA, 191–93, 229–30, 232
Batavia, OH, 165
Beauregard, P. G. T., Gen., CSA, 33
Beech Creek, 73
Beersheba Springs, TN, 36
Belsche's Mill, VA, 222
Bell, Tyree H., Brig. Gen., CSA: and Brice's Cross Roads, 187, 190–94; and Johnsonville, 226, 228, 234
Bennett, James, Col., CSA, 102
Bergholz, OH, 171
Berryville, VA, 205, 208
Bethel Station, TN, 87, 82
Bevis, IN, 165
Biffle, J. B., Col., CSA, 72, 75–77, 84

Big Miami River, 165
Big Round Top, 150–51
Big Sandy River, 228
Biles, Edwin, Lt. Col., USA, 69
Black Creek, 12
Blackford, William W., Lt. Col., CSA:
    and Chambersburg raid, 54, 59–64,
    67, 69; and Gettysburg, 145
Blackwater Swamp, 217–18, 222–23
Blennerhassett Island, 170
Bliss, A. H., 129
Blue Ridge Mountains, 46, 141, 143, 211
Bob (Stuart's servant), 47, 68
Bolivar, TN, 75, 87, 89, 95–97
Booneville, MS, 187
Borcke, Heros von, 47
Boston, KY, 110
Bouton, Edward, Col., USA, 186, 191,
    195–96
Bower, The, 47, 49–50
Bowling Green, KY, 23, 103, 105
Boydton Road, 217
Boyle, Jeremiah T., Brig. Gen., USA;
    citizens view of, 20; Morgan's first
    Kentucky raid, 23, 25, 27, 32;
    Morgan's second Kentucky raid,
    103, 105; position in Kentucky,
    19–20
Bradford, Jimmy, Bugler, CSA, 192
Bragg, Braxton, Gen., CSA, and Holly
    Springs raid, 88; and Murfreesboro,
    101, 110; and Murfreesboro raid,
    71–72, 78; and Ohio raid, 156; and
    Sequatchie Valley raid, 174–75, 183;
    and Stone's River, 112–26; and
    Tullahoma, 155; and Vicksburg, 100
Brandenburg, KY, 159, 161
Brandy Station, VA, 37
Brayman, Mason, Brig. Gen., USA, 75
Breathed, James, Capt., CSA, 4
Breckenridge, John C., Maj. Gen., CSA,
    124
Breckinridge, William, Col., CSA, 102
Brice's Cross Roads, MS: battle of,
    189–99; Brice's House, 191; area,
    188, 191–92, 195, 197
Briggs Section (artillery), CSA, 234
Brooke Turnpike, 5

Brooks, William T. H., Maj. Gen., USA,
    53
Brown, John, 2
Bruce, S. D., Col., USA, 105
Brynes, Edwin, Capt., CSA, 157, 161
Buckner, Simon Bolivar, Lt. Gen., CSA,
    155
Buell, Don Carlos, Maj. Gen., USA, 19,
    25, 27, 32–33, 44, 99
Buffington Island, 166, 169
Buford, Abraham, Brig. Gen., CSA: and
    Brice's Cross Roads, 187, 191,
    193–94, 197; and Johnsonville, 226,
    229, 234
Bull Run, 137
Bull Run Mountain, 143
Burbick, James, Capt., Ohio Militia,
    171–72
Burkesville, KY, 112, 156
Burnside, Ambrose E., Maj. Gen., USA:
    mentioned, 99; and Morgan's Ohio
    raid, 155, 160, 166, 168, 171; and
    Sequatchie Valley raid, 174–75,
    178–79
Butler, Matthew G. (Matt), Maj. Gen.,
    CSA, 216
Butler, W. C., Col., CSA, 51–51, 56,
    58, 167–68

Campbellsville, KY, 11–12
Caney Fork, 102
Carlisle, PA, 146, 148, 150, 154
Carroll, Charles, Col., CSA, 83
Carroll Station, TN, 75
Cashtown, PA, 59–60
Catoctin Mountain, 59
Cave City, KY, 108
Cave Run Bridge, 108
Cedar Creek, 204
Cemetery Hill, 151
Cemetery Ridge, 150–52
Centreville, VA, 127, 129, 131, 133,
    135–37
Chalmers, James R., Brig. Gen., CSA,
    226–27, 230–31
Chambersburg, PA: and Stuart's capture
    of, 50, 54–56, 65; and Stuart's
    march to Gettysburg, 145–46, 148

Chambliss, John R., Jr., Brig. Gen.,
   CSA, 142
Chancellor, Lorman, 130
Chancellorsville, Battle of, 140
Chantilly, VA, 127, 129–30, 136
Chapman, William, Capt., CSA, 208,
   210
Charles City Road, 14
Charles Town, VA, 204
Chattanooga, TN: and Forrest's
   Murfreesboro raid, 33–36; men-
   tioned, 19; and Wheeler's Sequatchie
   Valley raid, 175, 177–79, 183
Cheatham, Benjamin F., Maj. Gen.,
   CSA, 74, 116
Cheek's Ford, 202
Chenault, D. W., Lt. Col., CSA, 102,
   110
Cheshire, OH, 169
Chester, OH, 166
Chester Gap, VA, 204
Chester Road, 167
Chew's Battery, 222
Chickahominy River, 1, 3, 7, 9, 13,
   15–16
Chickasaw Bayou, 87, 98
Chillicothe, OH, 165
Christiana, TN, 180
Cincinnati, OH, 26, 29, 164, 165
City Point, VA, 215
Clarksburg, TN, 82
Clarksburg Road, 82
Clear Springs, MD, 52
Clifton, TN, 73, 80, 84
Cluke, R. S., Col., CSA, 101, 107
Cocke's Mill, VA, 218
Cocky, Mr., 63–64
Coggin's Point, VA, 215–16, 218,
   221
Cold Harbor, Battle of, 16
Cold Harbor Road, 8
Collierville, TN, 197
Collins River, 179
Columbia, KY, 111–12, 157
Columbia, TN, 180
Columbus, MS, 73, 78
Concocheague Bridge, 56, 58
Concocheague River, 50

Cooke, John Esten, Capt., CSA, 12–13,
   16, 150
Cooke, Philip St. George, Maj. Gen.,
   USA, 9, 10, 13
Cook's Bridge, 217, 222
Copperheads, 162
Corbett, C. C., Capt., CSA, 102, 107–8
Corinth, MS, 73, 75, 81, 187, 226
Cottonport, TN, 176
Couch, Darius N., Maj. Gen., USA, 52
Cowan, George, Lt., CSA, 195
Cox, Jacob D., Maj. Gen., USA, 29, 52
Cox, N. N., Col, CSA, 75, 76
Coxe's Riffle, 171
Cox's Regiment, CSA, 116, 122
Crab Orchard, KY, 31
Crittenden, John J., Sen., 37
Crittenden, Thomas L., Maj. Gen.,
   USA, 103, 117
Crittenden, Thomas T., Brig. Gen.,
   USA, 37–38, 41, 44
Crook, George, Maj. Gen., USA, 173,
   175, 177–82, 201
Crowell's Mill, TN, 180
Croydon, IN, 162
Cub Run, 137
Culpepper Courthouse, VA, 137–38
Culp's Hill, 150–51
Cumberland, MD, 55
Cumberland, OH, 171
Cumberland Gap, 18, 174
Cumberland Mountain Plateau, 36
Cumberland Mountains, 20–21, 26
Cumberland River, 22, 32, 102,
   111–12, 156
Cumberland River Valley, 21
Curtin, A. G., Gov., 55–56
Custer, George A., Maj. Gen., USA,
   152, 210
Cynthiana, KY, 26, 29, 31

Dabb's Farm, VA, 3
Dandridge, Stephen, 47
Darksville, VA, 50
Davidson, Henry B., Brig. Gen., CSA,
   174, 176, 180–82
Davies, Henry E., Maj. Gen., USA, 222,
   223

Davies, Thomas A., Brig. Gen., USA, 73, 78
Davis, Hasbrouck, Brig. Gen., USA, 55
Davis, Jefferson, Pres., CSA, 121, 175
Davis Mill, MS, 89, 93–94
Davis's Battalion, CSA, 116
Dawson, W. A., Col., CSA, 231
Dearing, James, Brig. Gen., CSA, 216, 218–20, 222–23
Dennison, Camp, OH, 165
Department of Alabama, Mississippi and East Louisana, CSA, 187, 226
Department of Mississippi, USA, 19
Department of Northern Virginia, 16
Department of Ohio, USA, 103
Department of West Virginia, USA, 204
de Polignac, Prince Camille Armand J. M., Maj. Gen., CSA, xvi
Devil's Den, The, 151
Dibrell, George G., Brig. Gen., CSA, 72, 75–77, 82–84
Dickey, T. L., Col., USA, 89
District of Central Kentucky, USA, 103
District of Jackson, USA, 73
District of Washington, USA, 202
District of Western Kentucky, USA, 103,
Dodge, Grenville M., Maj. Gen., USA, 73, 75, 80–81
Douglas, Edwin H., Lt., CSA, 84–85
Dover, PA, 149
Dranesville, VA, 129
Dresden, TN, 79
Duck River, 180
Duffie, Alfred N. A., Brig. Gen., USA, 64
Duff, W. L., Col., CSA, 190–92
Duffield, William, Col., USA, 37, 43
Duke, Basil W., Brig. Gen., CSA: military unit, 20; Morgan's first Kentucky raid, 20–21, 27; Morgan's second Kentucky raid, 101–2, 105–7, 109–10; Morgan's Ohio raid, 156, 158–60, 167–68; mentioned, 199; reaction to Ferguson, 21–22
Duke's Regiment, 20
Duncan, John, Pvt., CSA, 118

Dunham, Cyrus L., Col., USA, 80–84
Dunovant, John, Brig. Gen., CSA, 224
Dupont, IN, 163-64

Eagleport, OH, 170
Early, Jubal A., Lt. Gen., CSA: and Gettysburg campaign, 142, 146, 148–49; and Mosby's Berryville raid, 200-202, 204, 209
Eastern Highland Rim, 173
Eastin, George, Lt., CSA, 111–12
Ebenezer Church, VA, 217, 223
Edward's Ferry, 60
Eighth Confederate Cavalry, CSA, 116
VIII Corps, USA, 201
Eighth Kentucky Cavalry, CSA, 101, 157–58
Eighth Illinois Cavalry, USA, 201, 204
Eighth Michigan Cavalry, USA, 158
Eighth Tennessee Cavalry, CSA, 72
Eighth Texas Cavalry (Terry's Rangers), CSA, 34, 40–41, 43, 116, 122
Eight Mile Island, 169
XI Corps, USA, 150
Eleventh Kentucky Cavalry, CSA, 102, 157–58
Eleventh Michigan Battery, USA, 158
Eleventh Pennsylvania Cavalry, USA, 13, 221
Eleventh Virginia Cavalry, CSA, 220
Elizabeth Town, KY, 106
Elsworth, George (Lightnin'): and Morgan's first Kentucky raid, 23–24, 26, 32, 36; and Morgan's Ohio raid, 159–60, 162, 165
Emancipation Proclamation, 49
Emmittsburg, MD, 60–61
Emory, William H., Maj. Gen., USA, 10, 13
Englemann, Adolph, Col., USA, 76
Ewell, Richard S., Lt. Gen., CSA, 141, 146, 148–49, 151

Fairfax Courthouse, VA, 127–28, 131, 133–37, 144
Fairfax Station, VA, 135, 203
Fairview, MD, 52
Falls Church, VA, 200

Farmington, TN, 181–82
Farmington Road, 180
Ferguson, Champ, 21–22, 29, 31
Fifth Division, XIV Corps, USA, 103
Fifth Kentucky Cavalry, CSA, 157–59,
  166–67
Fifth Michigan Cavalry, USA, 210
Fifth New York Cavalry, USA, 130–32
Fifth New York Infantry, USA, 9
Fifty-first Alabama Cavalry, CSA, 116,
  118
Finnell, John, Col., USA, 26
First Alabama Cavalry, CSA, 116
First Cavalry, USA, 10
I Corps, USA, 150
First District Cavalry, USA, 218–20,
  222
First Infantry Division, USA, 201
First Michigan Cavalry, USA, 171
First United States Cavalry, USA, 10
First Virginia Cavalry, CSA, 4
First Virginia Partisan Rangers, 50
Flakes Store, TN, 81
Flat Foot Road, 217, 224
Ford, Antonia, 128, 139
Forge Bridge, 14
Forked Deer Creek, 76–77
Forrest, Nathan Bedford, Lt. Gen.,
  CSA: and Brice's Cross Roads,
  185–99; description, 33–34, 72,
  225; mentioned, 88, 98, 100, 114,
  213, 237; and Johnsonville raid,
  226–35; and Murfreesboro raid,
  35–44, 71; and Tennesse raid,
  72–86; and Wheeler's Sequatchie
  Valley raid, 174–76, 181
Forrest, William, Capt., CSA, 34, 82
Forrest's Cavalry Corps, CSA, 226
Forrest's Tennessee Cavalry Battalion,
  CSA, 34
Fort Donelson, 72–73
Fort Heiman, 73, 75, 226, 228
Fort Henry, 73, 75
Fort McHenry, 209
Fort Powhatan, VA, 218
Fort Tennallytown, 146
"Forty Thieves, The," 82
Fosterville, TN, 180

XVI Corps, USA, 72
Fourteenth Kentucky Cavalry, CSA,
  102
Fourth Alabama Cavalry, CSA, 72–74,
  78, 177–78
Fourth Division, Center, XIV Corps,
  USA, 112
Fourth Iowa Cavalry, USA, 195
Fourth Kentucky Cavalry, USA, 37
Fourth Missouri Cavalry, USA, 197
Fourth Ohio Cavalry, USA, 175
Fourth Tennessee Cavalry, CSA, 72, 75
Fourth United States Cavalry, USA, 122
Fourth Virgina Cavalry, CSA, 4
Frankfort, KY, 26, 29
Frankfort Road, 26
Franklin, William B., Maj. Gen., USA,
  55
Franklin, TN, 117
Frederick, MD, 55, 60–61, 145–47,
  201
Frederick Road, 145
Fredericksburg, VA, 141
Fredericksburg, Battle of, 99, 166
Fredericktown, MD, 142
Freeman's Battery, 72, 74, 77
Freeman's Ford, 223
Front Royal, VA, 204
Fry, Jacob, Col., USA, 77
Fry, James B., Brig. Gen., USA, 45
Fry, Speed S., Brig. Gen., USA, 103,
  105
Fuller, John W., Brig. Gen., USA,
  75–76, 80–81, 83–84

Gallatin, TN, 103, 105
Gano, Richard M., Brig. Gen., CSA, 22,
  25, 28, 101
Gano's Texans, 20, 22, 28–30
Garlick's Landing, VA, 11, 16
Garnettsville, KY, 160
Gartell, Henry, Capt., CSA, 192
Gartell's Georgians, 192
Gatling, George, 236
Gatling Gun, 236
Georgia, State of, 185
Georgetown, KY, 26–28
Gettysburg, Battle of, 148, 152–54, 162

Gettysburg, PA, 58–60, 146–50
Gettysburg Road, 147
Glasgow, KY, 23, 103–5, 111
Glasscock's Gap, 143
Glendale, IN, 165
Graceham, MD, 60
Gracey, Frank, Capt., CSA, 231, 233
Grand Gulf, MS, 141
Grand Junction, MS, 89, 95
Granger, Gordon, Maj. Gen., USA, 103, 105
Grant, Ulysses S., Lt. Gen., USA: and evaluaton of Rosecrans's Army, 183; and Forrest's Tennessee raid, 73–75, 81, 84, 86; and Hampton's cattle raid, 215–16, 221, 224; mentioned, 19, 198, 214, 235; and Mosby's Shenandoah Valley operations, 202, 209; and relief of Thomas, 183; and Van Dorn's Holly Springs raid, 89, 92, 93–98; and Vicksburg, 71, 87, 99, 100–101, 141, 152, 155
Gravelly Run, 217
Graves, W. H., Col., USA, 96
Green Bottom Bar, 232
Green River, 105, 157, 160
Gregg, David McM., Brig. Gen., USA, 147, 152
Gregg, Henry H., Capt., USA, 220
Grenada, MS, 88
Grenfell, George St. Leger, 20, 30–31
Grierson, Benjamin H., Maj. Gen., USA, 95–97, 186–88, 190–91
Griffith, John, Col., CSA, 87, 96
Griffith's Texas Brigade, 87, 90–91, 96
Groveton, VA, 137
Gunboats: *Key West*, 232: *Moose*, 168; *Tawah*, 231; *Undine*, 230–33
Gunnell, William Presley, Dr., 127
Guntown, MS, 187, 197
Guntown Road, 190
Gurley, Frank B., Capt., CSA, 73–74

Hagan, James, Col., CSA, 175
Hagerstown, MD, 54, 60
Hagerstown Road, 55, 60
Halisy, Dennis, Col., USA, 111, 112

Halleck, Henry W., Maj. Gen., USA: and Morgan's first Kentucky raid, 19, 25, 27, 32; and Stuart's Chambersburg raid, 49, 55–56; and Morgan's second Kentucky raid, 101; and Morgan's Ohio raid, 171; and Mosby's Shenandoah Valley operations, 208–9
Halltown, VA, 203, 209, 211
Hamden, OH, 170
Hammondsville, KY, 105
Hampton, Wade, Lt. Gen., CSA: and cattle raid, 213–24; mentioned, 47, 237; and Pleasonton's reconnaissance, 48; and Stuart's Chambersburg raid, 50, 52, 54–58, 66; and Stuart's march to Gettysburg, 143, 146–48, 152
Hampton's Legion, 213
Hancock, Winfield S., Maj. Gen., USA, 143–44
Hancock, MD, 55
Hanover, PA, 148–49
Hanover Court House, VA, 6
Hanson, Charles, Lt. Col., USA, 158–59
Hanson, E. H., Maj., USA, 197
Hardee, William J., Lt. Gen., CSA, 115, 118, 121–23, 125
Harlan, John, Col., USA, 105, 110–11
Harpers Ferry, WV, 47, 201–2, 204–5
Harrisburg, PA, 55
Harrison, IN, 164
Harrison's Georgia Regiment, CSA, 116
Harrodsburg, KY, 25, 159
Hart's Battery, CSA, 50
Haskell, Frank, Lt., USA, 152
Hatcher, Walt, 134
Hawes Shop, VA, 6
Hawkinsville, VA, 223–24
Haymarket, VA, 143
Haynie, Isham N., Brig. Gen., USA, 79–80
Hearn, John, 203–4
Hedgesville, VA, 51
Heintzelman, Samuel P., Maj. Gen., USA, 129, 135
Heth, Henry, Maj. Gen., CSA, 152
Hewett's Kentucky Battery, USA, 37

Hickory Creek, 179

Hill, Ambrose P., Lt. Gen., CSA, 46, 141

Hines Road, 218–19, 222

Hoad's Mill, MD, 147

Hobson, Edward H., Brig. Gen., USA, 157, 160–61, 164–68, 170–71

Hodge, George B., Brig. Gen., CSA, 174, 179, 181

Hoge, George B., Col., USA, 186, 191–92

Holly Springs, MS, 76, 86–87, 89–90, 92–93, 95, 97–98, 100

Home Guards, 22, 27–29, 32

Hooker, Joseph (Fighting Joe), Maj. Gen., USA, 15, 140–43

Hopedale, OH, 171

Horse Cave Gorge, KY, 33

Hoskins, Edward, Col., USA, 110–11

Houston, MS, 88

Howe, J. H., Col., USA, 198

Hoyer, Joseph S., Lt., USA, 11

Hudson's Battery, 253

Huffman, J. M., Lt. Col., CSA, 109

Humboldt, TN, 76–77

Hunt, A. A., Col., CSA, 20, 22

Hunter, David, Maj. Gen., USA, 183

Hunter, William L., Sgt., CSA, 134–37

Hunt's Georgia Battalion, CSA, 20, 27, 30

Huntington, TN, 81, 228

Hutcheson, John, Lt. Col., CSA, 101, 105–6

Hyattstown, MD 64–65

Imboden, John D., Brig. Gen., CSA, 50, 55

Indiana, Governor of, 25

Indiana, State of, 25, 161

Indiana Militia, 161–62, 164

Indianapolis, IN, 162–64

Ingersoll, Robert G., Col., USA, 73–74

Iron Scouts, 214

Island Ten, 78

Iuka, MS, 74

Jackson, Thomas J. (Stonewall), Lieutenant General, CSA, 3, 49, 133, 140–41, 151

Jackson, OH, 165

Jackson, TN, 73–76, 80–82, 226

Jackson's Tennessee Brigade, CSA, 87, 90

Jackson, William H. (Red), Brig. Gen., CSA, 87

Jacques, Mr., 52

James River, 15, 215–16, 220

Jasper, OH, 165

Jefferson, PA, 149

Jefferson, TN, 119

Jeff Davis Legion, CSA, 4

Jeruselam Plank Road, 217, 222

Johnson, Adam R., Col., CSA, 156, 165, 167, 169

Johnson, Andrew, Vice Pres., USA, 25, 179

Johnson, Bushrod R., Maj. Gen., CSA, 187, 190–92, 194

Johnson, Samuel D., Col., CSA, 102, 105, 110

Johnsonville, TN, 226, 230–35

Johnston, Joseph E., Gen., CSA, 185

Johnstone, Robert, Col., USA, 134–36, 138

Johnstone, Robert, Mrs., 135–36

Johnsville, MD, 62

Jones, Tom, Pvt., CSA, 75

Jones, Richard, Col., CSA, 183

Jones, William E. (Grumble), Brig. Gen., CSA, 50, 52, 56, 66, 143

Judah, Henry M., Brig. Gen., USA, 157, 160, 165–68

Kanawha Division, USA, 55

Kautz, August V., Brig. Gen., USA, 161, 166–67, 218, 222–23

Kelley, Benjamin F., Brig. Gen., USA, 204

Kelley, D. C., Col., CSA, 226, 231

Kelly, J. L. P., 1st. Sgt., CSA, 74

Kelly, John H., Col., USA, 55

Kenly, John R., Brig. Gen., USA, 52, 205–6

Kenton, TN, 79

Kentucky, State of, 19–22, 25, 27, 29, 32–33, 35–36, 73, 100–101, 103, 105, 112, 114, 156, 227

Kentucky River, 31
Kenyon, Albert, Sgt., USA, 220
Kernstown, VA, 201
Kilby's Station, VA, 4
Kilpatrick, H. Judson, Brig. Gen., USA, 147–49, 152
Knoxville, MD, 60
Knoxville, TN, 20, 44

La Grange, TN, 89
Landram, T. J., Lt. Col., USA, 29
Lanneau, John F., Lt., CSA, 217
Latane, William, Capt., CSA, 8
Laurel Brigade, CSA, 216
La Vergne, TN, 117, 119–20, 124
Lavinia, TN, 226
Lawton, J. K., Col., CSA, 39, 41
Lawton's Georgians, CSA, 40, 41
Layton's Road, 218
Lebanon, KY, 24–25, 110–11, 158–59
Lebanon, TN, 43
Lebanon and Columbia Road, 111
Lebanon Junction, KY, 24, 160
Lee, Fitzhugh, Maj. Gen., CSA: description, 4; and Stuart's Peninsula raid, 6, 8, 14, 15; and Stuart's march to Gettysburg, 143, 147–48, 150; and Stoughton's capture, 133, 137–38
Lee, "Light Horse Harry," 4
Lee, Robert E., Gen., CSA: appointed commander Army of Northern Virginia, 2; description, 2–3; and Gettysburg, 140–43, 147–48, 150–55; and Hampton's cattle raid, 213–15, 224; mentioned, 162, 200; and Stuart's Chambersburg raid, 46, 49–50, 68–69; and Stuart's Peninsula raid, 3–4, 7, 14, 16–17; and Wolsely's opinion of, 2
Lee, Stephen D., Lt. Gen., CSA, 187–89
Lee, T. C., Lt., CSA, 54–55
Lee, Thomas, Col., CSA, 145–46
Lee, W. H. F. (Rooney), Maj. Gen., CSA: description, 4–5; and Hampton's cattle raid, 216, 218, 220–21, 223; and Pleasonton's reconnaissance, 48; and Stuart's

Chambersburg raid, 50, 52, 56, 66, 69; and Stuart's Peninsula raid, 5–8, 14
Leesburg, VA, 60
Leesburg Pike, 143–44
Left Wing, XIV Corps, 103
Leib, Edward, Lt., USA, 6–8
Lester, Henry C., Col., USA, 37, 42–43
Lewisburgh Pike, 183
Lexington, IN, 163
Lexington, KY, 25–26, 28–29, 31, 36, 105
Lexington, TN, 73–75, 81, 84, 226
Liberty, MD, 63
Liberty Turnpike, 37
Licking River, 29
Light Division, 47
Lincoln, Abraham, Pres., USA: and, Hampton's cattle raid, 224; mentioned, 33, 99; and Morgan's first Kentucky raid, 25, 27; and Morgan's Ohio raid, 171; and Morgan's second Kentucky raid, 113; and Mosby's Shenandoah Valley operations, 202, 209; and Stoughton's capture, 139; and Stuart's Chambersburg raid, 49, 70; and Stuart's march to Gettysburg, 146, 153
Little Bighorn River, 198
Little Monocacy River, 65
Little River Turnpike, 130
Little Round Top, 150–51
Locust Grove, OH, 165
Logan, Thomas, Capt., USA, 52
Logan, Hugh, 58
Londonderry, OH, 171
Long, Tom, 27
Longstreet, James, Lt. Gen., CSA, 16–17, 141–42, 146, 174
Lookout Mountain, 174
Lough, Mr., 90
Louisville, KY, 23, 26–27, 31–32, 101, 103, 108, 159
Louisville Turnpike, 104
Loundon County, 204
Love, John, Col., USA, 163
Lowe, William W., Col., USA, 75, 80

Lyon, Hylan B., Brig. Gen., CSA, 187–92, 194, 197

Mabry's Brigade, CSA, 227
McArthur, OH, 170
McCalla, Jo, 219
McCook, Alexander, Maj. Gen., USA, 116–17
McClellan, George B. (Little Mac) (Mac the Unready) (Little Corporal of Unsought Fields), Maj. Gen., USA: after Antietam, 46–47, 49; described, 1–2; mentioned, 19, 51, 216; and Stuart's Chambersburg raid, 53, 55–56, 59–60, 62, 68, 69–70; and Stuart's Peninsula raid, 2–4, 8–10, 15–17
McClellan, H. B., Maj., CSA, 142
McClure, A. K., Col., PA Militia, 54–55, 57–58
McCook, Edward M., Brig. Gen., USA, 179–80
McCoy's Ford, 51–51, 55
McCullough, Robert (Black Bob), Brig. Gen., CSA, 88
McCullough's Missouri and Mississippi Brigade, 90–91, 227
McKenzie, TN, 80
McLemoresville Road, 82
McMillen, William L., Col., USA, 186–87, 191–92
McMinnville, TN, 36, 44, 176–77, 179–80
McNeil, John M., 204
Madison, IN, 163
Malone's Battalion, CSA, 116
Manassas, VA, 129
Mann, J. C., Capt., USA, 206–7
Marsh, C. C., Col., USA, 93, 95
Martin, William T., Maj. Gen., CSA: and Stuart's Peninsula raid, 5–6, 12; and Wheeler's Sequatchie Valley raid, 174, 176–77, 180, 182
Martinsburg, WV, 47–48, 201
Martinsburg-Darksville Turnpike, 48
Maryland, State of, 46–47, 50–51, 56, 60, 63, 145, 201–2

Massie, Col., CSA, 219
Mason, Mrs., 90
Meade, George G., Maj. Gen., USA: and Gettysburg, 146–48, 151, 153; and Hampton's cattle raid, 215, 218, 220, 222
Mechanicstown, MD, 60
Memphis, TN, 72–73, 98, 187
Mercersburg, PA, 52–54, 60
Metcalfe's Cavalry, 29
Michigan, Lake, 163
Middleburg, MS, 95–97
Middleburg, VA, 60, 129, 142
Middleport, OH, 65
Midway, KY, 26
Milan, IN, 164
Mill Creek, 116
Miller, George, Capt., CSA, 121
Mississippi, State of, 86, 97–98, 114, 185–86
Mississippi River, 19, 71, 87, 98, 155
Mitchell, IN, 162
Mitchell, Robert B., Brig. Gen., USA, 112, 179–80
Mizner, J. K., Col., USA, 89, 95, 97
Monocacy Junction, VA, 202
Monocacy River, 60–62, 84–65, 202
Montana, State of, 198, 210
Montgomery, IN, 165
Moore, Orlando H., Col., USA, 157
Moorefield, OH, 171
Morgan, John H., Brig. Gen., CSA: described, 18, 102; and first Kentucky raid, 19–32; mentioned 33, 35, 36–37, 114, 237; and Ohio raid, 155–72; and second Kentucky raid, 100–113
Morgan, John T., Brig. Gen., CSA, 178
Morgan, Tom, 159
Morgan, W. H., Col., USA, 94–95
Morrison's Georgians, CSA, 40–41
Morton, John W., Capt., CSA: and Brice's Cross Roads, 187, 190–95; and Forrest's Johnsonville raid, 226, 228, 231, 233, 235; and Forrest's Tennessee raid, 77, 84
Morton, Olive P., Gov., 162

Morton's Battery, 187, 226, 233

Mosby, John S., Col., CSA: and capture of Stoughton, 128–39; description, 127; mentioned, 15, 143, 237; and Shenandoah Valley Operations, 201–12

"Mosby's Confederacy," 130, 211

Mosby's Rangers, 204, 208

Moscow, KY, 75

Mudd, John J., Maj., USA, 93, 97

Muddy Branch, MD, 202

Muldraugh's Hill, 101, 108, 112

Munfordville, KY, 23, 105–6

Murfreesboro, TN: mentioned, 23, 101, 104, 180; Forrest's capture of, 36–41, 43–45; and battle of Stone's River, 105, 114–15, 118, 123, 125

Murphy, R. C., Col., USA, 89–90, 92, 94, 96

Muskingum River, 170

Mussel Shoals, 182

Napier, T. A., Lt. Col., CSA, 74, 78, 83

Nashville, TN, 36, 43, 45, 72, 101, 114–15, 121, 177

Nashville and Lebanon Pike, 41

Nashville Turnpike, 122, 124, 180

National Turnpike, 52, 162, 171

Neblitt's Millstream, VA, 223

Nelson, Joseph, 132, 134–35

Nelsonville, OH, 170

New Albany, IN, 162

New Albany, MS, 97

New Baltimore, OH, 165

New Baltimore, VA, 12–13, 143

New Burlington, OH, 165

New Kent, VA, 10, 12

New Loundon, VA, 63

New Market, KY, 110

New Market, VA, 63

Newspapers: Richmond Dispatch, The, 224; Washington Star, The, 224

"New York Rebel," 63

IXX Corps, USA, 201, 206

Ninth Kentucky Cavalry, CSA, 102, 107, 158

Ninth Michigan Cavalry, USA, 158

Ninth Michigan Infantry, USA, 37, 41, 43

Ninth Michigan Volunteers, USA, 37

Ninth Pennsylvania Cavalry, USA, 22

Ninth Tennessee Cavalry, CSA, 72, 156, 161

Ninth Virginia Cavalry, CSA, 4, 7–8, 59

Nolan's Ford, 202

Nolensville, TN, 116, 120–21

Nolensville Pike, 116

Nolin Stockade, KY, 106

Nottoway River, 223

Obion River, 79–80

Occoquon, VA, 127

Occoquan Creek, 144

O'Conner, L. L., Provost Marshall, USA, 128, 135

Ohio, Governor of, 25

Ohio, State of, 25, 169

Ohio Militia, 165–66, 169, 171

Ohio River, 156, 159, 161–63, 165–66, 170–71

Okolona, MS, 188

Old Carrollsville, MS, 191

Old Church, VA, 6–8, 10, 13

Old Washington, OH, 171

106th New York Infantry, USA, 203–4

Overall's Creek, 123

Oxford, MS, 87, 89

Paducah, KY, 79

Palmer, Baylor, Captain, CSA, 101, 107

Palmer's Battery, 102

Palmyra, TN, 162

Paris, IN, 163

Paris, KY, 26, 29, 31

Paris, TN, 80, 228

Paris Landing, TN, 228

Parker's Cross Roads, TN, 82, 84

Parkhurst, John G., Col., USA, 37, 43

Patterson, Michael L., Maj., USA, 179

Paul, James, 39

Peach Orchard, The, 151

Pegram, John, Brig. Gen., CSA, 116

Pelham, John, Lt. Col., CSA, 50, 66–67

Pelham's Battery, 50, 65

Pemberton, John C., Lt. Gen., CSA, 71, 87–88, 93, 98, 100, 141, 152
Pender, William D., 152
Pendleton, V. M., Capt., CSA, 110
Penisula, The, 70
Pennington, Alfred, Lt., USA, 64
Pennsylvania, State of, 50, 53, 56, 62, 67–68, 145, 162, 202
Petersburg, Battle of, 214
Petersburg, VA, 221, 224
Peyton, Samuel, Lt., CSA, 104
Pickett, George E., Maj. Gen., CSA, 152–53
Pierce, R. Butler, Col., USA, 129
Pierceville, IN, 164
Piketown, OH, 165
Pleasonton, Alfred, Brig. Gen., USA, 48–49, 55, 60–62, 64–69
Point-of-Rocks, MD, 201, 203
Polk, Leonidas, Lt. Gen., CSA, 115, 118, 121
Pemeroy, OH, 167
Pontotoc, MS, 88–89, 97
Pontotoc Road, 191
Poolesville, MD, 60, 65, 201
Porter, Fitz John, Brig. Gen., USA, 10
Port Gibson, MS, 141
Potomac River, 47–48, 51–51, 55, 60, 62, 65, 141, 143–44, 146, 153, 201
Powhatan Stage Road, 218, 220
Prentiss, Lt., USA, 132, 135
Price, Channing, Lt., CSA, 50, 58, 68–69

Quirk, Capt., CSA, 104–5

Railroads: Baltimore and Ohio, 147, 204; Central Mississippi, 100; Kentucky Central, 25; Louisville and Nashville, 101, 105, 108; Memphis and Chattanooga, 33; Mississippi Central, 71, 87, 95; Mobile and Ohio, 79, 100, 187; Nashville and Chattanooga, 37, 44; Norfolk and Petersburg, 217; Orange and Alexandria, 129; Richmond, Fredericksburg, and Potomac, 5

Rappahannock River, 157
Readyville, TN, 44
Rector's Crossroads, VA, 142
Reedsville, OH, 168
Reid, Frank, Sgt., CSA, 187–88
Reynolds, John F., Maj. Gen., USA, 13
Reynolds, J. J., Maj. Gen., USA, 103, 105
Reynoldsburg, TN, 80
Reynoldsburg Island, 232–33
Richards, A. E., Capt., CSA, 208
Richardson, William, Capt., CSA, 39, 42
Richmond, KY, 31
Richmond, VA: city 1, 5, 15–16, 49, 59, 140, 216, 221, 224
Richmond, VA (Confederate government), 123
Rienzi, MS, 187
Ripley, MS, 97, 187
Ripley, OH, 165
Ripley Road, 90, 191
Robertson, Beverly H., Brig. Gen., CSA, 143
Robins, W. T., Lt., CSA, 6–7, 11, 12, 16
Rock Martin's, TN, 36
Rock Springs, TN, 120
Rockville, MD, 145–46
Rolling Fork River, 24, 108–9
Rosecrans, William S., Maj. Gen., USA: mentioned, 72, 94, 155; in Middle Tennessee, 99, 100–101, and Morgan's first Kentucky raid, 103–5, 108, 110, 112; and Morgan's Ohio raid, 160, 171; and Stone's River, 114–26; and Wheeler's Sequatchie Valley raid, 174, 176–79, 183
Rosser, Thomas L., Maj. Gen., CSA, 216, 218–20, 222–23
Rounds, Oliver C., Capt., USA, 38, 40
Rowanty Creek, 217, 221
Rowser's Ford, 144
Royall, William B., Capt., USA, 7, 8
Rucker, Edmund W., Col., CSA, 187–92, 194, 197, 226, 230

Russell, Alfred A., Col., CSA, 72, 76, 78, 82–83
Russellville, AL, 187
Rush, Richard H., Col., USA, 13, 60–62
Rush's Lancers, 10, 13, 15
Rutherford Station, KY, 79
Rutland, OH, 79

Salem, IN, 162
Sand Shoals Ford, 102
Sardinia, OH, 165
Saulsbury, TN, 96–97
Schriver, William, 147
Scioto River, 165
Scott, John S., Col., CSA, 174, 181
Scott's Ferry, VA, 156
Scottsville Road, 105
Second Brigade, XXII Corps, USA, 127
II Corps, 143
Second Illinois Cavalry, USA, 91, 93, 97
Second Kentucky Cavalry, CSA, 20, 29–30, 101, 105–6, 158–59, 161, 171
Second New Jersey Cavalry, USA, 190
Second North Carolina Regiment, CSA, 148
Second South Carolina Cavalry, CSA, 54, 145
Second Tennessee Cavalry, CSA, 191, 229
Second Tennessee Cavalry, USA, 73–74
Second Vermont Brigade, 128
Secret Service, 138
Sedgewick, John, Maj. Gen., USA, 16
Selden, Cary, Pvt., CSA, 220
Seminary Ridge, 151
Seneca, MD, 201
Seneca Creek, 60
Senecaville, OH, 171
Sequatchie Valley, 36, 173, 176–77, 184
Sequatchie Valley Road, 174
Seventh Indiana Cavalry, USA, 190
Seventh Pennsylvania Cavalry, USA, 37, 39, 41
Seventh Tennessee Cavalry, CSA, 194
Seventh United States Cavalry, USA, 198

Seventh Virginia Cavalry, CSA, 219
Seventy-fifth Regiment, Illinois Infantry, USA, 122
Seventy-ninth Pennsylvania Infantry, 61
Seymour, IN, 162
Shackleford, James M., Brig. Gen., USA, 158, 168–72
Shadburne, George B., Sgt., CSA, 214–15, 218
Shady Grove, TN, 81
Sharonville, OH, 165
Shelbyville, TN, 43, 180
Shelbyville, KY, 159
Shenandoah Valley, 3, 141, 202, 204, 212
Shepherdstown, WV, 144
Shepherdsville, KY, 160
Sheridan, Phillip S., Maj. Gen., USA, 202–5, 208–10, 215–16, 221
Sherman, William T., Maj. Gen., USA: and Brice's Cross Roads, 185–87, 198; mentioned, xvi, 34; and Forrest's Johnsonville raid, 226–28, 235; and Vicksburg, 71, 87, 98
Shiloh, Battle of, 19
Shiloh, MS, 115
VI Corps, USA, 53, 201
Sixth Kentucky Cavalry, CSA, 158, 166–68
Sixth United States Cavalry, USA, 6, 8, 9
Slater, George, 137
Sleepy Creek, 204
Sligo, KY, 159
Smith, Andrew J., Maj. Gen., USA, 198
Smith, Baxter, Maj., CSA, 36, 41–43
Smith, E. Kirby, Lt. Gen., CSA, 18–19, 20, 29, 44, 103, 105
Smith, G. Clay, Brig. Gen., USA, 31
Smith, H. S., Lt. Col., USA, 106–8
Smith, John E., Maj. Gen., USA, 198
Smithfield, KY, 159
Smith's Ford 171
Smyrna, OH, 171
Snicker's Gap, VA, 204
Somerset, KY, 31–32
Songs: "Jine the Cavalry," 48, 224, 231; "Lorena," 224; "Rally 'Round the Flag Boys," 166

South Anna River, 5, 8
South Carolina Boykin Rangers, 4
Spangler's Spring, 151
Sparta, TN, 20, 22, 36
Spiller's Battalion, 36
Spring Creek, 76, 78
Springfield, KY, 25, 110, 159
Stagall's Ferry, 32
Stanton, Edwin M., Sec. of War, USA, 33, 55–56, 183, 198, 202
Starkweather, John, Brig. Gen., USA, 119
Starnes, James W., Col., CSA, 72, 76–77, 82–84
Steamboats: *Alice Dean* 161; *Anna* 229–30; *John B. Combs* 161; *J. W. Cheeseman* 230; *Mazeppa* 228–29; *Venus* 230–32
Stewart's Creek, 117–18
Stoneman, George, Maj. Gen., USA, 55, 60, 62, 64–66, 68–69
Stoner, R. G., Lt. Col., CSA, 102, 107
Stone's River, 37, 112, 114, 119, 125, 180
Stoney Creek, 117
Stoughton, Edwin H., Brig. Gen., USA, 127–35, 137–39
Stuart, James Ewell Brown (Jeb) (Beauty), Maj. Gen., CSA: and Chambersburg raid, 49–70; description, 3, 47; and march to Gettysburg, 141–54; mentioned, xv, 1, 18, 102, 213, 216, 237; and Peninsula raid, 5–19; and Pleasonton's reconnaissance, 48; and Stoughton's capture, 128, 130, 133, 138; at The Bower, 47–48
Stuart Horse Artillery, 4
Stubb's Farm, MS, 187
Sturgis, Samuel D., Brig. Gen., USA, 186–88, 192–93, 195–98
Sudley Ford, 137
Sugar Loaf Mountain, 64–65
Sullivan, Jeremiah C., Brig. Gen., USA, 73–76, 78, 80–85
Susquehanna River, 148
Swan, S. A., Capt., CSA, 7

Sweeney, Sam, 47, 237
Sycamore Church, VA, 218, 220, 222
Sykesville, MD, 147

Tallahatchie River, 90, 97, 188
Talleysville, VA, 12
Taneytown, MD, 60
Taylor, Richard, Lt. Gen., CSA, 226
Tebb's Bend, KY, 157
Tennessee, State of, 23, 35–36, 79, 88, 100, 114, 155, 160, 181, 185–86, 199, 225–27
Tennessee River, 35, 71–72, 80–81, 84, 100, 174–75, 180, 182, 226, 228, 233–34
Tennesse River Valley, 73, 173, 183
Tenth Kentucky Cavalry, CSA, 102, 157
Theaters of Operations: East 99; East Tennessee 172, 186; Middle Tennessee 35, 45, 99–100, 226; Southwest 155; West 76, 98–99; West Tennessee 71–72, 198–99
Third Alabama Cavalry, CSA, 116, 175
III Corps, CSA, 117
Third Division, Center, Army of the Cumberland, USA, 103
Third Division, VI Corps, USA, 53
Third Kentucky Cavalry, CSA, 101, 105
Third Kentucky Volunteer Cavalry, USA, 117
Third Minnesota Infantry, USA, 37
Third New York Cavalry, USA, 22
Thirteenth Pennsylvania Infantry, USA, 220
Thirty-fifth Battalion Virginia Cavalry (The Comanches), CSA, 216, 220
Thirty-ninth Iowa Infantry, USA, 82
Thomas, George H. (The Rock of Chickamauga), Maj. Gen., USA, 116–17, 183
Thrall, J. C., Capt., CSA, 233, 235
Thrall's Battery, 233, 235
Tishomingo Creek, 190, 194–95
Tompkinsville, KY, 22–23
Totopotomoy Creek, VA, 6–7
Trenton, TN, 76–78, 80–83, 86
Tribble, Alexander, Capt., CSA, 111

Triune, TN, 117
Tucker, T. J., Lt., CSA, 157
Tullahoma, TN, 125, 155
Tunstall's Station, VA, 9–13, 16
Tupelo, MS, 34, 186–87
Tupper Plain, OH, 169
Turkey Neck Bend, KY, 156
Turner's Tavern, VA, 5
Twelfth Illinois Cavalry, USA, 52
Twelfth Michigan Infantry, USA, 76
Twelfth Virginia Cavalry, CSA, 219–20
Twentieth Illinois Infantry, USA, 93, 95
Twentieth Kentucky Cavalry, USA, 158
Twenty-eighth Brigade, USA, 119
Twenty-fifth Michigan Infantry, 157
XXII Corps, USA, 202
Tyler, H. A., Capt., CSA, 189
Tyler, Robert, Brig. Gen., USA, 202
Tyler's Battalion, 191, 195

Union City, TN, 79
Union Mills, VA, 129, 147
Unionville, TN, 180
Upperville, VA, 142
Urbana, MD, 63–64

Van Buren, MS, 96
Van Dorn, Earl, Maj. Gen., CSA:
    description, 88; mentioned, 114,
    237; and raid on Holly Springs, 76,
    86, 88–98, 100
Venable, Reid, Maj., CSA, 223
Vernon, IN, 163
Versailles, IN, 164
Versailles, KY, 25
Vicksburg, MS, 19, 71, 85, 87, 98–100,
    152–53, 155
Vienna, IN, 162–63
Vienna, VA, 135
Vinton, OH, 170
Vinton County, OH, 170
Virginia, xiv, 1, 49, 56, 59, 60, 68–69,
    129–30, 138, 140–41, 164,
    200–201, 210, 213–14

Walden's Ridge, 35, 173, 176–77, 179
Wallace, Lewis, Brig. Gen., USA, 163,
    201

Walls Road, 218–20, 222
Walton, E. S., Capt., CSA, 226, 228
Walton's Battery, 226
Ward, William T., Brig. Gen., USA, 26,
    68
Waring, George E., Col., USA, 186,
    188–90, 193
Warner's Bridge, 180
Warren, Gouverneur K., Maj. Gen.,
    USA, 9, 10
Warrenton, VA, 137
Warrenton Turnpike, 131
Wartrace, TN, 180
Washburn, Cadwallader C., Maj. Gen.,
    USA, 186, 197
Washington, D.C., 27, 99, 141,
    144–46, 200–202, 214
Washington (US Government), 17, 25,
    27, 32, 46, 101, 198, 208–9
Weitbrecht, Robert, 132
Wells, Gideon, Sec. of Navy, USA, 32
West, W. C., Pvt., CSA, 229
Westminister, MD, 147
West Virginia, State of, 67, 168
Wharton, John A., Maj. Gen., CSA: and
    battle of Stone's River, 116–18,
    122–24; and Forrest's Murfreesboro
    raid, 39, 42; and Wheeler's
    Sequatchie Valley raid, 174, 176–77,
    179–80, 182
Wheatfield, The, 151
Wheaton, Henry, 201
Wheeler, Joseph (Fighting Joe) (The
    Warchild), Lt. Gen., CSA: and battle
    of Stone's River, 115–26; descrip-
    tion, 115, 184; mentioned, 237, and
    Sequatchie Valley raid, 173–84
White, B. S., Capt., CSA, 58, 102, 165
White, Elijah (Lige) V., Lt. Col., CSA,
    216, 220
White House, VA, 12
White Oak Swamp, 15
White River Country of Arkansas,
    235
White's Battery, 116
White's Ford, 60, 65, 69, 201
Whitewater River, 164
Wickham, Henry, Col., CSA, 5

Wilder, John T., Brig. Gen., USA, 179, 180
Wilkesville, OH, 165
Wilkins, A., Col., USA, 186, 191
Wilkinson's Bridge, 217, 223
Williams, Frank, 133
Williams, Lawrence, Maj., USA, 9, 10
Williamsburg, OH, 165
Williamsport, MD, 47, 52
Wilson's Creek Pike, 117
Winchester, KY, 31
Winchester, OH, 165
Winchester, VA, 47, 201, 204–5
Wing, Mr., 90
Winslow, Edward F., Col., USA, 186, 190, 193
Winston's Farm, 5
Wintersville, OH, 171
Wirtz, Union Surgeon, 92
Wise, John, Lt., CSA, 213
Wolf Creek, 94

Wolf Creek Bridge, 94
Wolf Run Shoals, 129, 144
Wolford, Frank, Col., USA, 31, 156–58, 167–68, 170, 172
Wolseley, General Viscount, 2, 44
Woodbury, TN, 36, 38, 44
Woodbury Pike, 41–42
Wood's Alabama Brigade, CSA, 117
Woodsborough, MD, 61–63
Wool, John E., Maj. Gen., USA, 55
Wright, Horatio, Maj. Gen, USA, 103–5, 110
Wright's Brigade, CSA, 151
Wyndham, Sir Percy, Col., USA, 127, 129–32, 134, 138

Yalabusha River, 88
Yazoo River, 87, 98
Yellow Tavern, VA, 213
York, PA, 142, 144, 146, 148–49
York Turnpike, 152

About the Authors

BRIG. GEN. WILLIAM R. BROOKSHER and LT. COL. DAVID K. SNIDER are retired U.S. Air Force officers. Both are frequent contributors to *Civil War Times Illustrated*, *Military History*, and *Military Review*. General Brooksher is also the author of *Bloody Hill: The Civil War Battle of Wilson's Creek* (Brassey's, 1995). Brooksher lives in Richland, Washington. Snider lives in Houston.